The Sascha team, victorious in the 1922 Targa Florio, is welcomed back to the Austro-Daimler factory. Behind the wheel of the first car is the famous Alfred Neubauer, and the third boy from the left is myself.

Ferry Porsche:
Cars Are My Life

Ferry Porsche: Cars Are My Life

Professor Dr. Ing. h.c. Ferry Porsche
with Günther Molter

Patrick Stephens Limited

First published in 1989

British Library Cataloguing in Publication Data

Porsche, Ferry
 Ferry Porsche: cars are my life.
 1. West Germany. Car industries. Porsche, Ferry, —
Biographies
 I. Title II. Molter, Günther
 338.7′6292222′0924

 ISBN 1-85260-259-7

Photo credits: Dr. Ing. h.c. F. Porsche AG (145); Daimler-Benz AG (18); Günther Molter (15); Auto Union AG (4); NASA (1); PAA (1); Luftbild A. Brugger, Freigegeben vom Reg. Präsidium Stuttgart Nr. 2/58783c (page 249).

Patrick Stephens Limited is part of the Thorsons Publishing Group, Wellingborough, Northamptonshire NN8 2RQ, England.

Printed in Great Britain by Butler & Tanner Limited, Frome, Somerset
Typeset by MJL Ltd, Hitchin, Hertfordshire

10 9 8 7 6 5 4 3 2 1

Contents

Introduction

The idea for this biography first saw the light of day in Badgastein, that Austrian spa where kings and emperors once sought rest and relaxation. Prince Bismarck visited it on several occasions and it was there, during a stay in the middle of August 1865, that he drew up the so-called 'Gastein Convention'. For many years after the Second World War, as long as his wife Dodo was still alive, Ferry Porsche, who as a child had spent holidays in Badgastein with his parents, used to go there with her to relax at the Hotel Elisabethpark.

I also go to Badgastein occasionally; the town lies at one end of a mountain valley and nestles closely against the towering Hohen Tauern mountains. It is not a very big place and one frequently bumps into people when out for a walk.

And so it was that a few years ago I met Ferry Porsche, whom I have known personally for more than 40 years. As a journalist, I have chronicled his rise to international fame as a businessman and designer of motor cars. We arranged to meet for dinner at the Elisabethpark. At that time I was still press officer at Daimler-Benz, and that evening, as so often before, we talked about cars, their future and the problems that would have to be overcome.

I very soon realized that, having lived for so long in the shadow of his famous father, he felt impelled to publish his own highly personal account of his life in the motor industry. On that evening in August 1983 we decided that after I retired from Daimler-Benz we would write his biography.

Many books have been written about Porsche, mainly about Dr Ferdinand Porsche, but also about his son and his world-famous company, but this one contains Ferry Porsche's own very personal account of his life and work.

This book emerged out of the many conversations that we had together in his house in the Feuerbacher Weg in Stuttgart, at his factory in Stuttgart-Zuffenhausen, where he still works every day, even at the age of 79, and at the family estate in Zell am See in Austria. It is on this estate that his parents, Frau Aloisia Porsche and Professor Ferdinand Porsche, his wife Dodo and his brother-in-law, Dr Anton Piëch, were laid to rest in a simple chapel.

It is the autobiography of an entrepreneur, an engineer and a designer, but also of the genial, modest man that Ferry Porsche is, written almost in his own words. It is the story of his life and work, and, in a sense, also his legacy.

Günther Molter
Stuttgart

There's going to be a war

The imposing figure standing in front of us was the man who had written the history of the motor car. The mass production techniques of which he was the pioneer had laid the foundations for the manufacture of reasonably priced motor cars which even people with limited means could afford. The man's name was Henry Ford; he was the creator of the famous Model T, a simple and robust four-seater with universal appeal which could be used with equal success as a farm vehicle or as a family car. More than 15 million Model Ts were produced, a figure which has still only been exceeded by Volkswagen.

We are writing of the year 1937. My father had taken me with him on a trip to the United States, where we were to study the latest production methods that we intended to use in the construction of an ultramodern automobile factory. The factory was destined for the mass production of the new Volkswagen which was just being developed. Our party included Ghislaine Kaes, my father's secretary, Jakob Werlin, the director of Daimler-Benz, Otto Dieckhoff, formerly with the automobile manufacturers Wanderer, now an expert in production engineering in our employment, and Dr Lafferentz of the German Labour Front (Deutsche Arbeitsfront).

A visit to Henry Ford in Dearborn was an essential part of our itinerary; even then he was one of the major figures in automobile history. Ford welcomed us at his factory, where after a lengthy tour of the production facilities, we met for a concluding discussion in his office. The discussion took place in a relaxed, informal atmosphere and centred of course on the dialogue between Henry Ford and my father, with Ghislaine Kaes acting as interpreter.

In the course of the conversation, Mr Ford asked how Europeans saw the future of the motor car. My father felt the question was addressed to him and started to give an answer; however, Ford interrupted him and said, pointing to me, 'Let's have an answer from the young man, he represents youth and the future!' I did not need long to consider my answer, since the car I had in mind corresponded in most respects to the Volkswagen philosophy. So I said,

'The car of the future, as we in Europe see it, should carry four people in comfort, irrespective of size, but it should also be com-

Myself at the age of 28 on board the transatlantic liner *Bremen* for my first trip to the United States in 1937, together with my father Ferdinand Porsche. In the background steams Cunard's *Aquitania*.

pact in design. It should be able to cruise on the motorway at a speed of about 62 mph [100 km/h] and have low fuel consumption. It will have to be an economical vehicle, since circumstances in Europe are different from those in the USA — Europeans have to economize!' Ford listened to me attentively, but made no comment on my remarks.

At the end of our discussion, my father invited Henry Ford to come to Europe and visit the German automobile industry, saying that he would be happy to make himself available to accompany him. However, Mr Ford made a gesture of refusal, saying, 'Unfortunately that won't be possible, because there's going to be a war!' His tone was very persuasive and his words did not fail to have an effect on us; in 1937, who was thinking of war?

I was 28 years old at the time of the visit to North America and it made a deep impression on me, giving me plenty of food for thought. I thought to myself that Hitler should be sent on a two-year trip round the world. Our trip had given me a feeling of freedom and shown me the opportunities offered by a free economy, emphasizing how different it all was at home. For example, very severe restrictions were placed on us in the development of the Volkswagen. At that time, Germany had only very limited foreign currency reserves and there were shortages of raw materials. In any case, rearmament took precedence, so in developing the Volkswagen, we had very little room for manoeuvre from the technical point of view. For example, we had virtually no copper or rubber, and even had to be cautious in our use of licences, since they also cost foreign currency.

After the new government which came to power in 1933 had abolished taxation on motor cars, the industry experienced an upturn, which of course led to further shortages of raw materials.

At that time, the Teves company was producing a hydraulic brake manufactured under licence from an English company and based on patents held by Lockheed. For each brake manufactured in Germany and fitted to a car, a licence fee had to be paid to England, causing a further drain on foreign currency reserves. Rubber, copper and other raw materials had to be purchased from abroad. In producing the Volkswagen, we had to avoid everything that cost foreign currency; thus we had to use a mechanical brake and had to be economical in our use of rubber in, for example, the engine mounting. This was a great handicap for us.

When as a young man I had my first experience of America with all its liberality and tolerance, its industrial and technical capabilities and its infinite vastness, I was immediately filled with enthusiasm. If I had not already been married and had a son, I would have seriously considered staying over there.

The Nazis had suspected something of the sort before our departure and had not been at all keen on my plans to visit America. It was only with the support of Dr Lafferentz of the German Labour Front that the obstacles placed in our way by official party policy could be removed.

Many years later, when we had built our own factory and were able to operate in accordance with the principles of the free economy, I often used to cast my mind back to that visit in 1937. However, there was a long, hard road to struggle along before we reached our current level of achievement. From a very early age, my whole life was very closely bound up with the motor car, and my career was very much influenced by my father, from whom I learnt a great deal. Nevertheless, a lot of what was done at that time bears my own mark.

I am often asked how it is possible to come out from behind the shadow of such a famous father. I would like simply to cite an episode that occurred during the period when the Volkswagen was being developed. A technical predecessor of the VW was the Porsche Type 32, which we had developed for NSU. In collaboration with Wilhelm Sebastian, I worked in our garage in the Feuerbacher Weg in Stuttgart on the engine for this car, which we dismantled. I joined in enthusiastically and was not afraid to get my hands dirty. As I worked, I noticed that Sebastian was watching me closely. After a while, speaking in the local dialect and shaking his head, he said, 'You're not at all like the description I was given of you. You can really get stuck into work, and what you're doing is really fantastic!' That showed me quite clearly how closely the 'son of Professor Ferdinand Porsche' was being observed by the employees.

But it all began in the secure atmosphere of the Austro-Hungarian monarchy in the year 1909, or to be more precise in Wiener-Neustadt in Lower Austria.

2

The world was still a safe place

At the beginning of the twentieth century the world was still a safe place. Stefan Zweig describes that time in his biography *The World of Yesteryear — Memoirs of a European*:

'It was the golden age of safety. Everything in our Austrian monarchy, which had lasted for almost a thousand years, seemed destined to last for ever and the state itself was the highest guarantor of this permanence. The rights that it granted to its citizens were ratified by Parliament, the freely elected representatives of the people, and each duty was precisely defined... Everything in this extensive kingdom was fixed and immovable... Nobody gave any thought to war, revolution or subversion. Everything radical or violent seemed impossible in this age of reason!'

Great progress had been made in industrial development and the people had grown more prosperous. There had even been advances in social matters and the process of development was continuing. It was possible to travel freely around Europe without having to overcome bureaucratic obstacles, since neither passport nor visa was required and currencies could be freely converted.

This traditional Europe came together once again for the festivities held in 1908 in Vienna to mark the sixtieth year of the reign of Kaiser Franz Joseph. Many different races and peoples were united under the Habsburg crown in a supranational empire, the

The first automobile of my father, Ferdinand Porsche. Built in 1900 when he was working for Lohner, it was called the Lohner-Wagen. It was powered by two electric engines each developing 2.5 PS (1 PS = 0.9863 HP), and located in and directly driving the front wheels. The range was short because of the problem of storing sufficient energy capacity.

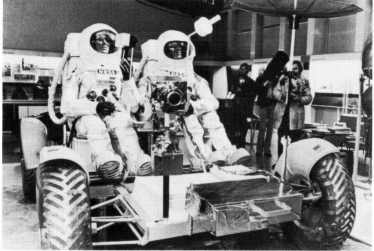

Four electrical wheel hub motors were the characteristic mode of propulsion of the Lohner-Porsche racing car designed by my father. This car was acquired in September 1900 by the English gentleman E.W. Hart for 15,000 French Francs. The photo shows my father, the designer, and Mr Hart at the controls. The same mode of propulsion was applied to the American 'moon car' driven on the moon by astronauts Scott and Irwin in July 1971.

like of which was never to be achieved again. For me personally, the Austro-Hungarian Empire as it existed at that time was a sort of precursor of a United States of Europe. Unfortunately the politicians responsible for the Treaties of Versailles and St Germain did not understand that. In any event, it was in what I would call the secure atmosphere of the period before the First World War that I was born on 19 September 1909 in Wiener–Neustadt.

At that time my father held the position of technical director at the Austro Daimler company; he was later to be appointed to the board of this company. Austro Daimler had grown out of a mechanical engineering company founded in 1865 by the Fischer brothers. Gottlieb Daimler himself conducted the preliminary negotiations which led eventually to the foundation of the Aus-

Right and below right
To improve the range of his cars, my father used a 28 PS Mercedes petrol engine driving a dynamo producing the energy for the electrical engines in the front wheels. The photo shows him behind the steering wheel of his car in 1902 during the Exelberg hill-climb in Austria, in which he won his class, and came third overall. His co-driver was Mr Lohner.

Below My father in 1909, the year in which I, his only son, was born. He was director of the Austrian subsidiary of Daimler-Motoren-Gesellschaft mbH. The factory was located at Wiener-Neustadt.

trian Daimler Motor Company Bierenz, Fischer & Co, which was set up to 'introduce the production of automobiles into the factories of Fischer Brothers in Wiener–Neustadt'. That was in 1899. In 1900 Gottlieb Daimler died.

His son Paul took over as technical manager of this Austrian company, until in 1906 he was succeeded by my father, at which time the company began to undertake its own development projects. As technical director, my father strengthened the company's commitment to automobiles, but he also got involved in the construction of racing cars, which for him was a real challenge for the engineer.

The most important model of the automobile programme at that time was a four-cylinder, 30 hp car known by the beautiful name of Maja. This model had of course nothing to do with Bonsel's

Above An important model in the Austro-Daimler range was the 'Maja' with a four-cylinder engine of 30 PS. The car was designed by my father in 1906.

Left Ferdinand Porsche behind the steering wheel of the Austro-Daimler he designed for the Prinz-Heinrich-Fahrt in 1910. He won the race against strong opposition from the original Daimler company.

famous book *The Maya Bee*; rather it was named after the daughter of the Austrian businessman Consul Emil Jellinek, who lived in Nice and sold cars to rich people on the Côte d'Azur. Emil Jellinek was a major buyer of Daimler and Austro Daimler cars. He also took part in motor races, driving under the pseudonym 'Mercedes'; his youngest and favourite daughter was Mercedes Adrienne Manuela Romana Jellinek. On 7 July 1903, he was even granted official permission by the Municipal District Office for the First Borough of the Imperial and Royal City of Vienna to call himself Jellinek-Mercedes. He then began to use his daughter's first name as a trademark for the Daimler cars that he imported. Even the Daimler Motor Company in Stuttgart-Untertürkheim took over this designation for the vehicles that it produced itself, which were henceforth known as Mercedes. After the merger of Daimler and

Benz the cars produced by the new company were known as Mercedes-Benz, a trademark which has been maintained until the present day.

Maja, on the other hand, was one of Jellinek-Mercedes's older daughters, but the name never gained widespread acceptance as a designation for the cars produced by Austro Daimler. This was hardly surprising after the father had officially added the name of his youngest daughter to his own name, the family name! In 1909, my father used the Maja as the basis for a new 32 hp model fitted with a four-speed gearbox.

On Sunday 19 September, my father was driving this car, which succeeded the Maja, in the Semmering Hillclimb, a famous racing event of the period, and consequently was not able to be present at my birth. He finished first in his class that day, although the overall winner was the famous Swabian Christian Lautenschlager in a Mercedes. However, on his return home, my father was greeted by a much more valuable prize, a son, who was christened Ferdinand Anton Ernst: Ferdinand was my father's name, Anton was my grandfather's name and Ernst was my mother's brother.

In the same year, my father had also driven the successor to the Maja in the famous Prince Henry Trials. He was one member of a team which also included Fischer, the director of Austro Daimler, and Hugo Boos-Waldeck, who was an Austrian like Fischer. This race had been brought into being by Prince Heinrich of Prussia, who was a motor racing enthusiast. In 1909 the race started in Berlin and went via Wroclaw, Tatrafüred, Budapest, Vienna and Salzburg to Munich, a total distance of 1,149.4 miles (1,849.3 km). Although the Austro Daimler team did not actually win the race, it finished without any penalty points but was still placed well down the field. This was no comfort to my father. He went to Untertürkheim and suggested to the Daimler engineers that since the Daimler Motor Company still had an interest in Austro Daimler they should jointly build a car for the 1910 race. Shortly after the 1909 failure my father had already produced some new ideas for a new car. However, the Daimler engineers rode the high horse and said, 'No, no, we'll develop our own car and you design *your* own!'

My father returned to Wiener–Neustadt and designed a four-seater touring car which had an 86 hp engine and a top speed of 87 mph (140 km/h). For the Prince Henry trials, which favoured sporty touring cars, 17 special trials were announed in which the decisive criterion was to be the speed attained. The race lasted from 2 to 8 June and was contested over a distance of 1,215.3 miles (1,955.4 km). There was nothing less than a sensation when the Austro Daimler team, which consisted of my father, Herr Fischer and Heinrich Graf Schönfeld, took the first three places in that order in the overall classification. Pilette, in seventh position, was the best Mercedes driver and Fritz Erle for Benz was fifth. This victory had a very favourable effect on sales of Austro Daimler cars. Incidentally, the first prize in this important event still occupies a place of honour in my house.

It was in this world of the automobile that I grew up. Even as a small boy I felt attracted to cars. When we went out for a ride, my father drove and I sat on my mother's lap next to him in the co-driver's seat, picturing myself steering with an imaginary wheel in front of me. The reader might think that a little crazy, but it does indicate an early fixation with cars!

All in all, I had a wonderful childhood, on which I look back with pleasure. We lived very close to the Austro Daimler factory and scarcely a day went past when I did not wander around the factory.

I enjoyed almost complete freedom of movement in a world which interested, indeed fascinated, me from a very early age. I much preferred to spend my time in the factory rather than doing my schoolwork. I was very friendly with all the foremen and had access to all the workshops. On Sundays, for example, my father always used to go to the drawing office in the factory and he would often take me with him. Most people would have assumed that a little boy of my age would have preferred to go out to play on a Sunday, but these visits to the factory never bored me at all, although the adults who used to discuss technical matters with my father were of the opinion that 'the lad doesn't understand a word'. In fact, I understood a great deal of what was discussed. By dint of listening and examining, I eventually learned to 'read' a technical drawing, and consequently, I never actually had to study the skill formally. I could just do it and was capable of saying precisely this is an engine cross-section, that's a piston rod, that's the piston, the crankshaft and so on. I just absorbed it all through my daily contact with engineering. This proximity to the factory also meant that I gradually acquired a good eye for practical solutions, an ability which was to benefit me greatly in later life.

I was the youngest member of the family, with a sister five years older than me named Louise, after my mother. I had been given my father's name, Ferdinand, but I was known to everyone as Ferdy, a name which my governess, a Viennese lady called Edith Reichmann, did not like at all. Many years later, my future wife, whom I had already met, said to an Austrian girl friend, 'I've met an Austrian called Ferdy!', to which her friend replied, 'Every shoemaker's lad in our area is called Ferdy!' Thus the objections of Edith Reichmann and the experience of my future wife led to Ferdy being changed to Ferry, which it has remained to this very day.

Despite my fixation with my father, whose work meant he could offer everything that might inspire a young lad, I was very closely attached to my mother, particularly when I was very young. I was what is generally called a 'mummy's boy'. I loved my mother very much, and that remained true throughout the rest of my life.

I must admit that I did not enjoy school. When the time came for my name to be put down for this institution, my mother took me there and since we were a very well-known family in the town it was the headmaster himself who dealt with us. A birth certificate was of course required for the purposes of registration, which my mother gave to the headmaster, who said, 'Very good, Frau Porsche, just leave this with me and I'll lock it up until school begins.' However, I misunderstood the headmaster and thought he was referring to me! Since school did not begin for another four weeks, I was stricken by panic at the thought of having to endure a whole month in this austere, unwelcoming school building and began to sob uncontrollably. Neither my mother nor the headmaster had the slightest idea why the tears were suddenly flowing, and it was some time before they were able to ascertain the reason for my distress.

When I started school, the First World War had already broken out. I was too young to experience this tragic era in any conscious way, but the increased military activity could not fail to make an impression on me. I can remember that we could hear the thundering of artillery on the Austro-Italian front while on holiday in Badgastein, and the thunder of more artillery could indeed be heard from the southern mountain ridges in Naßfeld above the Gastein valley. The war even made itself felt in school as an increasing number of teachers were called up for military service. This led very soon to a teacher shortage, and in the end two classes had to be combined in the same classroom, which of course created problems. It once happened, for example, that Class Four had an essay to write while Class Five had geography on the timetable; the subject of their lesson was Hamburg. I myself had an essay to write. For this purpose, there was a picture of a dancing bear, the subject of our essay, hanging on the blackboard. We had to write a letter to a friend relating an encounter with a dancing bear on the way home from school. However, Hamburg fascinated me much more than the dancing bear, and I completely forgot about the essay until the last minute. With great presence of mind I wrote,

'Dear Max,
On the way home from school I saw a dancing bear. I'll tell you more about it in my next letter!
Yours Ferry.'

My teacher naturally considered this a little brief and I was given a very low mark. Max incidentally was our gardener's son.

This shows that I was more interested in geography than German. As a small boy I found atlases fascinating, preferring them to any picture book, and I used to pore over the various maps, visualizing in my imagination all the far-away places depicted there. However, my favourite subject was mathematics. I found it very easy and was always able to finish my homework before the end of school.

I have particularly strong memories of two events that took place during the war. In the vicinity of Wiener–Neustadt there was a munitions factory which was blown up twice, taking off the roofs and shattering the window panes into tiny pieces. The next catastrophe to hit the town was a whirlwind which caused great loss of life and much damage to property.

In 1918, when the war came to an end, we all faced a new situation as Austria became a republic. The victorious powers demanded reparations, which led to considerable restrictions. The production lines at the factory had to be converted from military to civilian use. However, this led to considerable job losses; in the last year of the war there were 6,000 people working at the factory, although some of these were prisoners of war. Incidentally, the future Yugoslavian president Tito worked at Austro Daimler, under his civilian name of Josip Broz. He joined the company in 1912 and was employed as a driver running in cars. In his autobiography Tito gives a positive assessment of this period and speaks with great respect of my father. He was conscripted at the beginning of 1913.

The great Austro-Hungarian Empire had been replaced by a small country whose industry was now dependent to a considerable extent on exports. Immediately after the end of the war there were still a lot of exciting experiences for a boy of my age. The factory was occupied by the so-called Arbeiterwehr or Workers' Resistance, but since my father had always had good relations with his workers he had no problems. On the contrary, the Workers' Resistance even put a guard on our house in order to guarantee our safety in this turbulent period. Members of the Workers' Resistance wore armbands in the Austrian national colours of red, white and red, worn in such a way that only the red was visible. This was a clear indication of the direction in which politics was heading.

My father's birthplace, Maffersdorf in Bohemia, was now in the state of Czechoslovakia which had been newly created by the peace treaties of Versailles and St Germain. This was actually a purely German area which had previously belonged to Austria-Hungary. I should also point out that in pre-war times there was no overt nationalism. There were, for example, school exchange programmes which enabled young Czechs to spend their school holidays in German families and young Germans to stay with Czech families. My father also spent his school holiday in a Czech

Myself, Ferdinand Anton Ernst, known as Ferry, in 1914 in a Scottish costume which my father brought me as a present from one of his trips to Britain.

family where he learned their language. Prejudices and barriers on both sides were broken down, and the extravagant, often radical, nationalism of the post-war period was a phenomenon that my father could not understand at all.

If my father had refused to become a Czechoslovakian citizen, not only would his parents' property have been sequestered, but he would also have lost the opportunity of travelling abroad again immediately after the war. As an Austrian, he would have been one of those who had lost the war. Thus, for example, it would not have been possible for him to go to Paris, where the most important international automobile exhibition, the Paris Salon, took place in the Grand Palais. For the technical director and, since 1917, general manager of an automobile factory, but particularly for an engineer as closely involved as my father was with the development of the motor car, the opportunity to attend such an important exhibition was absolutely essential. Moreover, my father felt that Maffersdorf was his native territory, the place where he felt at home, and that he should not change his allegiance to this part of the former Austro-Hungarian Empire as he might change his shirt.

The first passenger car that Austro Daimler put into series production after the war was a six-cylinder model with a cubic capacity of 4.4 litres and an output of 60 hp; it was a sporty car that sold well abroad and brought in precious foreign currency. This foreign currency was the cause of the first serious tensions between the shareholders and my father which were to lead later to a parting of the ways. My father held the view that the foreign

Alfred Neubauer (later to become the well-known racing director of Daimler-Benz), when working for Austro-Daimler after the First World War, behind the steering wheel of the elegant Austro-Daimler model 17/60 PS, designed by my father.

Myself at the age of 11 in my own automobile, built for me by my father for Christmas 1920.

currency belonged to the company. This was understandable, since the accumulation of capital was a prerequisite for further investment. However, the shareholders were of the opinion that this foreign currency belonged to them.

It was during this period that my dream of having my own car was fulfilled. I had of course already secretly learned to drive, since there were always opportunities for 'manoeuvring' a car on the factory premises or in the garage at home. The great surprise came at Christmas 1920, when I was eleven. My father had had a small car made for me, an open two-seater with an air-cooled, two-cylinder, four-stroke engine. The family had naturally been secretive about it, and whenever I broached the subject of cars, they would always explain, 'You're not getting a car, you're having a goat and cart!' Everybody except me knew all about it. But then it happened: the car was placed in the entrance hall of our house where the Christmas tree was. The wheels had to be taken off before it could be taken through the front door, a task entrusted to Josef Goldinger, my father's driver and a sort of factotum for all of us. As he was taking the wheels off, the wrench fell out of his hands. My sister and I were of course forbidden to go into the entrance hall, where the presents were heaped up, until the time came for them to be distributed. But we pricked up our ears, and the sound of the falling wrench was a sign for me that the eagerly coveted car was indeed awaiting me, but all I said was, 'Aha, they're assembling the goat cart.'

On the day after the distribution of the presents, the first day of Christmas, the two-seater was taken outside again, the wheels put back on, the engine started, and, much to my father's astonishment, I drove off immediately in my new car. He certainly hadn't reckoned on that!

The car had its peculiarities. There were no car tyres made that

21

would fit the size of wheel used, so motor cycle tyres had to be fitted. However, these tyres did not behave on the wheel rims in the same way as car tyres. The two-seater had no differential, which meant that the two powered rear wheels always revolved on bends at the same speed, with the result that the front wheels pushed outwards, forcing the tyres off the wheels. I tried to correct this by using six tyre stretchers instead of the customary three. This did improve the behaviour of the car when cornering, but total success remained elusive. However, the absent differential had another advantage. My father used to go hunting, and we had a hunting cabin in the mountains. Whenever we went there in winter, the other ordinary cars became stuck in the snow, while my small car was able to grind its way through the snow to the cabin.

Since my car had to be fitted with the best equipment there was, the ribbed racing spark plugs naturally impressed me a great deal and I wanted to have them fitted to my 3.5 hp engine. However, racing spark plugs are designed for considerably higher operating temperatures than my engine attained, with the result that the racing spark plugs were constantly oiling up. My car, which was fitted with a two-speed gear box, had a leather cone clutch that often leaked at the flywheel and then began to slip. I increased the friction by the simple expedient of putting sand into the clutch, which made it work properly again. Incidentally, the gear box had no reverse.

My car was not registered and therefore had no number plate, but I drove it not only round the factory but also in Wiener–Neustadt and policemen used to turn away whenever I went past. Everything was very relaxed in Austria, and I certainly noticed

The Austro-Daimler Sascha, a small car designed by my father and described by Neubauer as a forerunner of the Volkswagen. This car was only ever built for racing, because Porsche could not get permission to make it into a production car.

In its first year, on 2 April 1922, the Sascha was very successful in the famous Targa Florio in Sicily. Here the team is welcomed at the factory on returning from the race. The third boy from the left is myself.

the difference later when I went to Germany.

The Austro Daimler company continued to produce large, prestigious cars, but my father was developing the idea of a small car, a type of vehicle which was growing in popularity in post-war Europe. The reasons for this were partly economic, but there was also a desire to make the motor car accessible to a wider range of people. The Austro Daimler management was not prepared to change its model policy, but eventually expressed its readiness to allow my father to produce a small series of this vehicle in the form of a racing and sports car. This was the origin of the Sascha,

Count Alexander 'Sascha' Kolowrat seated in the small car he inspired Porsche to design.

which had a 1.1 litre, four-cylinder engine. The Sascha was named after a good friend of my father, Count Sascha Kolowrat, who worked in the film industry and was very enthusiastic about my father's idea of producing a small car. It was he who suggested the development of a sports car along the same lines, and the small racing and sports car which finally appeared in 1922 bore his name.

In its first year of manufacture, the Sascha took part in the famous Targa Florio in Sicily, which was at the time probably the most demanding road race, where it was small in comparison with the competition. A former artillery officer in the Austro-Hungarian army by the name of Alfred Neubauer drove a version of the Sascha, with its cubic capacity increased to 1.5 litres, in the racing car class; he finished in sixth place in this class against the 4.5 litre 1914 Grand Prix Mercedes driven by the winner Masetti. Neubauer came eighteenth in the overall classification, ahead of his team-mates Kuhn and Pöcher who won the category for production cars up to 1,100 cm in the 1.1. litre Sascha. In the overall classification, Kuhn came twentieth and Pöcher twenty-second. This was undoubtedly a great success for the new model.

Neubauer's organisational talent had persuaded my father to take him on at Austro Daimler. He was later to become famous as the Daimler-Benz racing manager.

Incidentally, Alfred Neubauer later publicly expressed the opinion that the Sascha was a sort of forerunner of the Volkswagen. From the point of view of the basic idea underlying this vehicle, he may well have been right.

The four-cylinder engine had an overhead camshaft driven by a vertical shaft and spur gears and in the racing version must have achieved a maximum power output of about 50 hp. Its top speed was 90 mph (144.8 km/h), measured over 1 km with a flying start. Just as it is today, motor racing at that time not only challenged engineers to produce their best but was also a common practice which helped the manufacturers' names to become internationally known. Mercedes, Fiat and Peugeot were just three of the manufacturers involved in motor racing.

Although the Sascha was a success as a racing and sports car, the touring version that my father developed was never produced. At that time, the economic situation in Austria was very critical, inflation was rampant, and the small country, which would have liked to rely on Germany, its larger neighbour, had to grapple with some serious problems. Even Austro Daimler was not unaffected by these difficulties, and the creative and technical freedom that my father had enjoyed hitherto was to be considerably curtailed. However, my father was not the type to allow himself to be constrained within narrow limits. The matter of the precious foreign currency, which had in his view been wrongly used, finally pushed him into leaving Austro Daimler.

At the Daimler-Motoren-Gesellschaft (Daimler Motor Company) in Stuttgart, Paul Daimler, the son of Gottlieb Daimler and head of the central drawing office, had fallen out with the supervisory board and left the company at short notice. This was happening at about the same time that my father was having difficulties with the supervisory board of Austro Daimler. The Daimler Motor Company then offered him the post of technical director in charge of the central drawing office, together with a seat on the board. My father accepted the offer, although he was not able to free himself from his obligations at Austro Daimler and take up his new job in Germany until April 1923.

This of course meant a move for the whole family from Wiener–Neustadt to Stuttgart. I was just 13 years old when I went to Stuttgart for the first time in January 1923, and in the September of that year the whole family finally settled there. We lived in a small house that my father had rented in the Parler Straße, close to the Feuerbacher Weg, where we were very soon to purchase our own house. The move was not without difficulties for me. For a start, I was not allowed to drive my little car in Stuttgart: German thoroughness meant it was unthinkable to make an exception for me. In any case, I had already been granted a special licence for a small motor cycle, which was not normally given until the age of 17.

School was another problem. The curricula in Wiener–Neustadt and the Stuttgart area were completely different. I went to school in Bad Cannstatt on the recommendation of an acquaintance of my father, a retired teacher at the Gottlieb Daimler School in Cannstatt. The curriculum at the Daimler school included English, which had not featured at all on the curriculum in Wiener–Neustadt, so I had private tuition in order to be able to catch up on what I had missed.

Cannstatt was quite a long way from the Parler Straße and my father always took me to school on his way to the factory in Unter-türkheim. One day we had a problem with one of the tyres on the car and I was late for school. When I apologized for my lateness, the teacher said sarcastically, 'If you had come by tram instead of by car there would have been no problem!'

He was my 'favourite' teacher, of all people, but from now on we were at daggers drawn. A week later, the class was on time for their lesson: only the teacher — my favourite teacher — was missing. He was very late in arriving, and when he came in he said, 'You must excuse my lateness, but there was a power cut and the tram could not move! Please sit down.' Everybody sat down, except me; I remained standing and stared at him. Then he said, 'Porsche, I know exactly what you're thinking. Sit down!' Even then, there were always people who saw greater advantages in suburban transport systems than in cars, with all the independence they offer.

They were difficult times. Inflation was soaring unchecked. In July 1923 one dollar was worth 354.00 Marks; by August it had risen to 4.6 million and when inflation reached its peak in October 1923 one US dollar cost no less than 25 billion Marks. One day I was given 10 million Marks for my tram fare to school. That was enough to get me into town but I did not have enough money for the return journey and had to walk home.

In the meantime, the builders were making good progress with our house in the Feuerbacher Weg. It had been designed by the architects Paul Bonatz and Fritz Scholer, who had also drawn up the plans for the new central station in Stuttgart. We moved into the new house on 13 December, and although we were not exactly superstitious, we moved in over two days so that the whole move

Below and bottom
When Technical Director of Daimler in Stuttgart from 1923 onwards, my father carried out improvements to the supercharged 120 PS, with which Christian Werner won the famous Targa Florio in 1924.

did not take place on the 13th.

My father was already working flat out at the Daimler Motor Company in Untertürkheim when on 30 May 1924 a Daimler works team took part in the famous 500 mile race at Indianapolis in the USA. My father had not of course had any influence on the technical development of the cars used in the race, since the team was already on its way to America when he took up his job. Unfortunately the team did not achieve the success that had been expected. There had been problems with the exhaust valves on the supercharged 2 litre car, so although Max Sailer was the best-placed European, his Mercedes only achieved eighth position in the overall classification, while his team colleague Christian Werner finished in eleventh place.

This was disappointing for Daimler, since Mercedes had already won at Indianapolis: in 1915, during the war, the Italian Ameri-

Left and below left The Großmutter (Grandmother), the 1914 Mercedes Grand Prix car, with which Lautenschlager won the French Grand Prix in 1914. My father fitted the car with a supercharger, and Rosenberger raced it with great success in the 1920s.

27

Above and below Also at Daimler, my father designed the eight-cylinder 2 litre Mercedes as a Grand Prix car and/or a sports car. With this car the famous Rudolf Caracciola won the German Grand Prix on the AVUS at Berlin in 1926.

can Ralph de Palma had taken first place in a 1914 Grand Prix car. He won the 500 mile race with an average speed of 72 mph (115.8 km/h), while Sailer's average speed in 1923 was still only about 80 mph (129 km/h).

My father immediately started further development work on the 2 litre supercharged racing car, and in 1924 the Mercedes took the first three places in the overall classification in the Targo Florio; Christian Werner was first, Christian Lautenschlager second and Alfred Neubauer third.

He was particularly pleased by the car's performance in the Semmering race on 14 September of the same year. Not only did Werner take first place, achieving the best time on the day and setting a new record, but there were also victories in the touring car class over 4.5 litres and the racing car class over 3 litres. This last victory was won by Otto Salzer in the Grandmother, the nick-

name given to the 1914 Grand Prix racing car whose four-cylinder engine with four valves per cylinder produced 115 hp. He also set a new record for the class. The Grandmother, fitted with a supercharger, was to emerge again three years later.

The new Rentenmark had been introduced on 15 November 1923, immediately becoming legal tender at an exchange rate of 4.2 billion paper Marks to 1 Rentenmark. This provided the foundation on which the German economy slowly began to recover.

During his time at Daimler my father developed a number of outstanding sports cars which were to become famous throughout the world. The first of these, an eight-cylinder supercharged racing car, appeared in 1923, to be followed a year later by a six-cylinder touring car, also with supercharger. Subsequent models included the Type 200 Stuttgart and Mannheim and the six-cylinder K sports car with supercharger. With the supercharged

Another famous car designed by my father for Daimler was the Mercedes-Benz S with a six-cylinder super-charged engine of 6.8 litres.

The eight-cylinder in-line engine with supercharger designed by my father when working as Technical Director for Daimler.

29

Above The Mercedes-Benz S, designed by my father, on the start of the first race on the Nürburgring in June 1927. Winner Caracciola drove car number 1, and Adolf Rosenberger in car number 2 finished second.

Below Another famous Mercedes-Benz designed by my father was the model SSK, a sports car with a supercharged engine of 225 PS.

Model S, my father laid the foundation for a series which eventually led via the Types SS and SSK to the SSKL, which appeared in 1931. The S series was particularly successful in racing and, with drivers such as Rudolf Caracciola, Christian Werner, Otto Merz, Manfred von Brauchitsch, Adolf Rosenberger and Hans Stuck, achieved many important international successes for Daimler and, subsequently, Daimler-Benz.

In 1927 my father brought the Grandmother back to life as a Mercedes racing car. In 1914 this racing car, designed by Paul Daimler, had taken the first three places in the Grand Prix of the French Automobile Club, with Christian Lautenschlager taking first place. My father fitted the 4.5 litre four-cylinder engine with a supercharger and entered it in several mountain races. Adolf Rosenberger achieved several victories with this car, including, on 22 May 1927, the Hercules Mountain Race (best time of the day), the Hohe Wurzel race on 26 May and on 6 and 7 August the

ADAC's Freiburg Bergrekord on the Schauinsland; for this last race, the 4.5 litre supercharged engine was fitted in the chassis of the 2 litre racing car and recorded the day's best time. Finally, on 13 and 14 August, he won the Klausenpass Race in Switzerland, setting a new record in the process.

This gave me the opportunity of personally driving many of these interesting cars and getting to know their technical peculiarities. When I took my driving test on 11 November 1925 — I had reached the age of 16 on 19 September — the examiner left out the technical questions. All I had to do was drive a short stretch with the official driving instructor next to me, which of course I did without any difficulty at all. Indeed, the examiner stated I had a talent for driving. Of course this driving licence also was granted to me only with special permission since I was still under 18.

Today, more than 60 years later, I can at last admit that I did indeed drive a car before I had passed my driving test. It was on one of these outings that I had my first accident, although luckily little harm was done. I had been on good terms with Alfred Neubauer, the future Mercedes racing manager, when he was head of the running-in department in Wiener–Neustadt. Naturally I continued to cultivate this friendship even after he moved to Mercedes in Stuttgart, in order to be invited to the test drives for which he was also responsible at Daimler.

One day, I think it was in 1924, it was announced that test drives would be held at Kniebis in the Black Forest. A 45 hp Mercedes, prepared for competition, in which the petrol supply operated by means of negative pressure, had suffered engine damage caused by the formation of vapour bubbles in the fuel system. The aim of the test drives was to determine the cause of the problem.

One of the highlights of my father's career was when Mercedes finished first, second and third in 1926 with the model SSK in his local race on the Semmering. Winner in this hill-climb was Caracciola shown here.

31

Neubauer took me with him on the drive and on the way home allowed me to take the steering wheel. On the way we had several problems with the tyres, with the result that all four wheels were shod with studded tyres. On the sharp cobblestones of which roads at that time were made these tyres slid about as if on ice, and extreme caution was required.

Between Böblingen and Stuttgart we came out of a bend and saw in front of us an empty timber transporter coming towards us on the wrong side of the road. Since the trailer was not carrying any wood, the wheels were pushed together so that a long shaft projected from the back of the cart. When the driver saw us coming he pulled his horses across to the right-hand side of the road, blocking the road completely. I braked very gingerly, but in his anxiety Neubauer grabbed hold of the steering wheel and steered the car off the road to our right. At the side of the road, however, there was a high earth bank which merged into a field overgrown with grass and crossed by deep drainage channels. Neubauer's sudden movement caused the car to turn round, hit the bank at the side of the road and turn over. Fortunately we landed in one of the drainage channels and were unhurt, and even the windscreen, which we had put down shortly before, remained intact. So we put the car back on its wheels and drove home. Neubauer believed of course that his intervention had saved the situation, but I thought that if he had not seized hold of the steering wheel, we would not have turned over.

This reminds me of an experience with my sister Louise, who was herself an enthusiastic driver and at that time even took part in events with the Daimler team. I once brought home an interesting Mercedes which my sister was keen to drive. I gave her the key and said, 'You must be careful when you're driving that car, the carburettor's got a hole in it!', to which she replied, 'Is anything likely to happen?' Well, nothing happened, but even then carburettors were already creating problems.

The boards of the Daimler Motor Company and Benz & Co Ltd, which had combined in 1924 in order to exploit a 'community of interests', decided on 5 May 1925 to set up a joint design office. This new institution was headed jointly by Hans Nibel, the long-serving design chief at the Benz factories in Mannheim and my father, the technical director at Daimler. Nibel was a native of Moravia while my father came from Bohemia, so the two were virtually compatriots. It was always unlikely that two such strong-willed personalities with sometimes divergent opinions on technical matters could work together successfully for any length of time.

On 28 June 1926 the two firms Benz and Daimler merged to form Daimler-Benz AG. My father did not extend his contract with the new company and left Daimler-Benz AG on 31 December 1928.

He did not accept the consultancy contract that was offered to him, although he never actually severed his connections with the Stuttgart company.

In the meantime, my father had received an offer from the Austrian company Steyr to become technical manager, with a seat on the board. At that time the Steyr factory was the largest automobile factory in Austria. It had developed out of the J.u.F. Werndl company which had started out as an armaments manufacturer; at the suggestion of government departments the company had started in 1916 to produce aero engines. Even during the war, Werndl, probably as a result of its involvement in aero engines, had begun to show an interest in cars. After the end of the war the idea was developed further and the company eventually entered the automobile industry. Their first car came onto the market in 1920, and in the meantime Steyr had even outstripped Austro Daimler. The company produced everything, from castings to coachwork, in-house, which gave it a considerable competitive advantage over its rivals.

My father's move from Daimler-Benz to Steyr was greeted with great enthusiasm by the Austrian media, particularly the technical press.

For my part, I had left the school in Bad Cannstatt after the first public examination and begun a practical training course with the Bosch company in Stuttgart, which I enjoyed very much. While at Bosch I met Manfred Behr, a young man of my own age who had the same interest in engineering that I had. We understood each other so well that we formed a close friendship that has lasted until the present day. His father had set up his own company, the Süddeutsche Kühlerfabrik Julius Fr. Behr, Stuttgart, which produces air-conditioning plant, radiators and similar equipment, principally for the motor industry.

Manfred Behr and I also shared sporting interests, such as skiing. We developed a special form of this sport which involved being towed on our skis by a car at speeds in excess of 40 mph (64 km/h). In this way we developed a sort of ski-joring by car. My training with Bosch lasted a year, by which time I had turned 18 and could now acquire a normal licence for cars and motor cycles. This gave me the opportunity to change over from the large touring car which was at our disposition to a sportier form of transport, namely a 500 cc BMW motorcycle.

My father's new job with Steyr meant of course a change of residence for the family. We rented our house in the Feuerbacher Weg to Dr Hans Nibel, my father's successor at Daimler-Benz AG.

My father insisted that I should complete a proper course of training, and to this end I was to attend the Institute of Technology in Vienna. Firstly, however, I had to pass the final school-leaving examination, and in order to do so I went to a private school in

Myself on a test drive with the very advanced Steyr XXX (30) in 1929, in which light alloy was used for the 2 litre six-cylinder engine. Also new technically was the self-supporting body.

Vienna where I lodged with my sister Louise, who had married the Viennese lawyer Dr Anton Piëch in 1928.

As I have already said, I never particularly liked school, but since the Steyr factory was not very far from Vienna I could spend every weekend there and share in my father's work. This made my studying in Vienna easier for me, since working in a car factory has always fascinated me.

Under my father's management, Steyr brought out a new model in 1929. It was a 2-litre car with an overhead-valve engine and independent wheel suspension. This was followed by a 5.3 litre eight-cylinder model, also with an overhead-valve engine which produced 100 hp.

My father himself drove this elegant five-seater drophead coupé to the Paris Salon which took place in October in the Grand Palais in the French capital.

While my father was in Paris, interesting things had been happening in Vienna. In the wake of the financial collapse in New

York, the Österreichische Boden-Credit-Anstalt, which was virtually the Steyr house bank, had gone into bankruptcy and been taken over by the Credit-Anstalt. This was the bank with which Austro Daimler had an association, but the representatives of this bank were the real reason why my father had left Austro Daimler in 1922. Inevitably, my father's room for manoeuvre was considerably reduced. The result was that Steyr was able only to pursue a limited programme, namely the manufacture of cheaper cars, while Austro Daimler produced the larger models. This of course heralded the end of such fine cars as the eight-cylinder drophead coupé, which, incidentally, had been sold under the name of Austria.

However, my father was not a man to allow himself to be hemmed in in this way and he terminated his three-year contract with Steyr after just one year. At all events, my weekend visits to my father at Steyr had been important for my later development. The fact that Steyr produced so much in-house naturally offered such a committed technical designer as my father great opportunities for new developments. During the period that my father was responsible for technical development, Steyr began to produce light-metal castings in ingot moulds. Thus the crankcase for the 2 litre six-cylinder engine was manufactured by Steyr in this way. This also opened the door for the use of light metals in mass production. Similarly, the Steyr Type XXX was a forerunner of a new design, namely the self-supporting method of construction; although the car had a frame to which the bodywork was attached, there was no longer an actual chassis frame. This was a fundamentally new concept in automobile design.

3

The return to Stuttgart

After his departure from Steyr, my father naturally thought very carefully about the path he should now pursue. He received offers from Skoda, the well-known Czech company, and from General Motors, but in the end he decided to go it alone and set up his own design company. My father of course discussed his plans with his former colleagues, particularly with our designer Karl Rabe, his oldest colleague, whom he had taken on at Austro Daimler in 1913. Herr Rabe thought it was a good idea for my father to set up his own business and he declared himself ready to join him in the new venture.

Father also consulted me and in the course of our discussions Stuttgart was mentioned as a location for the new company, which, with Mannheim, was after all the birthplace of the automobile. Stuttgart had many things in its favour. Firstly, it occupied a fairly central position in Europe, and all the important industrial countries were readily accessible. Also, at that time there were many factories there manufacturing either cars or parts for the motor industry. They were all potential customers and offered the possibility of rapid solutions to development problems.

For me personally, there was another reason for preferring Stuttgart. In 1927 I had met my future wife there. She was a native of Stuttgart and her name was Dorothea Reitz; I called her Dodo.

The decision was eventually made in favour of Stuttgart, where we already owned a house on the Feuerbacher Weg. We found premises for the offices and design department of the new company at 24 Kronenstraße in the north of Stuttgart. We moved in at the end of 1930, and on 25 April 1931 the new company was entered in the commercial register as Dr. Ing. h.c. F. Porsche GmbH, Konstruktionen und Beratungen für Motoren und Fahrzeugbau (Dr (honoris causa) Porsche Ltd, Design Office for Engines and Motor Vehicles), with its registered office in Stuttgart.

In addition to my father, who was managing director, and myself, the partners in the business included Adolf Rosenberger, the sales manager, senior engineer Karl Rabe, who was chief designer, Karl Fröhlich, who was in charge of gears and transmissions, Josef Kales (engines), Josef Zahradnik (chassis), Ghislaine Kaes (my father's secretary), Josef Goldinger (chief driver)

and Franz Sieberer (blueprints and duplication); later additions included Erwin Komenda (bodywork) and Josef Mickl (calculations).

The premises at 24 Kronenstraße, in the so-called Ulrichs-Haus, had a further advantage as far as I was concerned: in the immediate vicinity was the Lehrenkraus Café, which belonged to Dodo's mother, and later became a favourite meeting place for our engineers. Herr Mickl was a particularly frequent customer, since he discovered that the tables in the café were ideal for sketching new designs.

I had first met Dodo a few years earlier, in the summer of 1927, as I was travelling on a tram. I was on the rear platform of the first coach, and opposite me, on the platform of the second carriage, I saw two pretty young girls. One of them attracted me immediately. As soon as I set eyes on her, it was love at first sight. It was Dodo!

Later, she told me about her impressions of that first meeting. She had said at the time to her friend, pointing to me, 'Is that a Negro in front there?' Indeed I must have looked like an African on that day, since I had just come back from the Wörther See, where I had spent my summer holidays, and I was very suntanned.

Some time elapsed after this episode on the tram before I saw my adored one again. I met her one day by chance walking up

My father established a design office at Stuttgart with several of his old collaborators from Austro-Daimler and Steyr. Front row from left to right: Erwin Komenda, myself, Karl Rabe, Franz Reimspieß; second row from left: Franz Sieberer, Emil Saukup, Leopold Jänschke, Egon Forstner.

For the Wanderer company, in a very short time the new Porsche office designed the Wanderer W22 with a six-cylinder engine of 1.7 or 2 litres giving 35 or 40 PS respectively.

from the Helfferichstrasse to the Feuerbacher Weg, and I did something that I had never done before, something that at that time was even considered improper: I spoke to her. At any event, our first meeting on the tram must have made some impression on her, because she did not rebuff me. After we had walked a little way together, we parted without having arranged to see each other. I was determined to meet her again at the first opportunity, and lo and behold, one day I was driving my car into the city when I saw her walking down the Tazzelwurm (a street near the Feuerbacher Weg), violin case in hand. I stopped near her to ask whether I could give her a lift, and discovered she was on her way to school. She got in and I drove her to the Waldorfschule in the Kanonenweg. Naturally I enquired when school finished and was waiting at the appointed hour to pick her up. When she appeared, I suggested we should go to the funfair, but she said, 'I can't, I have to go home'; to which I replied, 'It'll take you three-quarters of an hour to get home by tram, so we can use that time to go to the fair and I'll drive you straight home!' She agreed to come with me. From then on we met regularly and became inseparable. In that year, 1927, Dodo was just 16 years old and I was 18.

But we must return to the design office in the Kronenstraße, where life was continuing.

My father had met up again with our chief designer, senior engineer Karl Rabe, when he went to Steyr. When he moved to Stuttgart to join the new company, he was never to leave us again; he continued to work for us until retirement and was a very valuable colleague of my father and later of myself.

In all, my father brought 12 of his old colleagues with him from Austria to Stuttgart. They formed a dedicated and highly-skilled team and under my father's proven management were ready to tackle even the most difficult tasks. Our team was further augmented by my brother-in-law, Dr Anton Piëch, who took over responsibility for the company's legal affairs.

The commencement of work in the Kronenstraße ushered in a new phase of my life, and from the very first day I devoted all my energies to the company. In addition, I was still receiving private tuition from Walter Boxan, an engineer who had also worked for the Steyr Group, who taught me the basic concepts of mechanics, physics and so on; in short everything that a designer needed and that I should actually have learnt at the Institute of Technology in Vienna. I had had to abandon my studies there because of my father's early departure from Steyr. From the very beginning in the Kronenstraße I stood at my drawing board and designed, so that I was involved in all the development work that was handled there.

Most of my colleagues were Austrians who were all to play an important role in the history of the Porsche company. The only person missing from our team was Alfred Neubauer, who had accompanied my father from Austro Daimler to Daimler and had remained at Daimler-Benz in Untertürkheim when my father left at the end of 1928.

The new Porsche company had already received one commission when my father's plan to start out on his own had become public knowledge. This commission came from the Wanderer company which had its headquarters in Chemnitz in Saxony, and for which we were to develop a medium-size car with a six-cylinder engine of between 1.7 and 2 litres cubic capacity and an output of 35 to 40 hp. One week before Christmas in 1930 we began the engineering drawings for this model and we were able to deliver them to Wanderer in Chemnitz, complete with parts list, on 1 April 1931.

Since our house at 48 Feuerbacher Weg was still rented to Daimler-Benz and Dr Hans Nibel was still living there, we leased a house in the Schoderstraße, which was not far from our own property. At the same time we were designing another model for Wanderer with an in-line eight-cylinder engine and a cubic capacity of 3.25 litres; this order had come at the same time as that for the 2 litre, six-cylinder car. We also developed a supercharged version of the eight-cylinder model. However, while prototypes of the first two models were built and the 2 litre car actually went into production, the supercharged version was never built.

In the meantime, Wanderer, Horch, Audi and DKW had merged to form Auto Union AG, in which new group, it was Horch that built the larger cars, while the production of medium-size models

The new office also designed the Porsche model 12, a small car for the German Zündapp company. It was also a forerunner of the Volkswagen although it had a water-cooled, five-cylinder radial engine.

was allocated to Wanderer. Horch already had engineering plans for a prestigious eight-cylinder car; they had been drawn up by Paul Daimler, who had gone to Horch after leaving the Daimler Motor Company in Stuttgart-Untertürkheim.

Given the prevailing economic situation, the business in the Kronenstraße had got off to a relatively good start. One of the commissions was to develop a small car for Zündapp, who at that time produced only motor cycles but were keen to enter the automobile business because of a sharp fall in motor cycle sales. The car Zündapp had in mind was a sort of 'Volksauto', or 'people's car', as Herr Neumeyer, the owner of Zündapp, described it. The vehicle that we subsequently developed had a rear-mounted engine, with the gearbox in front of the rear axle, a streamlined body and a central chassis frame; I like to see it as a forerunner of the Volkswagen. The engine that my father proposed was a three- or four-cylinder, air-cooled opposed piston engine, but Zündapp gave preference to a five-cylinder, water-cooled radial engine which was rather too elaborate for a low-cost 'people's car'. Radial engines, albeit in an air-cooled version, are much used in aircraft. In the Zündapp, which was known as the Type 12 in the Porsche programme, the engine was fitted at an angle in order to keep the coefficient of drag as low as possible.

The engineering drawings for this 'people's car' were started before the end of 1931 and were finished by the spring of 1932, and three prototypes were then built for the trial stage. However, the economic situation in 1932 was extremely difficult, and it became apparent in the course of the year that Zündapp would not be able to raise the finance required to put the car into mass production. In the following year there was an upturn in the automobile industry, which had a knock-on effect on the motor cycle business. As a result, Zündapp decided to scrap its plans to go into automobile production.

Incidentally, in carrying out our first commissions as an independent design company, we hit upon some interesting solutions. The Wanderer six-cylinder engine and gearbox, for example, had a common oil supply, with the surplus oil from the gearbox being delivered back to the engine via the flywheel, which was shaped in such a way that when the oil was returned it had a centrifugal cleaning effect. If the engine was dismantled, it was possible to establish exactly how much dirt had been spun out by the centrifuge.

The Wanderer's clutch was not a dry clutch but was immersed in oil. On the one hand, this had the disadvantage that greater foot pressure was required to operate it, but on the other hand it did have the advantage of a longer service life. A lot of interesting things were developed at that time only to emerge again here and there years later. This reminds me of a saying of my father: 'Basically, you know, everything has always existed, you just have to look for it!'

My father was of course the central figure in the new company, and was able to motivate his colleagues. He could spend hours at the drawing board designing a new vehicle, and if he was particularly interested in solving a problem, he would not ask how late it was but would spend the whole night with his colleagues at the drawing board.

In public he was the dominant figure. His leadership was at that time undisputed. Even I had to get used to that. However, when we were alone I could contradict him and even suggest different solutions. He would listen patiently and take due note of my proposal if it was better than the design in progress.

In 1932 something happened which could have had a very decisive influence on the course of my life. Quite unexpectedly, my father received an invitation to go on a fact-finding trip to the Soviet Union. At first the invitation seemed so fantastic that we had great difficulty in taking it seriously. However, it was very soon made clear to us that it was all meant to be taken very seriously indeed. My father accepted the invitation and went on an exhaustive visit to the centres of the Soviet motor industry, including a tractor factory in Stalingrad. He was allowed to visit any factory that interested him, including aircraft factories as well as automobile plants. Never before had a foreigner been afforded such an insight into the new Soviet industry.

In Moscow, at the end of his trip, the Russians offered my father the position of national director of development and design for the Soviet motor industry. This was unquestionably a fascinating offer, particularly since all the advantages of a privileged person were attached to it. My father was to be allowed to take his family with him and would be given wide-ranging powers. However,

Much more in the style of Porsche was this model 32, another small car designed and developed for the German NSU factory. Even more of a Volkswagen forerunner, the photo shows the car in front of the building in the Kronenstraße, Stuttgart, where my father had established his new firm.

after much thought, my father declined the offer. The main reason behind his decision was the language barrier, which, combined with the enormous responsibilities of a very difficult job, seemed to him at the age of 57 insuperable. It is now well known that Stalin was at the time making strenuous efforts to advance the industrialization of the Soviet Union.

Before my father's visit to the Soviet Union, we had received another commission for the design of a small car from NSU in Neckarsulm, whose managing director at the time was Fritz von Falkenhayn. The commission laid down no limits on our technical ingenuity, which meant that we were able to put our own ideas into practice, provided, of course, that we kept within the agreed budget.

Thus the NSU car had an air-cooled flat-four engine with a cubic capacity of 1.5 litres which was mounted at the rear of the car. This Porsche Type 32 designed for NSU was larger than the Type 12 designed for Zündapp and it also offered more passenger space. The car was fitted with a torsion bar suspension system, which was a new feature developed by the Porsche design team, and *not* based on French patents, as has been wrongly reported. The facts are as follows: we wanted to patent the principle of a torsion bar suspension system, but when we made our application it

24

transpired that there was a patent in existence for something which, while being completely different from this spring suspension system, did feature a torsion bar being used in a spring suspension system. There was thus no patent for this type of suspension, and the accompanying drawing simply reflected the workings of an engineer's imagination.

This torsion bar suspension system was subsequently to be used in many designs, both at home and abroad. Historians of the motor industry have seen it as an important stage in the history of automobile technology.

The body of the NSU car also had a low coefficient of drag, which meant it was very streamlined. In designing the body, we collaborated from the outset with two car-body works, Reutter in the Augustenstraße in Stuttgart and Drauz in Heilbronn. Reutter made an all-steel body for the Type 32, while Drauz made one with a wooden frame as the load-bearing element and an outer skin of artificial leather. This commission from NSU was virtually completed in 1933, but that is a new chapter.

Incidentally, in 1937 Reutter built a new factory in Stuttgart-Zuffenhausen close to our own premises.

4

A new concept in racing cars

In 1932 the German motor industry had reached its nadir. In 1931, a total of 62,563 cars had been produced in Germany; in 1932, this figure sank to 43,448. Although there were signs of an upturn towards the end of 1932, it was not until 1933 that the German automobile industry made a decisive recovery.

The new Chancellor of the German Reich, Adolf Hitler, had announced the first measures to aid the German motor industry at the opening of the International Automobile and Motor Cycle Exhibition on 11 February 1933 in Berlin. However, the aim was not only to breathe life back into this important industrial sector but also to develop the notion of 'motoring for the people', which meant making the motor car accessible to a much wider range of people. One of the measures taken to this end was to exempt from taxation all new cars registered for the first time on or after 1 April 1933. Cars registered before this date could be exempted from taxation on payment of a non-recurring fee.

The motor industry was further stimulated by the extension and renovation of the German road network, and also indirectly by the plans for the construction of a motorway system. These basic conditions undoubtedly made a significant contribution to the upturn experienced by the German motor industry during 1933. By the end of 1933, output had risen to a total of 92,226 units, more than double the figure for the previous year.

However, I do not want to anticipate developments. The trials of the new NSU car were conducted with the three prototypes that had been built in the course of the year. I was very much involved in the trials; moreover, my father placed great value on my judgement, since he was impressed by the way in which I drove and assessed a car. This gave me a special position, which meant that I had to spend my time not only in the design office but also in the places where the cars were manufactured and then underwent intensive trials. It is during the trials that the most important improvements and progress are made. Let me give one small example. I had done the drawings for the steering on the NSU car. The design was very simple and for reasons of cost could not include any expensive bearings. The steering shaft, for example, was not mounted on ball or roller bearings but on cheaper plain bearings. While I was testing the car at Solitude, the famous forest circuit just outside Stuttgart on which many great races had taken place, I was taking a sharp right-hand bend when the steering jammed on me. It had been designed in such a way that the upper plain bearing lay above the lubricating oil supply and had consequently seized up. However, this could be ascertained only as a result of practical trials. Even today I am actually still proud that I had the opportunity to play a leading role in trials of this kind, particularly because they made it possible for me to study the relationship between theory and practice.

The NSU car, which to a much greater extent than the Zündapp must be seen as a forerunner of the Volkswagen, was also unfortunately not put into series production. Just as with Zündapp, NSU's motor cycle business experienced such an upturn in 1933 that there was no spare capacity for automobile production.

In this connection, it is of interest to point out that virtually all the improvements that were subsequently introduced in the Volkswagen were based on the experience gained in the trials conducted with the NSU car.

Another change in our young company took place in 1933. Adolf Rosenberger, our business manager, wanted to quit the firm and leave Germany. Rosenberger was Jewish and quite understandably saw no future for himself in Germany under the new political system. Since we were not exactly blessed with great reserves of capital, we had to find somebody who was willing to commit themselves to the company in Rosenberger's place. We were very sympathetic to Rosenberger's desire to leave.

My brother-in-law, Dr Anton Piëch, was eventually able to persuade a wealthy amateur racing driver from Austria by the name of Hans von Veyder-Malberg to take over Rosenberger's shares. Von Veyder-Malberg had, incidentally, raced in Austro Daimler cars.

Then to crown it all, Adolf Rosenberger was imprisoned and we had to exert all our influence before he was finally set free. Rosenberger then emigrated to America, where he lived under an assumed name until his death. However, before he left us he was involved in one important decision which particularly affected him as a racing driver.

The International Sporting Commission in Paris, on the occasion of their autumn meeting in October 1932, had formally adopted a new formula for Grand Prix races which was to remain in force from 1934 to 1936 inclusive, but which was subsequently extended to 1937. This formula laid down only a maximum weight for the car of 750 kg (165.4 lb), without coolant, oil and tyres; there were no other restrictions. This meant that the designer could use either a normally aspirated or a supercharged engine. There were no restrictions on the choice of fuel and the only other regulation was that the width of the body should not exceed 85 cm (33.5 in). My father found this formula virtually ideal, since it allowed the engineer considerable room for manoeuvre, both in the area of lightweight construction and in the design of the power unit.

In November 1932 we met to discuss the opportunities presented by the new formula. My father was there, as of course were Karl Rabe, our chief designer, Josef Kales, our engine expert, and Adolf Rosenberger, the successful racing driver from Pforzheim. Rabe, who had done the basic calculations, had the first blueprint for the new racing car by 15 November. A team of engineers was put together, headed by Karl Rabe. Josef Kales was responsible for the engine, Karl Fröhlich for the chassis unit and Erwin Komenda was in charge of designing the body — all of them were old comrades from Steyr. This design had a V16 4.4 litre engine which was to be mounted at the rear of the car in front of the rear axle. As a result of the great experience that my father had already had with superchargers, particularly at Daimler, the engine was to be supercharged by means of a Roots blower.

It is no secret that from his earliest days as a designer of motor cars my father had been particularly interested in the design of high-performance cars for use in motor sport. So it was that he broached the subject with Wanderer when, towards the end of 1930, he had received the commission to develop private cars for the company. Racing cars were an extremely effective means of demonstrating the technical achievements of an automobile company. When my father met Klee, the general manager of Wanderer, at the Paris Salon in 1931, they discussed a commission to develop a racing car. However, he could not begin serious work on the project until the new racing formula had been approved in the autumn of 1932.

As has already been mentioned, Wanderer had in the meantime become part of Auto Union AG which was formed on 29 June 1932, although with retrospective effect from 1 November. Thus the new customer was Auto Union.

Since the racing car project was a very expensive business, involving a great deal of financial risk on the one hand and a high capital requirement on the other, and in view of the limited capital reserves available to Dr. Ing. h.c. F. Porsche GmbH, a new company was set up. Thus on 8 November 1932 the Hochleistungs-Fahrzeug-Bau GmbH (High-Performance Motor Car Company) was born, and on 19 November 1932 the new company was entered in the commercial register. The purpose of this new company was the construction and sale of racing and sports cars.

The next task was to raise the capital required to build the racing cars. We also thought about obtaining support from public funds, which the automobile clubs of the time, the ADAC (Allgemeiner Deutscher Automobilclub) and the AvD (Automobilclub von Deutschland) were calling for. The results were only modest, which in view of the generally poor situation was only to be expected.

The newly founded Auto Union, with the four rings as its trademark, and based in Chemnitz in Saxony, was concerned to draw international attention to itself, and one effective way of doing this was to get involved in motor racing. Discussions were held between my father and Auto Union, which ended on 17 March 1933 in the signing of an agreement. As a result, the Auto Union company took over Porsche design number 22 — which was the new racing car — as the Auto-Union-P car (P for Porsche) and began to build the new car with the aid of the engineering drawings supplied by us.

However, the decisive factor in the completion of this agreement was the fact that Auto Union received the state subsidy that Hitler had promised for the furtherance of motor sport in Germany. The new government was very well aware of the fact that success in international competition would help to boost the reputation of German engineering both at home and abroad.

Daimler-Benz, as the sole representative of the German automobile industry involved in Grand Prix racing, had hitherto been the recipient of this financial assistance. On the strength of their agreement, my father and Auto Union applied to Hitler. Hitler had actually intended to give the money to only one company, namely Daimler-Benz, which had already been successful in international motor sport, but my father was also able to produce evidence of success in this field. During his time as technical director at Daimler-Benz he had worked on the development of a new racing car with an eight-cylinder supercharged engine, which later formed the basis for the W25, which came into service in 1934.

The Ministry of Transport had made provision for a sum of 1.1 million Reichsmark to be used to subsidize motor sport. Hitler's suggestion of giving it all to one company was finally rejected by the Ministry of Transport. Daimler-Benz received 500,000 Reichsmark of the sum allocated, while Auto Union were given 300,000 Reichsmark. As a result, the two firms had become rivals.

In 1934 the two companies received the same amount of money, namely 300,000 Reichsmark. This was increased from 1935 to 400,000 Reichsmark for each company, and the subsidy remained at the same level until 1939. In addition, so-called success bonuses were paid from 1935 onwards.

However, the costs of running a racing team were much higher, since the subsidies and bonuses granted by government departments represented only a fifth of the actual expenditure.

The Auto Union racing department was set up in Zwickau in Saxony. Horch had already settled there in 1904; in 1909 he had left his company and founded the Audi automobile factory. Both

The famous Auto Union Grand Prix car with its 16-cylinder, supercharged engine located behind the driver! A sensation at the time, this Porsche model 22 started racing in 1934.

companies were part of Auto Union.

Good progress was being made with the construction of the Auto-Union-P car. Here again is the technical specification of the car: the engine was a 16-cylinder design, consisting of two eight-cylinder blocks arranged at an angle of 45° to each other. The engine housing was made of light metal and was cast in silumin with steel cylinder sleeves bathed in coolant.

The inlet valves were 35 mm and the exhaust valves 32 mm in diameter. The valves were driven, via pushrods and rockers, by an overhead camshaft. The camshaft was driven by a main shaft which also drove the Roots supercharger and the Bosch magneto. The engine had one sparking plug per cylinder and a cubic capacity of 4.4 litres.

The crankshaft had ten bearings. One particularly interesting feature of this engine was that it had only one camshaft which

The chassis of the Auto Union Grand Prix car with two tubes in which the cooling water was taken from the engine in the rear to the radiator at the front. Immediately behind the engine is the Roots supercharger; the gearbox is behind the rear axle.

was centrally located and controlled the valves on both sides. This was achieved by using fingers to operate the inlet valves and transverse push rods for the exhaust valves.

The V16 cylinder was designed in such a way that it could be bored out to 6 litres without a new housing being required. The engine plus flywheel weighed 210 kg (463 lb).

The chassis consisted of two parallel tubes with individually mounted wheels which were suspended by torsion bars and a rear transverse leaf spring. The parallel central tubes had a further special function. One of the tubes carried coolant from the engine to the front-mounted radiator, while the other tube carried it back to the engine. The engine was located in front of the rear wheel suspension; this meant that the car was laid out as a mid-engine design, its weight distribution favouring the driven wheels.

The first engine was built in the autumn of 1933. Since we were involved in an advisory capacity in the construction of the racing cars, I often went to Zwickau where the racing department had its headquarters in Auto Union's Horch factory. It goes without saying that the first test runs were not without problems. For example, the engineers were surprised that when the engine had reached its operating temperature the crankshaft turned blue at the ends and threatened to seize up. I thought about this and very soon came up with an explanation. 'Has it occurred to you that the crankshaft is made of steel, while the housing is a light metal casting? They have different expansion coefficients. As it heats up, the crankshaft expands more rapidly than the housing; consequently, the crankshaft pins have no more space to move and all the end-play is eliminated!'

Eberan von Eberhorst, one of the leading engineers at Auto Union under whose direction the D type was being developed for 1938, just said, 'Rubbish!' I replied, 'Let me show you then!' I took the crankshaft to the hardening room, where I put it in baths of differing temperatures and then measured its length. Herr von Eberhorst had to concede that this proved me right.

The trial runs with the Roots supercharger, which works on the same principle as geared pumps, gave me another opportunity to show that I had acquired my own technical knowledge and was not just the son of the famous professor. Excessively high temperatures were being generated in the supercharger, and in order to carry out a systematic examination of it I did some drawings of the rotor blades enlarged by a factor of ten. By this means I was able to ascertain that, when the two rotor blades were in certain positions relative to each other, compression developed in the housing. This compression, which heated the air and hence the whole supercharger unit, had not been foreseen. The overheating problem was solved by not allowing the excess pressure to occur in the first place. This was duly achieved in a way similar to that used in geared oil pumps, namely by cutting a notch in the housing through which the excess pressure could be released.

I was the youngest person in this circle and it took some time for me to be taken seriously and for my views to gain acceptance. At the same time, however, these incidents prove that I was very committed to all aspects of automobile engineering.

In the late autumn of 1933 (I believe it was the beginning of November), I was able to drive the new racing car for the first time, on a country road near Zwickau. I found this test run very impressive. The performance that could be obtained from this modern racing car was fantastic. However, it proved to be so fast that country roads, that were not even blocked off, were not suitable for use as test tracks, so we used the Nürburgring.

A poster on which Auto Union announced the record-breaking drive of Hans Stuck on 6 March 1934, when three world speed records were taken with the Auto-Union-P car over 100 miles, 200 km and one hour.

3 Weltrekorde für Deutschland

DER AUTO UNION RENNWAGEN

stellte am 6.III.34 auf der Avus bei Berlin folgende neue Weltbestzeiten auf:

für 100 MEILEN ..... 216,869 KILOMETER
für 200 KILOMETER... 217,085 KILOMETER
in 1 STUNDE ..... 217,106.79 km

When I got out of the racing car into my own car, which was a Wanderer with a 3.2 litre eight-cylinder engine, I thought, as I accelerated away, that the accelerator pedal had come away from its mounting. That was not of course the case, but my car certainly seemed very slow in comparison with the racing car.

The first version of the V16 engine used in the racing car produced about 295 hp at 4,500 rpm with a compression ratio of 7:1. These were moderate values for a racing engine, which left a great deal of room for further development. The engine was powered by special fuel.

After the test runs in November on the Nürburgring, the car went back to the factory. Further tests were carried out in January, this time at the AVUS in Berlin. On 6 March, Hans Stuck, who was leader of the Auto Union Grand Prix team of which the other members were the Prince of Leiningen and August Momberger, set three new world records at the AVUS. He achieved the following best performances:

1 hour at 217.106 km/h (134.93 mph)
200 km at 217.085 km/h (134.87 mph)
100 miles at 216.869 km/h (134.29 mph)

In achieving these times, the car reached top speeds of around 156 mph (251 km/h), although the real top speed was about 180 mph (290 km/h). So it was that we fulfilled the commission that had been officially placed on 17 March 1932.

With the passage of time I had developed the ability to identify problems by instinct and then to find simple solutions for them. I was thus, at a relatively early age, able to put my knowledge of technical procedures to the test. For example, I remember the time when my father was still working at Daimler-Benz. At that time, endurance runs were held at the Nürburgring with the Mercedes-Benz Nürburg 460. As the car drove past at the start and finish, I noticed that something was not quite right and I said to my father, 'It's not firing on all cylinders, I can hear it quite plainly.' Inspection revealed that I was right.

Years later, when test runs were being conducted with the Auto Union V16 racing car at the Nürburgring, the drivers were not achieving the lap times that they were looking for. I went over to Eberan von Eberhorst and the team leader, Willy Walb, and said, 'Check the rev counter; I've got the feeling the engine is running at 7 or 8,000 revs rather than 4,500!' As the car was driven past, I had noticed that the engine had a quite different note from its usual sound, and indeed the engine was running at speeds at which there was a significant fall-off in performance. The rev counter was wrongly calibrated and was showing 4,500 rpm although the engine was running at over 7,000 rpm. Since the drivers were driving in accordance with the revs indicated, they were not recording very good times.

I also have very clear memories of an incident in the 1950s. We had just developed a hill-climbing racing car whose road-holding characteristics left a lot to be desired. Herr Hild, our racing engineer, said, 'We've measured it, it's absolutely accurate!', to which I replied, 'Give me a rope!' The rope was forthcoming and I used it to take the diagonal measurements from the offside front wheel to the nearside rear wheel and from the nearside front wheel to the offside rear wheel. Sure enough the measurements did not tally. The chassis had been pulled out of shape. After this had been corrected the car held the road as well as any other. Later in the series I insisted on not simply relying on measurements, but also on checking that the left-hand side tallied exactly with the right-hand side and that the car really ran true.

I had learnt this lesson from my experience with bicycles; if the front and rear wheel are not accurately lined up, it is impossible to ride with no hands. This shows how important it is to look for simple solutions.

However, let us return to 1934. The design of the Auto Union racing car had inspired us to devise an interesting vehicle, the Type 52. This was a three-seater sports coupé with a streamlined body and was a more 'civilized' version of the Auto Union racing car. The maximum output of the V16 supercharged engine was reduced to 200 hp for the Type 52; it was fitted with a five-speed gearbox that was so designed that, at an engine speed of 3,650 rpm, speeds of 47 mph (75.6 km/h) in first gear, 60 mph (96.5 km/h) in second, 76 mph (122.3 km/h) in third, 95 mph (152.8 km/h) in fourth and 119 mph (191.5 km/h) in fifth were achieved, with a top speed of 125 mph (201.1 km/h). The driver sat in the middle, with the two passengers on either side of him. The car had an unladen weight of 1,300 kg (2,866.5 lb), and was intended to be driven at a weight of 1,750 kg (3,859 lb) when laden with three people, 70 kg (154 lb) of luggage and 150 kg (331 lb) of running

Inspired by the mechanical elements of the Auto-Union-P car, the Porsche bureau designed a sports coupé, the Porsche model 52. But this beautiful coupé with the 16-cylinder engine of the Grand Prix car, was never produced.

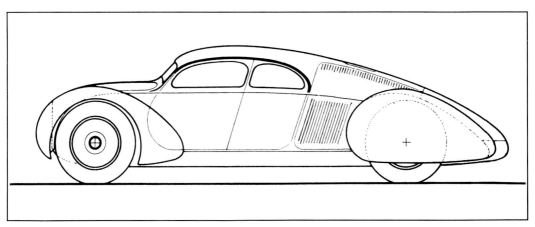

gear. It would have been an ideal vehicle for the new motorways, but unfortunately the Type 52 was never built.

In its first year, the Auto Union racing car had some impressive successes and was acclaimed in the international specialist press as a revolutionary engineering design. In its first race on 27 May 1934 at the AVUS in Berlin, August Momberger finished in third place, behind the winner Guy Moll and Achille Varzi in second place, both driving Alfa Romeos. In 1934, Hans Stuck recorded three Grand Prix wins in the new car, including the German Grand Prix at the Nürburgring, the Swiss Grand Prix at the Bremgarten circuit in Bern and the Czech Grand Prix at the Masarykring in Brno.

I personally very much enjoyed working on the Auto Union racing car, and particularly driving this high-performance vehicle. The driving instructor who had been in charge of my driving test in Stuttgart had not been so very wide of the mark when he had described me as having 'a talent for driving'. My father very quickly noticed how much I enjoyed driving the Grand Prix car and made no attempt to conceal his disapproval of any secret ambitions I might have harboured in the direction of motor racing. Although he acknowledged my talent as a driver, he made it absolutely clear to me that I should keep away from the racing car. He held the view that his only son should seek to develop a career in automobile engineering rather than in motor racing. Like all young people who have got an idea into their head, I was of course very disappointed. However, after giving the matter careful consideration, I eventually found something positive in my father's decision, since what he had said to me undoubtedly meant that I was to become even more involved in the work of the Porsche design office. This was indeed what happened, since in the meantime our engineering team had been given a new and very important task which was to be given absolutely top priority: we were to develop a new Volkswagen, or 'people's car'.

5

Hitler calls for a people's car

In his speech at the opening of the Berlin Motor Show in 1934, Hitler called upon the motor industry to develop an economical small car that would provide adequate and affordable transport for all. Anyone who had saved enough money to buy a motor cycle should be able to afford this car. Economical to run and to repair, it was to be a true people's car.

The work that we had done for Zündapp and NSU meant of course that we had already laid the foundations for a design that could be envisaged as a people's car, which from the outset my father believed had to be a fully adequate utility car. The experience that we had gained meant that we were able very quickly to draw up suitable proposals. This led to the conception of a utility vehicle with a rear-mounted, air-cooled, flat, opposed-piston engine with a cubic capacity of 1,250 cc and an output of 26 hp at 3,500 rpm. With a wheelbase of 2.5 m (2.7 yd) and a track width of 1.2 m (1.3 yd), it was to provide space for four people and have an unladen weight of 650 kg (1,433 lb). Its top speed, which was also to be considered its cruising speed, was to be about 100 km/h (62 mph) and it was to be able to climb a 1 in 3 hill in first gear. Fuel consumption was 8 litres/100 km (35 mpg). Another design feature was the modern chassis with independent wheel suspension at the rear and a Porsche front-wheel suspension with torsion bars. The purchase price of this car was to be in the region of 1,500 Reichsmark (about £75).

Jakob Werlin, a member of the board of Daimler-Benz AG, arranged a meeting in the spring of 1934 in the Chancellory between Hitler and my father. Also present was Herr Werlin, who in 1942 was to be appointed general inspector of the automobile industry by Hitler. At this meeting my father presented his plans for the people's car to Hitler, who agreed with his technical design; however, he requested that the sale price of the vehicle should not exceed 1,000 Reichsmark. A basic decision had thus been taken, and our design office immediately began work, although there was still no agreement in writing. The new project went into the company's files as the Type 60.

The German Automobile Manufacturers' Association was naturally far from pleased that they had been presented to all intents and purposes with a *fait accompli*. This was understandable, since some of the companies that belonged to the Association had small cars in their production schedule and they saw the Type 60 as posing a real threat to them after the economically difficult period they had been through. However, agreement was finally reached and on 22 June 1934 my father received the commission for the Volkswagen from the Automobile Manufacturers' Association. The contract stipulated that the car was to be developed within ten months for a monthly fee of 20,000 Reichsmark (about £1,000).

As my father left the building in which the contract had just been signed, he was accompanied by one of the industrialists who together with his colleagues had just voted for the project. He said, 'Herr Porsche, if you spend the money and then say that it can't be done, that will be exactly what we expect from you!' To this my father replied, 'Then you've given the contract to the wrong man, because it can be done!' The industrialist then declared, 'But Herr Porsche, the people's car is a bus; what does each worker need his own car for?'

The monthly fee was very low for the development of a completely new car, but every member of our design team accepted the challenge with great enthusiasm.

In view of the limited financial resources at our disposal, we had to do a great deal of the work ourselves. To this end we set up a workshop in the garage of our house in the Feuerbacher Weg,

My father's house on the Feuerbacher Weg 48-50 in Stuttgart. In the two garages on the left, the first Volkswagen models were assembled.

This is one of the very first drawings for the Volkswagen (Porsche model 60), designed and built by Porsche to the order of the German Society of Car Manufacturers. On the drawing it says 'Geheim' meaning secret.

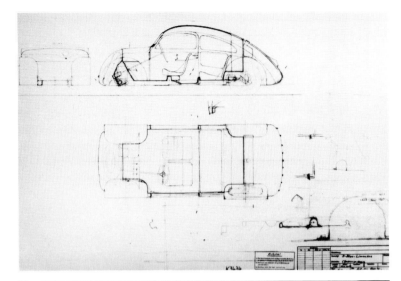

My father and myself at the drawing board discussing the Volkswagen design.

which I normally used for model-making. A drilling and a milling machine were already installed there, and a further two lathes were set up. Twelve men then set to work in this confined space.

The new car was assembled in our garage. The entire accessories industry in the Stuttgart and Württemberg areas made a significant contribution to the production of parts from our drawings. The small jobs which arose during the assembly process were carried out in our own workshop.

The question of the engine had been decided only shortly beforehand. We had studied various units, including two- and four-stroke engines, two- and four-cylinder engines and in-line and flat opposed-piston engines. We eventually settled on an air-cooled flat four with a cubic capacity of 985 cc and overhead valves, which produced 23.5 hp at 3,000 rpm.

Both money and time were in short supply, and even today I am still amazed that we actually managed to complete the project. Initially two pre-prototypes V1 and V2 were built, one an open-top and the other a saloon version, which were used in the preliminary trials. In December 1934 we were given authorization to build three test cars, known as the V3 prototype series, which were to be used for the road trials. These vehicles were later referred to by the Roman numerals I, II and III.

To a certain extent this was a sort of pre-series; the cars had independent suspension on all four wheels, with spring torsion bars in the front axle tubes and, at the rear, a floating axle with a longitudinal control arm on either side and transverse spring torsion bars in the axle tube. There was a central tubular frame, and the engine was mounted behind and the four-speed gearbox in front of the rear axle.

The bodies of cars I and II were constructed of a mixture of wood and sheet metal, while car III had an all-steel body with the familiar streamlined shape. Because of their composite construction, the first two cars were heavier than the third one, which by virtue of its all-steel construction almost reached the prescribed weight and, consequently, came close to the required performance.

These three cars did not of course have the definitive body shape. Thus, for example, the headlights were not yet positioned in the mudguards and there were vision slots at the back instead of the rear window. Komenda had designed the body. On 18 January 1936 he sketched the definitive shape with the headlights in the mudguards and the divided rear window. The all-steel type III was subsequently amended accordingly.

In the meantime, something had happened which still makes me smile today when I think of it. Good 'friends' had drawn Hitler's attention to the fact that 'his' people's car was being built by Czechs, since my father and I did indeed still hold our Czechoslovakian passports. However, Hitler did not appear to take any notice of this. As a former Austrian, he must have been aware of the special circumstances that faced citizens of the old dual monarchy of Austria-Hungary. In any event, we were granted German passports shortly afterwards.

In his speech at the opening of the 1935 Motor Show, for the first time Hitler made public mention of my father in connection with the people's car. He said,

'I am pleased that the outstanding designer Porsche, with the assistance of his staff, has succeeded in drawing up the preliminary designs for the German people's car; the first versions will be available for trials in the middle of this year. It must be possible to offer the German people a car that does not cost any more than an average motor cycle used to cost!'

Of course, given the conditions under which we had to work, it was not possible to start the trials in the middle of 1935. It is true that cars I and II had done 5,000 and 3,125 miles respectively (8,045 and 5,028 km), but the actual main trials did not start until 12 October 1936. They were conducted in two shifts, because we wanted to complete most of the planned 31,000 miles (49,079 km) before winter set in.

It is interesting to mention briefly the course used for the trials, since it gives a good impression of the demands made on the test car. The starting point was our house in the Feuerbacher Weg where maintenance work on the cars was also done. From there, the route went via Pforzheim to the Dobel and thence to Baden-Baden and then along the Rhine valley to Offenburg; from Offenburg, the circuit went via Biberach, Harmersbachtal, Oppenau, Alexanderschanze, Freudenstadt and Horb to Tübingen and then through the Neckar valley back to Stuttgart.

We were not responsible for conducting the trials, which were handled by the technical department of the Automobile Manufacturers' Association as a way of checking whether the information we had supplied was in fact correct. I was responsible for our side.

After my father had banned me from driving the Auto Union racing car, I started looking for another form of motor sport and eventually took up cross-country and long-distance driving, to which my father made no objection.

In 1934, for example, I took part in a three-day event in the Harz mountains, which could be described as a sort of cross-country race, organized by the National Socialist Motor Corps of which Hühnlein was boss. I drove a 2 litre Wanderer and was the only driver to complete the difficult course without any penalty points. Each competitor who was slower than the fastest in his class collected penalty points. According to the regulations I should have been awarded the gold medal. However, this did not suit Hühnlein and he decided that a medal should be given to all competitors who had not collected more than 10 penalty points.

Competitions like this were intended rather to be a sort of mass sport and a part of pre-military training.

I also took part in the 2,000 km (1,243 miles) endurance drive through Germany which started and finished in Baden-Baden, having taken in Munich, Berlin, Dresden and Cologne. Some famous racing drivers took part in the race which was followed enthusiastically by hundreds of thousands of people.

I was so excited at the thought of my first 2,000 km race that I was almost trembling, and I had difficulty in controlling the accelerator pedal. It was either right down on the board or up in the air. As I was driving down the mountain towards Gernsbach, round a sharp right-hand bend, the crowd scattered rapidly, which gave me the impression that I was driving very fast. The average speed laid down for my class was 64 km/h (40 mph), but I reached Baden-Baden in third place at an average speed of 74 km/h (46 mph) for the 2,000 km course. I must say I was very satisfied with this.

Despite all this exciting activity, I still had time for private matters. The work of our design company in the Kronenstraße had slowly borne fruit and the financial situation was gradually improving, so that Dodo and I were able at last to do what we had been planning to do for a long time, namely to get married. The great event took place on 10 January 1935. After a short honeymoon in the Allgäu, I had to return to work. Our first child, a son, was born on 11 December 1935. We christened him Ferdinand Alexander, but he soon acquired the nickname Butzi and was to be known by that name from then on.

Let us return, however, to the trials with the three prototypes of the people's car. The trials were not of course conducted solely on the Black Forest route, but in the afternoon a further circuit had also to be completed. It led along country roads to Bruchsal and then on to the new autobahn as far as Bad Nauheim and back again to Stuttgart. The Black Forest route was 215 miles (346 km) in length and average speeds of between 31 and 37 mph (46 and 60 km/h) were achieved. In the afternoon, a further 278 miles (447 km) had to be covered, and the average speed was 50 and then 53 mph (80, then 85 km/h).

In addition to our drivers, there were three cars carrying technical observers working for the Automobile Manufacturers' Association. They came from the departments of automotive engineering at the Institutes of Technology in Stuttgart and Berlin.

Thus the cars were doing 500 miles (805 km) per day, which was a heavy load for the driving crews. One of those involved as an observer was Professor Werner Rixmann, who travelled in car No I with Herr Ringel, one of our employees. He later became editor-in-chief of the technical journal *ATZ* (*Automobiltechnische Zeitschrift*, or *Journal of Automotive Engineering*) and the following

The chassis of one of the first three experimental Volkswagens. One can see the platform frame with the centre tube, the fully independent wheel suspension, the four-cylinder horizontally opposed, air-cooled engine behind the rear axle, and the four-speed gearbox in front of the rear suspension.

is an extract from a report he published in that journal:

'The trials began on 12 October 1936, and despite numerous breakdowns and many a hazardous situation the basic soundness of the car's design soon became evident. The cars covered their 500 miles on time almost every day. I remember with pleasure many trouble-free morning drives in the magnificent autumn scenery of the Black Forest. The 185 mile [298 km] trip on the motorway at an average speed of 50 to 53 mph [80 to 85 km/h] was less interesting. Our free time was often spent evaluating the reports in order to keep ourselves constantly up-to-date. Breakdowns sometimes led to delays when the overnight repairs were not finished. Occasionally a car was out of

One of the series 30 Volkswagens (left) and one of the first three experimental VWs assembled in the garage of the Porsche house, which is seen behind the two cars.

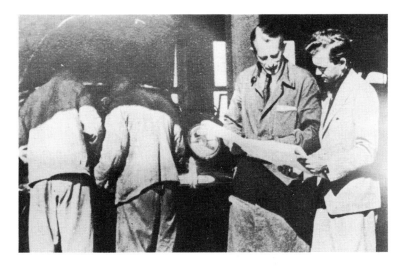

As a young man I was fully engaged in the development of the new Volkswagen. In this photograph (on the far right in the light coloured suit) I discuss the test route with one of the engineers.

use for several days. However, after 18,750 miles [30,161 km] car No I had developed only the following faults requiring repair:

- Cracks in the front axle mounting, repaired by welding. Alterations were made to the design.
- Burnt-out exhaust valve (damage to the seating).
- Damaged brakes (distorted drum plate).

'After 31,000 miles [49,079 km] the following additional problems emerged:

- Burnt-out cable in the engine compartment.
- Slight collision with a stationary lorry on an icy gradient (no further hindrance). Collision with a young deer on the motorway near Bruchsal.
- One torsion bar broken, but the car could be driven on.
- Broken piston rod in the 4th cylinder (at 29,375 miles [47,264 km]), replacement engine used temporarily.

'By 18 December 1936 car No I had been driven for a total of 31,250 miles [50,281 km]. It can be seen that most of the problems were caused by material defects and only a few by design faults and accidents. This was a really satisfactory result for a prototype at that time.

'Similar results were recorded for cars II and III and the same faults often recurred; these included, among others, burnt-out valves, a second broken piston rod and brake damage. In addition, on car II, various cast-iron crankshafts broke; this fault was cured by fitting a steel crankshaft. In addition, some front-wheel wobble was noted, caused by too much play and elasticity and a poorly adjusted camber.

'Many of the breakdowns, such as those caused by the break-

61

ing of a cast-iron crankshaft or a piston rod, led to a great deal of time being lost, since in some cases the cars had to be collected from a long way away; the services of Dr Porsche's driver Goldinger were very useful in this connection.

'By 19 December 1936 all the cars reached the target of 31,250 miles; some reached that figure even earlier, depending on the amount of time lost. The breakdowns and mechanical failures recorded do not show any fundamental deficiencies. They are a consequence of inadequate preliminary testing of the parts and of the finished vehicles, and partly also of the largely makeshift nature of the parts and the assembly. That it all ended satisfactorily is a tribute to the untiring efforts and skill of the Porsche team. All the observers' reports praised the car's driving qualities, road-handling, stability on corners and feeling of safety, particularly when one had got used to driving it. In this respect, the then very modern wheel suspension, the low centre of gravity and the design of the suspension were particularly important.'

This clearly reveals the opinion of Professor Rixmann, who can be considered an impartial witness since he acted as an observer during the trials and had no connection with the Porsche company.

The report compiled by the Automobile Manufacturers' Association, which was almost 100 pages long, gives a positive assessment of the trial results. Among other things, the report said that:

- The design had proved suitable.
- The trial cars had in general completed the 31,250 mile trial successfully. There had, it was true, been a number of breakdowns and some faults had been discovered. However, none of them was caused by fundamental design flaws and they could all probably be corrected without any great difficulty. Various components, such as, for example, the front axle and brakes, still required exhaustive trials for further development.
- Fuel consumption was kept within satisfactory limits.
- The car's handling and performance were good.
- The car had revealed qualities which make further development recommendable.

This extract from the Association's report shows that we undoubtedly had grounds to be very satisfied with the assessment, particularly if the circumstances in which we had built the three trial cars were taken into account.

In the meantime, however, further development work had been carried out with the Grand Prix car. As usual, our technical advice was being sought and I can still remember very clearly what took place at that time. During training runs at the Nürburgring, I was standing one day with my father at the lowest point of the circuit where the cars come down the Wehrseifen and go over the bridge at Breitscheid. After the bridge there is a difficult ascending right-hand bend. It struck me that as the cars took the bend the tyre on the wheel closest to the inside of the bend was giving off great clouds of smoke. I thought, 'Why don't they have a limited-slip differential?' I remembered that I had already fitted the NSU car such a differential, so I suggested it to my father, who agreed. We drove up to the starting line and I telephoned Rabe. 'Look, Herr Rabe, we need to get a limited-slip differential from ZF for the racing car. Can you get in touch with them immediately?'

That happened in 1935. In 1936 the Auto Union racing cars appeared with a limited-slip differential. It was Auto Union's most successful season, with the young Bernd Rosemeyer winning the European championship.

Rosemeyer was indeed a great talent. He did not join the Auto Union racing team until 1934 and rode the 500 cc DKW. He very soon became a top-class performer. When the racing car was built, Rosemeyer gave no one any peace until he was eventually able in the autumn of 1934 to take part in the trials for up-and-coming drivers. He immediately recorded good lap times and was given a contract to race the car in 1935.

His first big event came in 1935 at the International Eifel race at the Nürburgring. The young man created a sensation when he led the field into the last lap. It was typical Eifel weather, with

The famous Bernd Rosemeyer at the Nürburgring driving in his brilliant style the Auto Union V16 cylinder Grand Prix car, designed by Porsche.

Start of the
Internationales
Eifelrennen on 16 June
1935 on the famous
Nürburgring. Von
Brauchitsch is taking
the lead in a Mercedes
(7), followed by the
Auto Unions of Stuck
(left) and Varzi (2).
Caracciola is in car 5.

rain and differing temperatures on the circuit, but this did not
prevent Rosemeyer from driving like an old hand. Not until the
final lap did Rudolf Caracciola in a Mercedes-Benz catch him up
and beat him into second place. The result shows how close the
race was: Caracciola won with an average speed of 73.6 mph (117.8
km/h), while Rosemeyer came second with an average speed of
73.43 mph (117.5 km/h). Rosemeyer finished the 1935 season with
a victory at the Masaryk race in Brno in Czechoslovakia.

Incidentally, it was later stated that the Auto Union racing car
was very difficult to drive and oversteered sharply. There is no
truth in this. The car's engine was mounted in front of the rear
axle and the fuel tank was located directly on the centre of gravity.
This meant that the distribution of weight did not change even
as the fuel supply was used up. After the 'drop-shaped Benz' of
1923, the Auto-Union-P car was the second racing car design with
the engine mounted in front of the rear axle and a very successful forerunner of a development which has now become a common feature of racing car design.

Bernd Rosemeyer was an amazing phenomenon, a daredevil
and an exceptional driver who right from the start drove the Auto
Union car very quickly indeed. Part of the reason for this may
have been that he had never driven a racing car before and that
the Auto Union was the first Grand Prix car he had ever raced.
As a result, he was able to attune himself completely to this new
design, since he was totally unfamiliar with conventional designs
with the engine at the front and rear-wheel drive, although he
would probably have been very quick in this type of car as well.
He was a very talented driver, but he was also prepared to take
great risks and was constantly striving to achieve a better lap time
simply because he enjoyed driving. Incidentally, his daredevil
character and his desire to go ever quicker aroused the anger of

the older and more established racing drivers — I do not want to name any names here — who grumbled, 'Why does he always have to keep going faster and faster? We're already driving fast enough!' The same happened later to Hermann Lang, who also left all his rivals standing, particularly in 1939.

It may also be that Rosemeyer's willingness to take risks was the main reason why he sadly lost his life at such a young age. On 28 January 1938 he set out on an attempted record-breaking drive on the motorway near Frankfurt, despite strong, gusty winds. Given the prevailing conditions, he probably took one risk too many, but more of that later.

At the end of this very successful season, Caracciola paid us a visit and told us that the people at Daimler had for a long time been racking their brains to find out why the Auto Union racing car showed a clean pair of heels to the Mercedes on every bend. Eventually, it occurred to them that the answer lay in the limited-slip differential, which allowed higher speeds on bends; at certain engine speeds, moreover, the V16 engine developed greater power than the Mercedes eight-cylinder, in-line engine. The 6.1 litre engine used in the Type C Auto Union in 1936 produced 520 hp.

In the meantime, considerable progress had been made with the people's car project, and on 11 June 1936, my father presented two of the three test cars to Hitler. Werlin, the director of Daimler-Benz, was also present. When Hitler decreed that a further 30 test cars should be built in order that more extensive trials could be carried out, my father suggested they should be built at Daimler-Benz. That company had already been involved in some of the preliminary work, and since they had their headquarters in the

My father showing Hitler a model of the Volkswagen. In the middle is Dr Robert Ley, the chief of the Deutsche Arbeitsfront, and responsible for the KdF-Wagen project. Hitler asked my father on this occasion to lower the front part of the car, but he did not do so.

same place as we had ours, my father expected the entire project to be completed with less difficulty. Hitler agreed to this. He personally issued the order for the test cars and explained that he would pay for them himself.

The 30 test cars were assembled under the designation W30 at the Daimler-Benz factory at Sindelfingen and were then subjected to exhaustive trials. These trials were carried out over a total of 2.4 million km (1.5 million miles), with individual vehicles covering more than 62,500 miles (100,563 km). Thirty members of the SS were used as drivers; they were not engineers but average drivers chosen at random to represent cross-section of the kind of drivers who would use the car for every day driving. A party organization was chosen in order to keep the project secret. At the same time, however, the organization was to check that the data supplied by the Porsche design team and the car's technical standard corresponded to reality. As a 'neutral' political organization, it was to guarantee the objectivity of the test data. I was responsible for the conduct of the trials; as an engineer, I naturally took the opportunity to gather a great deal of important data on the running of the car, its oil and fuel consumption and general wear and tear. The information thus acquired was used to make appropriate changes to the vehicle.

In that same year my father travelled to the USA, where he was particularly interested by the mass production of motor cars. The people's car could only be sold at a suitable price if it could be produced in large quantities. The price was of course still in excess of 1,000 Reichsmark. However, at that time taxes accounted for at least 20 per cent of the selling price of a car, to which distribu-

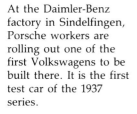

At the Daimler-Benz factory in Sindelfingen, Porsche workers are rolling out one of the first Volkswagens to be built there. It is the first test car of the 1937 series.

Left and below left
One of the Volkswagens from the 30 series ready for test driving. Note that the head lamps are not yet fully integrated into the front wings.

My father stands next to one of the Volkswagens from the 30 car test series built in 1937. Note that the doors still open forward. After returning from the United States, inspired by American cars, he modified the design so that they opened in the other direction.

Right Rear view of the 30 series Volkswagen. There was still no rear window.

Below Volkswagens of the 30 series which marked the beginning of the Beetle era. Following successful testing, the German government gave the go-ahead for further development and the construction of the factory, but it was more than 10 years before the first production car rolled off the Wolfsburg assembly line.

tion costs also had to be added; thus it was not difficult to see where considerable savings could be made.

My father was also interested in a race that was held every year over a distance of 300 miles (482.7 km) on Long Island near New York. The winner was awarded the Vanderbilt Cup and my father wanted to check whether it would be possible, from a purely tech-

nical point of view, for Auto Union to enter the race.

In autumn 1936 we again met Hitler to discuss the people's car project. The Automobile Manufacturers' Association had in the meantime declared itself willing to produce the car at a unit price of 1,000 Reichsmark provided that the state paid a subsidy of 200 Reichsmark per car.

Hitler suggested that instead of paying a subsidy per car the money would be better spent on constructing a factory in which to build the new car. If it were assumed that a million units were to be built, then a state subsidy of 200 Reichsmark per vehicle would provide 200 million Reichsmark of investment capital. With that money, said Hitler, it would be possible to build a factory for the people's car. In talks in Berlin with Dr Robert Ley, who headed the German Labour Front, and with Herr Werlin, Hitler gave Robert Ley and his Labour Front responsibility for the people's car project and for building the factory. Of all Hitler's organizations, the Labour Front, with its subsidiary organization 'Strength Through Joy', had access to the greatest sums of money. Strength Through Joy had already had large seagoing vessels built, including the *Wilhelm Gustloff*, which was the flagship of their own fleet. Every German worker had to pay a compulsory levy to the German Labour Front, membership of which was obligatory. As a result, far greater sums were raised than those paid as dues to individual trade unions today. Hitler was of the opinion that the subsidy of 200 Reichsmark per vehicle would be lost for ever if it was paid to the motor industry. However, if it was invested in a factory, he would always have that in return.

The cost of the factory was not to appear in the estimates as investment in buildings and machinery, but was rather to be considered as a non-recurring grant. The Labour Front was to work on a non-profit-making basis, which would of course reduce costs further and make a selling price of 1,000 Reichsmark a realistic possibility. On the strength of this, the Automobile Manufacturers' Association decided at an official meeting to hand over the people's car project to the state. And thus on 28 May 1937 the Gesellschaft zur Vorbereitung des Volkswagens m.b.H. (VW Development Company) was established. The German Labour Front, as the company's backer, provided it with a capital stock of 50 million Reichsmark.

The new company had three directors: Dr Bodo Lafferentz, commercial manager and representative of the German Labour Front, my father, who was technical director, and Jakob Werlin.

The next task was to find a suitable site for the factory. Dr Lafferentz and his colleagues used an aeroplane in order to reconnoitre the terrain. Hitler had suggested that the factory should be built in central Germany, with adequate communication links by rail, canal or motorway to facilitate the transport of the necessary materials and equipment. Eventually a suitable site was found not far from the Mittelland Canal near Wolfsburg. The land required belonged almost entirely to the Count of Schulenburg, who advanced a number of arguments against giving the land over to industrial uses, which today would all have been sufficiently persuasive at least to delay the building work for a long time and possibly to prevent it altogether. Apart from the fact that the land had been in the possession of the Count's family for almost 500 years, with the fourteenth-century Wolfsburg as its central point, there were several thousand oak trees on it, many of them about 100 years old. However, the arguments were to no avail; the state, or, to be precise, a Nazi organization, was the client, and the decision very soon went in favour of the site found by Dr Lafferentz. The new factory was to be built near the village of Fallersleben right on the Mittelland Canal and the Hannover-Berlin motorway.

It was in the same year, 1937, that we went on the trip to the USA that I mentioned at the beginning of my story. However, the visit to Henry Ford was not the only item on our programme; we also visited several factories and had discussions with people, mainly German immigrants now living in the USA and working in the motor industry. They were specialists, mainly in modern mass production methods, whom we hoped to attract to the new Volkswagen factory. I well remember one interesting experience in this connection. At Chrysler we met an Austrian from Graz in Styria who now managed an automobile plant in America. He was one of the group of experts who was of importance to us, but he declined our offer, saying, 'You know, it's the difference in mentality that makes me reluctant to accept this offer. For example, in Europe, if I make eight suggestions for improvements and two of them are turned down, I get the sack. In America in the same situation, I get commended and receive a bonus!' This answer gave me a great deal of food for thought.

However, it was not only the Volkswagen and the new factory that kept us busy in 1937. The racing season was in full swing, and there were also record-breaking attempts for which a special version of the Auto Union racing car was used. The 1937 season began with a victory by Ernst von Delius who beat Rosemeyer in the Auto Union Type C in the First Grosvenor Grand Prix (the Cape Town Grand Prix).

In the race at the Berlin AVUS, which for the first time included the newly built, steeply cambered North Bend, the winner was Hermann Lang in a Mercedes at an average speed of 261.648 km/h (162.61 mph); Ernst von Delius came second, but Bernd Rosemeyer, in the fully streamlined Auto Union, recorded the fastest lap time of 276.4 km/h (171.78 mph). Thirteen days later, on 13 June, Bernd Rosemeyer won the International Eifel Race on the north loop of the Nürburgring, beating Caracciola in the Mercedes-Benz

W125, which in 1937 was considered to be the strongest Grand Prix car of all. It was said to produce 600 hp, and a test motor which was never actually put into use achieved as much as 646 hp. Our V16 engine fitted in the Type D Auto Union, with its cubic capacity of 6.1 litres, was not as powerful.

Tests carried out after the AVUS race had showed that the fully streamlined body that had been developed for that contest was capable of breaking world records and best performances in class B (5,000 to 8,000 cc) that had been set by Caracciola in a Mercedes-Benz in October and November 1936 on the Frankfurt-Darmstadt motorway. As a result, Auto Union applied to the National Sporting Authority for permission, which was duly granted. The engine chosen for the record attempt was the one in which Rosemeyer had just won the Eifel race. It was sealed under official supervision and then dismantled and transported to Zwickau, where it was built into the fully streamlined body. On 16 June, just three days after the Eifel race, Bernd Rosemeyer set the following records:

    1 km with flying start at 389.61 km/h (242.14 mph)
    1 mile with flying start at 242.31 mph (389.88 km/h)
    5 km with flying start at 376.25 km/h (233.84 mph)
    5 miles with flying start at 229.02 mph (368.50 km/h)
    10 km with flying start at 357.21 km/h (222 mph)
    10 miles with flying start at an average speed of 223.90 mph
      (360.27 km/h)

These results were of particular interest to us because they represented a very promising starting position for the week of record-breaking attempts planned by the National Sporting Authority between 25 and 30 October 1937 on the Frankfurt-Darmstadt motorway.

Before that, however, a very important mission had to be fulfilled. Bernd Rosemeyer and Ernst von Delius were to drive the Auto Union car in the race for the Vanderbilt Cup at the Roosevelt Raceway on Long Island. The track was relatively short and was actually more like a circuit, so that a good view of the whole race could be had from the stands. Since 1936, two straights of about 1 km (0.6215 mile) in length had been added, but it was still more like a track than the Grand Prix courses to which we were accustomed in Europe. Incidentally, the track, which had been built at the instigation of some rich Americans who wanted to bring European-type racing to America, was situated on the airfield from which on 21 May 1927 Charles Lindbergh had started out in his single-engined *Spirit of St Louis* in his successful attempt to become the first man to fly solo across the Atlantic from west to east.

The Americans, and particularly the press, showed great interest in the German racing cars. Rudolf Uhlenhaut, an engineer with

Above Bernd Rosemeyer with the Auto Union during practice for the Vanderbilt Cup Race on the Roosevelt Raceway on Long Island in the USA in 1937. I am on the far left watching the discussion with continental tyre specialist, Dietrich.

Below My father enjoying a glass of beer and a sausage during practice for a race.

the Mercedes team, gained first-hand experience of this in the most positive way, as he subsequently told me. He was on the way in a car from New York to Long Island and was not paying very much attention to the speed limit. He was stopped by a traffic policeman who announced his intention of giving him a ticket for speeding. Uhlenhaut discovered to his horror that he had forgotten his papers and tried to talk his way out of the situation. 'You know,' he said, 'I'm with the German motor racing team, the Mercedes team that's taking part in the Long Island race. I'm in a hurry to get there!' The officer replied, 'Which company are you from then, the one with the engine in front or the one with the engine at the rear?' Uhlenhaut enlightened the good man and there ensued a conversation on the subject of racing cars. When the policeman's thirst for knowledge had been quenched, he wished Uhlenhaut a good journey, forgot the ticket and said, 'Good luck, but it would be better if you stick to the speed limit on the way back!' So saying, he swung himself on to his motor bike and roared off.

The race for the Vanderbilt Cup covered a distance of 300 miles (482.7 km) and was to take place on 3 July. Incidentally, the cup was over 3 ft (1 m) high, and the victor received only a copy of it. Shortly before the start it began to rain. At that time in America races were not held in rain, and so the event was put back from the Saturday to the Monday, since races could not be held on Sundays, and in any case, that particular Sunday was Independence Day.

Right from the start, a bitter struggle developed between Bernd Rosemeyer, the young daredevil, and the old fox Rudolf Caracciola, vying for the lead. However, the duel came to a premature end when Caracciola had to abandon the race on lap 17 because

of compressor trouble.

It was the up-and-coming English driver Dick Seaman in a Mercedes who now began to press Rosemeyer hard. Shortly before the finish, however, his engine began to splutter because of a lack of fuel and Seaman had to go into the pits to fill up, leaving the way to victory open for Rosemeyer; Seaman was second.

For Auto Union this was of course a useful victory, because the USA is an important market for top class cars. Moreover, the youthful, good-looking Rosemeyer was always a worthwhile subject for American journalists and enhanced his success on the track with good public relations off it. The Rosemeyers were on their honeymoon, Bernd having married the famous pilot Elly Beinhorn, and the mere fact that he had married an internationally famous woman ensured a great deal of media attention.

Above Start for the Vanderbilt Cup Race in the USA on 5 July 1937, which Rosemeyer won in front of Dick Seaman in a Mercedes. In 12 is Caracciola (Mercedes), left of him is Rosemeyer in an Auto Union (4). In the second row on the right is the British driver Seaman in his Mercedes.

Left Rosemeyer's Auto Union (4) ready for the Vanderbilt Cup Race. In the cockpit is his mechanic, Ludwig Sebastian. Behind him, with the hat, is my father, while right from him is Dr Feuereisen, the Rennleiter (racing director) of the Auto Union team.

After the Vanderbilt Cup race we continued our American trip with the visit to Henry Ford. On our arrival in America we had bought a Ford car with a 2.6 litre V8 engine which interested us a great deal from the technical point of view. It was a great surprise to us that, to company directors, we were not 'socially acceptable' in that car. We had been accepted to travel in a Cadillac or a Lincoln. One of the people we met said that visiting companies in the Ford was comparable to using a bicycle for business trips in Germany! Well, we survived...!

We brought back another important modification to the Volkswagen from the USA. When you look at photographs of the first 30 pre-series Volkswagens which were built at the Daimler-Benz factory, you will notice that the doors are hinged to the centre post and open towards the front of the car. We noticed in America that car doors there opened towards the back, which was not only safer, since the doors could not fly open when the car was in motion, but it also made it easier for women to get in and out. Although our design was cheaper, we adopted the American design for the mass production vehicle.

While the Auto Union racing team was sailing back to Germany on board the *Europa*, owned by North German Lloyd, another Auto Union victory was achieved by Rudi Hasse, who on 11 July won the Belgian Grand Prix at the Spa-Francorchamps circuit in the Ardennes. Hans Stuck was second, also in an Auto Union. The team met up again on 13 July in Germany. Shortly afterwards we also set out on the journey home on the *Bremen*, the sister ship of the *Europa*.

The 1937 motor racing season brought several more successes: Rosemeyer won the Coppa Acerbo in Pescara (Italy) and the Donington Grand Prix in England, while Stuck won the Grosser Bergpreis (Mountain Grand Prix) on the Schauinsland near Freiburg.

Our involvement with the Auto Union racing team ended on an impressive note with the week of record-breaking attempts on the Frankfurt motorway, where Rosemeyer became the first person to reach over 400 km/h (248.6 mph) on a public highway. On 25 October 1937 Rosemeyer recorded an average speed of 252.51 mph (406.3 km/h) for 1 km with a flying start, and 252.50 mph (406.28 km/h) for 1 mile with a flying start.

These were new world records for the 5,000 to 8,000 cc class. Between 25 and 27 October Rosemeyer set a total of 16 new records in the 3,000 to 5,000 cc and the 5,000 to 8,000 cc classes, from 1 km with both flying and standing starts to 10 km and 10 miles.

Our contract with Auto Union officially ended on 31 December. From 1 January 1938 we were under contract to Daimler-Benz AG, although we had already started collaborating with the company. Our first task was to produce the drawings and calculations for the twin compressor for the new 3 litre V12 Mercedes Grand Prix car. The car had the designation W154 and was designed for the new racing formula which came into force in 1938.

Although Daimler-Benz kept us constantly busy, the commissions were on a smaller scale; we simply never got the really big orders. It always seemed to me that the principal motive behind our contract with Daimler-Benz was to bring to an end our association with Auto Union. Of course it was very important for us to keep the work flowing in, and a very attractive commission, the T80, did indeed soon come our way, as I shall report later. Nor would I wish to appear ungrateful, since it was the Daimler people who later recommended us to other customers, for example to the tank commission at the beginning of the war.

6

Rosemeyer meets his death

The year 1938 began tragically: on 28 January Bernd Rosemeyer was killed attempting to set further records on the Frankfurt motorway. The death of this personable young man hit my father very hard; he and Rosemeyer had been particularly close, almost like father and son, and Bernd had always valued my father's judgement and advice very highly indeed. It was also the first time that my father had not been present at the Auto Union record attempts. Although the V16 racing car we had designed was being used for the record attempts, we were by that time no longer under contract to Auto Union. I myself did not arrive at the scene of the record attempts until after the accident.

The car used for the record attempts had a body shape that had been tested in the wind tunnel during the period of our involvement but which my father had rejected because of its excessive susceptibility to side winds. My father said later that under no circumstances would he have allowed Rosemeyer to set off in the side wind prevailing at the time. On the other hand, the Berlin Motor Show was imminent. In view of the intense competition that had developed between Auto Union and Daimler-Benz, particularly on the race track, Auto Union naturally wanted to regain the record that had just been set by Caracciola in order to be able to celebrate the success at the very important Berlin Show. It is tragic that Rosemeyer met his death on a test run that was intended simply to put the car through its paces once again. The accident occurred at a very high speed which must have been in excess of 250 mph (402 km/h).

Since I did not personally witness the accident, I would like to quote the words of someone who did. Carlo Wiedemann, an internationally registered time-keeper, was in attendance and produced the following report:

'Even during Bernd Rosemeyer's first run, I had the impression that the car was not holding the road as well as Caracciola's (Caracciola had that morning achieved an average speed of 432.69 km/h [268.91 mph] for the kilometre in the Mercedes). On the fatal run, the car was travelling in a westerly direction towards Darmstadt. I was standing at the 9.2 km mark, from which I could see for between 500 to 700 metres down the carriageway. Thus I watched the run from the 8.4 km mark, that is from the moment Rosemeyer passed the arch of the bridge located at that point. When Rosemeyer had passed the arch of the bridge, the car moved a little to the right away from the centre of the carriageway. At about the 8.8 km mark, where a forest lane joins the motorway from the right, the car was hit by a side wind from the south-west which carried it at an obtuse angle into the central reservation, so that the wheels on the left-hand side mounted the grassed surface of the central reservation. It would seem that from there Rosemeyer applied opposite lock, because the car suddenly moved to the right again, hit the carriageway at an angle and turned over the left-hand front wheel on to its side. At this point, therefore, the car was lying not quite at right angles to the direction in which it had been travelling. When the car turned over for the first time, it hit the carriageway with its wheels uppermost; it then turned over a second time and I heard an explosion. The car body flew high into the air and landed in pieces on the carriageway just in front of me. The chassis and the remains of the body turned over again and landed at the edge of the forest. In my view, it was only then that the driver was hurled out of the car, because he was lying in the same direction about 50 metres away in the forest. The chassis rebounded off the trees and changed direction again, flying towards me along the edge of the forest; it hurtled over my head and finally landed on the slope of the embankment at the flyover at the 9.2 km mark. The chassis lay there, its wheels in the air, completely wrecked and bereft of all bodywork.

Although the accident happened in a split second, I have the impression that when Rosemeyer hit the central reservation he was aware that the arch of the bridge was only 400 m away and that he was trying with all his might to get the car through it by braking and steering in the opposite direction (witness the skid marks on the carriageway). Whether the sudden change between the damp surface of the central reservation and the rought cement surface of the carriageway, together with the sudden braking, caused the car to overturn, I shall leave to you to decide.'

So much for the eye-witness account. The inquiries that were carried out showed that the car must have been hurled against the central reservation by the sudden side wind from the forest lane and as a result went out of control.

On 13 March 1938 Germany annexed Austria, and on 26 May a great celebration was held at which Hitler laid the foundation stone of the Volkswagen factory. To the great surprise of all of us,

Myself behind the steering wheel of the experimental Volkswagens. This was the first convertible.

Hitler renamed the VW the KdF car after the Strength Through Joy (Kraft durch Freude) section of the German Labour Front which had taken the place of the trade unions. I was horrified by this renaming, since numerous press reports had ensured that the VW trademark was already internationally known. Volkswagen, or People's Car, was a readily understandable name, while the same could hardly be said of KdF. Even then, we were fairly certain that the VW would become a very successful export, and given the foreign currency situation prevailing at the time, it was extremely important to earn foreign currency. However, Hitler had committed himself in public and we could not do anything to change his mind.

Together with some colleagues, I had brought three Volkswagens to Wolfsburg for the laying of the foundation stone, one saloon with folding roof, one saloon and one convertible. These three cars were standing at the spot at which the foundation stone was to be laid and were thoroughly inspected by Hitler and his party chiefs. When the ceremony was over, I had the task of driving Hitler in the convertible car to a special train at a station about 3 km (2 miles) away. My father got into the back of the car and Hitler sat next to me. The road to the Fallersleben station was lined by thousands of cheering people who kept throwing flowers into our car. My father kept telling me to drive more slowly, although I was only travelling at about 20 mph (32 km/h). Even at that slow speed, however, you could still feel it if a bunch of flowers hit you on the head. But Hitler did not seem to be bothered by this; he just beamed and waved to the cheering crowd.

Hitler's words at the ceremony had made the people sit up and

After the foundation laying ceremony on 26 May 1938, I drove Hitler to the station at Fallersleben in a VW convertible. I am in civilian clothes among the many uniforms.

take notice and aroused in them the hope that they would very soon get their own cars. The KdF car was to be sold at a price of 990 Reichsmark. To this end, the so-called KdF car savings card was created, on to which savings stamps in units of 5 Reichsmark could be stuck. The savings card guaranteed its owner's claim to a KdF car, a car which could carry four or five people as well as their luggage. Its 23.5 hp engine enabled it to cruise at about 62 mph (100 km/h) on the motorway and to travel 47 miles (75 km) on 1 gallon (4.5 litres) of petrol.

The drive with Hitler to the Fallersleben station had other consequences for me. The convertible Volkswagen carrying Hitler was of course constantly photographed as it made its way through the crowd, and many of the pictures made the cover pages of illustrated magazines and newspapers both at home and abroad. As a result, the young man seen on the photographs acting as the Führer's chauffeur received a large number of letters and even some proposals of marriage. However, I had to disappoint the ladies; I was already married, and on 5 June our second son was born. He was christened Gerhard Anton and known to the family as Gerd. Incidentally, I think that my father and I were the only people in civilian clothes among the uniformed officials at the laying of the foundation stone, yet it was the two civilians who sat with Hitler in an open-top car for everyone to see.

The new commissions meant that our company had expanded considerably. The original 19 employees had increased in number to more than 100 as a result of which we had to look for new premises.

In 1936 we had acquired a site in Stuttgart-Zuffenhausen, at 2

Spitalwaldstraße. A modest hut was built which served as the starting point for the trial runs that were carried out with new developments. Over the years these premises were gradually expanded, and in June 1938 the whole operation moved to the Spitalwaldstraße site where vehicles could now be produced. Our No 1 works now stands on this site.

In the meantime we had built a further series of 30 Volkswagens with bodies manufactured to our order by Reutter in Zuffenhausen. These vehicles were intended mainly for use as demonstration models and exhibits at motor shows.

We had also found room at Zuffenhausen for the newly hired American specialists who were waiting for the Volkswagen to be completed. We had engaged them to assist in certain key positions in the development of a modern mass production system for the KdF car, as it was now known. At the end of the planning phase, 'our' Americans had calculated that each vehicle would take 54 man-hours to produce. Assuming an hourly wage of 1 Reichsmark, this meant that the wage cost per vehicle would be 54 Reichsmark. My father was particularly proud of the fact that this figure of 54 man-hours per VW was actually achieved within two years of the commencement of production at Wolfsburg after the war.

Hitler ordered Porsche to develop a so-called people's tractor for farmers. Here is the prototype of the Porsche type 110, without body, driven by a 12 PS air-cooled diesel engine.

We had also received a new commission from Hitler, who was extremely interested in engineering and particularly in automobile engineering. Hitler wanted agriculture to be motorized. At that time, smaller farms mainly used horses or oxen to pull the plough and other agricultural machinery. Larger farms did use tractors, but they were relatively expensive. Hitler suggested that a light but powerful tractor should be produced in large quantities, just like the Volkswagen, so that it could be sold at a low price.

We had already begun to develop a similar machine in 1937; it was designated the Porsche Type 110, and in the months that followed it was developed further into the Type 111 and then the Type 113. This so-called Volkstraktor, or people's tractor, was designed not only to pull ploughs or harrows, but also to serve as a sort of universal agricultural machine that could handle all the jobs that occur on a farm. Whereas the Type 110 had a 12 hp diesel engine, the Type 111 had a 16 hp diesel engine, also air-cooled. The tractor was developed, incidentally, in collaboration with the agricultural college at Hohenheim near Stuttgart, where trials were also carried out.

It was planned to produce this tractor in a new factory to be built at Waldbröl near Cologne, which would be capable of turning out about 300,000 units per year. There is no doubt that this

Here is the final version of the people's tractor, with the fuel tank now in front of the driver. The vehicle was tested by the University of Hohenheim near Stuttgart.

project formed part of Hitler's plans for the management of the agricultural *Lebensraum* that he intended to create for himself in Eastern Europe. However, at the time the tractor was being developed, none of us had any inkling of such a venture. In the meantime we also delivered an open-top Volkswagen to Hitler at his residence on the Obersalzberg near Berchtesgaden.

While the Volkswagen factory was being built in Wolfsburg under close supervision from my father, another project was coming to maturity, one which my father had been thinking about for a long time and which had already taken shape during discussions between my father and engineer Josef Mickl. It involved nothing less than the development of a car which would bring the absolute world speed record for cars to Germany. This project entered automobile history under the designation Daimler-Benz T80.

7

Special record car for Daimler-Benz

The plan to build a special record car to bring the absolute world speed record to Untertürkheim was actually latent at Daimler-Benz. From the very beginnings of motor sport, Mercedes and Benz cars had written themselves into the record books. Even before the First World War, drivers such as Victor Hémery, Barney Oldfield and Robert Burman broke the 125 mph (200 km/h) barrier in the famous Blitzen-Benz. On 23 April 1911 at Daytona Beach in the USA, Bob Burman set a new absolute world speed record in the 200 hp Blitzen-Benz. He attained an average speed of 228.096 km/h (141.76 mph) for 1 km with a flying start. This record stood until 19 February 1919, when it was beaten by the Italian-American Ralph de Palma in a Packard 905 Liberty Racer, also at Daytona Beach, who achieved a speed of 242.261 km/h (150.566 mph) for 1 mile with flying start. The Blitzen-Benz, which can be seen today in the Daimler-Benz museum in Stuttgart, had a four-cylinder engine with a cubic capacity of 21.5 litres which produced its maximum output of 200 hp at 1,600 rpm

During the 1920s, the absolute world record increasingly became the preserve of the English. In 1939, the record stood at 369.82 mph (595.041 km/h); it had been set by the Englishman John R. Cobb in a Railton Special on the Bonneville Salt Flats in Utah, USA. The actual impetus for the construction of a German car to make an attempt on the world record came from the racing driver Hans Stuck, who had already set international class records and world best performances in speed boats and the Auto Union racing car. In 1938, Stuck was still driving successfully for Auto Union — particularly in mountain races. However, his career as a racing driver was already past its peak, and he wanted to finish his active career by setting world records for cars and speed boats; the latter were to be powered by the Auto Union V16 engine that we had designed.

My father had begun development work on a car for the record attempt and he and Mickl jointly held a patent on a design. As early as the spring of 1937, speculative reports about plans for a new record attempt had appeared in the international press, reports which were duly noted at Daimler-Benz.

Stuck held discussions with my father and they decided to collaborate. At that time, the English drivers were using souped-up aero engines in their record-breaking cars. Two engines were fitted into a specially designed chassis and power outputs in excess of 5,000 hp were achieved. However, the fitting of two engines led to a considerable increase in the car's weight to between four and six tons. My father and Mickl had different ideas, based on a single engine and a considerably lower vehicle weight of the order of 3,000 kg (6,615 lb). In order to make full use of the powerful engine, they planned to use aerodynamic aids on the bodywork. The design target was a speed of 435 mph (700 km/h), which would require an output of 3,000 hp. A Daimler-Benz aero engine seemed suited to the job.

In the early 1930s, Daimler had developed a new aero engine series, the DB600, a V12 engine with inverted cylinders arranged at an angle of 60° to each other. This formed the basis of a whole series of increasingly powerful engines. One of these was the 44.5 litre DB603, which had four valves per cylinder, direct fuel injection and two spark plugs per cylinder; the exhaust valves were filled with sodium chloride in order to improve heat dissipation. The engine was supercharged by a Daimler-Benz centrifugal blower, driven directly by the engine.

Trial sample No 3 of the engine that was developed was made available for the new car. This sample had already produced 2,800 hp on the test bench, with a possible short-term increase to 3,500 hp. There was only one problem, and that was that these aero engines were being developed and built on behalf of the Ministry of Aviation whose property they were. However, Ernst Udet, the former stunt pilot now promoted to the rank of general, declared his willingness to lend an engine to his old friend Hans Stuck. Thereupon Hans Stuck entered into an agreement with the chairman of Daimler-Benz AG, Dr Kissel, and, on the basis of the pre-existing contract and patents and their previous experience, the Porsche company was commissioned to design the new car. The engineering drawings were duly submitted on 2 February 1939. The Mercedes-Benz T80 record-breaking racing car had the following technical characteristics:

A twin-tube chassis with tubular cross members; Porsche system front-wheel suspension by lever parallelogram rocking in direction of travel; torsion-bar spring mounting; additional suspension in the middle by means of flexion springs; hydraulic shock absorbers combined with friction discs; rear-wheel suspension by means of oscillating axle with supporting struts; torsion bar suspension with oscillation equalization between both rear wheels; hydraulic shock absorbers combined with friction discs; high-pressure grease lubrication.

The car had four rear wheels, which were all driven. Rear wheel thrust was transferred by struts.

The two front wheels were steered by a Porsche cam-and-peg steering system which had a steering lock angle of 9° to either side. A 9° turn of the steering at the front wheel corresponded to 270° at the steering wheel. The transmission ratio was 1:30. The steering system was mounted in the centre of the car. The car's turning circle was 32 m (35 yd).

A hydraulic inner shoe brake with four shoes per wheel operated on all six wheels. There was an hydraulic brake compensating device, no handbrake was fitted. We used wire spoke wheels with Rudge hubs and a central gap, together with special tyres by Continental. The DB603 engine was mounted in front of the rear axle and had a glycol cooling system which operated at a temperature of 105°C. This car was also a mid-engine design. Twin Bosch magnetos and a Bosch inertia starters were two further technical characteristics. Behind the rear axle was the 80 litre (17.6 gallon) fuel tank.

The car had no gearbox; power was transmitted by a triple disc heat accumulating clutch with automatic centrifugal force adjustment and servo-assisted hydraulic operation by oil pressure. The six rubbing surfaces of the clutch, which ran in oil vapour, were coated with wire cloth with asbestos filling. The clutch was let in by slippage by means of a centrifugal force regulator until the plates were aligned by oil pressure with the rigid power transmission.

One of the special devices fitted to the car was an automatic torque adjuster which regulated engine torque by means of a geared differential between the front and rear wheels in the event of the drive wheels slipping. The centrifugal force adjuster connected to it came into action as soon as the difference in rpm reached five revolutions. This was quite important for safety, since the thin rubber surface of the special tyres might have been

With a Daimler-Benz aero engine type DB 603 as the powerplant, Porsche developed the T80 record car for Daimler-Benz. Here is the V12 engine with direct fuel injection. This engine powered the Messerschmitt Me 109 fighter in large numbers.

33143

33142

damaged if the wheels had slipped when the car started up. An accident at high speed would then have been well within the bounds of possibility.

Another special feature was the pneumatically operated jacks located at four points on the vehicle operated from one central connection for the compressed air.

The light-metal, fully streamlined body was equipped on both sides with fins which had a negative profile for downward pressure. They automatically produced the pressure required to transmit the 3,500 hp to the ground and made it possible to have a lighter vehicle. The contact pressure with the ground increased with vehicle speed.

The car carried 25 litres (5.5 gallons) of oil, which was cooled by an oil cooler next to the water cooler. The dynamic pressure in the cooler was used for the supercharger.

The body was held to the chassis by eight quick-release locks and could be completely lifted off for maintenance work.

The special fuel that was used consisted of equal proportions of two different mixtures containing methyl alcohol, benzole, ethyl alcohol, light petrol, ether, nitrobenzole and acetone. At the top speed of about 400 mph (643.6 km/h) fuel consumption was 225 grams per hp per hour.

The chassis was completely assembled by October 1939; on 12 October it ran on a roller bench. The engine, a DB603, trial sample No 3, was not yet producing its full power and went back to the flight-testing department. (Daimler-Benz had its own test flight department as part of the large-scale aero engine programme.) The trial run on the test bench showed that some changes were required; unfortunately, however, the war brought the work to a halt and the engine remained in the flight-testing department.

Alfred Neubauer, who as racing manager at that time was also involved in the preparations for record attempts, was in a position to give further details of the plans of those days. I consider

Opposite top The Mercedes-Benz world record car T80 designed by Porsche had a planned top speed of 650 km/h (more than 400 mph), but the war stopped the project. The car had short wings with a negative angle to press the car down on the road at high speed.

Opposite middle The T80 had six wheels with the four rear wheels being driven. Note the huge brake drums with their cooling ribs.

Opposite bottom Front view of the T80. The driver (Hans Stuck) sat in front of the aircraft engine, which developed 3500 PS for a short run.

Above this photograph shows the very light and very stiff streamlined frame for the aluminium body.

it important to hear what he had to say, because there were, and still are, a lot of rumours about the planned attempt on the world record. According to Neubauer, it was planned to make the record attempts on the Bonneville Salt Flats in the USA. However, I should perhaps explain what the Salt Flats actually are. If you leave Salt Lake City, Utah, on the Western Highway, you soon come to a desert-like high valley where, not far from the village of Wendover, the Great Salt Lake lies at about 4,265 ft (1,300 m) above sea level. In summer, the top layer of this lake dries out and for a few weeks the salt crust is so firm that it can be used as a track for record attempts; and indeed, record attempts are held there every year in high summer. The stretch that would have been available in 1940 for the record attempt in the T80 was 22 km (13.67 miles) in length; however, according to the calculations of the British record-holder, Captain Eyston, 40 km (24.86 miles) would have been needed for a speed of 400 mph (643.6 km/h).

As a result, according to Neubauer, a section of the motorway between Halle and Dessau was to be laid out for record attempts. However, this plan could not be implemented since the work would have interfered with the opening up of a brown coal seam, which did not seem a good idea. For this reason, the central reservation was concreted over a distance of 10 km (6.2 miles) only, which was not long enough for the absolute record. Nevertheless, 1939 saw another record attempt by Daimler-Benz with an approximately prepared racing car, during which Caracciola reached a speed of almost 250 mph (402 km/h).

Thus an interesting technical achievement was not brought to full fruition; however, evidence of it can still be seen in the Daimler-Benz Museum.

Incidentally, Stuck had had his record plans officially blessed. To this end, he had sought and been granted an audience with Hitler. According to Stuck, he showed Hitler his plans, who then slapped him spontaneously on the shoulder and declared, with a smile, 'Absolute records on land and sea are part of our propaganda. You have our wholehearted support. Good luck, Herr Stuck!'

Unlike Neubauer and Captain Eyston, I still believe even today that the distance available on the Bonneville Salt Flats would have been sufficient for the record. My father shared this view. It was really Hitler who wanted the records to be set in Germany.

Despite the demands of the VW programme, we had of course never abandoned our own racing plans. Indeed, the VW provided an almost perfect basis for further developments in this direction. In the wake of the political co-operation between National Socialist Germany and Fascist Italy — the so-called Berlin-Rome axis — a great race from Berlin to Rome was to be held in 1939. Long before this, we had been making plans to produce our own cars, and

For the publicity race from Berlin to Rome in 1939, Porsche developed this streamlined coupé based on the Volkswagen; a type 60K10 with tuned VW engine and aluminium body. It had a top speed of about 145 km/h (90 mph).

our people were investigating the possibilities and had developed a sports car study based on VW components. In this way, the VW, known to us as the Type 60, led initially to the VW Type 64. This was to be fitted with an engine bored out to 1.5 litres and an aluminium body with a low coefficient of drag.

We had of course submitted our plans for making sports versions of the VW to the leaders of the German Labour Front, but they rejected them out of hand. They were unable to go along with plans of that kind. Later, we hit upon the idea of making our own cars based on VW components, which could have been supplied to us by the Wolfsburg factory, but this proposal was not favourably received either. Sports versions of the VW were rejected principally because they were developments of the Volkswagen concept. As an entirely state-run enterprise, VW did not want to make available components from the KdF car for private initiatives.

However, the Berlin-Rome race at least offered us the opportunity of working on the production of a few of the cars we had in mind, since this after all was an official sporting event organized for propaganda purposes under the auspices of the National Sports Authority. Since the course was to include part of the new Berlin-Munich motorway, then lead from Munich through the Brenner Pass into Austria and thence on to closed-off Italian motorways, a total distance of 1,300 km (808 miles), the race was at the same time an advertisement for the new motorway.

Thus the Porsche Type 60K10 was developed on the basis of the Types 60 and 64; the K indicated that the body was made of aluminium. The engine was also of course made more powerful. Three of these sports coupés were built; they had a top speed of over 87 mph (140 km/h) and in terms of handling and performance represented a considerable step forward.

The Berlin-Rome race was to take place in September 1939, but, like so many other things intended to serve peaceful ends, it too fell victim to the war. We enjoyed driving the 60K10, and my father in particular used it very often for his trips, with Goldinger as his chauffeur. They even set a few records. I remember that my father and Goldinger once made the journey from the Hotel Bristol in Berlin to the Volkswagen factory at Fallersleben at an average speed of 81.25 mph (130.73 km/h). Even despite the motorway, this was a considerable achievement at the time.

Thus at a very early stage we were already involved in the production of sports cars which is today the sector in which our company operates.

8

The Americans questioned

This was a time of extreme political tension and mass hysteria. It sometimes seemed to me that most people were living in a sort of frenzy, whipped up, it is true, by a skilfully orchestrated propaganda campaign. However, for those of our countrymen who had retained some clarity of vision and were able to make occasional visits abroad, as I myself did, the future looked bleak. I had always been a confirmed civilian, and the importance of our company's work for Hitler's Reich prevented me from having to serve in the armed forces. I had got to know Hitler, since it was I who had presented the Volkswagen to him whenever progress had been made in the vehicle's development. Hitler had accepted me in this capacity. At the dedication ceremony for the Volkswagen factory his assessment of the new car had been very positive. Consequently he had been presented with one of the first Volkswagens for his own personal use, which I delivered to him. At the Fallersleben station he had thanked his 'chauffeur', me, most profusely.

Despite all the technically very interesting problems that we had to overcome and which left us with scarcely any time to draw breath, I harboured secret doubts about how long the rest of the world could continue to observe developments in Germany without taking action to curb Hitler's increasingly excessive demands. Even the things my father reported gave me food for thought. My father was basically a completely apolitical person who at that time was enjoying opportunities for work that he had never imagined even in his wildest dreams. Great honours had been bestowed upon him. On 6 September 1938 he had been awarded the German National Prize, which was worth RM 100,000, for the creation of the KdF car. As early as 1924, he had been given the honorary title of Doctor of Engineering by the Stuttgart Institute of Technology.

With the 100,000 Marks of prize money we bought a house on the Wörther See in Austria. This had become possible after the Anschluß and it gave us the opportunity to visit our native country more often. However, my father also spoke of difficulties created by each and every administrative department in connection with the building of the Volkswagen plant. The problems all

Above Hitler is looking at the Volkswagen chassis, with my father on his left doing the explaining. Behind Hitler, the tall man in uniform is Dr Bodo Lafferentz, responsible to the Deutsche Arbeitsfront for the KdF car.

Right The car I drove in 1938 was an Alfa Romeo 6C 2300 with a body designed by Pininfarina. The car shown here was exhibited at the Berlin Motor Show in 1938, where I bought it directly from the stand.

had a common theme, namely that consideration should be given to the military usefulness of the factory in the event of war. Matters went so far that my father said to Hitler one day, 'Am I supposed to be building an armaments factory or one in which to build the Volkswagen?' The answer was, 'Your commission, Dr Porsche, is to build a factory for the Volkswagen, and nothing more!'

Since my father had to spend a lot of time in Wolfsburg, he had a small house built there, a sort of cabin in which he could live and also accommodate guests.

During my trip to the USA in 1937 on board the *Bremen*, I am seen here with the group who were to join my father and the German teams for the Vanderbilt Cup Race. From left: Mrs Werlin, Mr Werlin, Dr Lafferentz, Bernd Rosemeyer, Ernst von Delius, journalist Hundt, and myself.

Many of the ideas and proposals that he had formulated during his visit to America were introduced into the design of the factory, which was to have a daily output of 1,000 and an annual output of 250,000 units.

As well as my father, I was invited by Dr Robert Ley, head of the German Labour Front, to attend the 1938 Party Congress. We were accommodated in Nuremberg in a tent village for guests, where the only place to wash was a temporary wash place set up in the open air for this mass event. Nothing in my experience had prepared me for anything like this. In the evening I was invited to eat at Ley's table, where he was sitting with his wife. One of the topics of conversation, of course, was the Volkswagen, but we also discussed the political situation, the Party Congress and many other things besides.

The next day, the great parade took place in the presence of Hitler. Afterwards, I asked my father, 'Do you need me tomorrow?' My father's reply was short and to the point: 'Why?' I replied, 'Well, Dodo is in Bad Mergentheim because of her gall-bladder trouble, and I'd like to go and see her.'

My father thought he could do without me. I got into my car and hurried to get out of Nuremberg, with all its uniforms and marching, military music and marching songs. When I had left the city behind me, I stopped at the first opportunity and lit a cigarette. I had the same feeling as I used to get during my school days at the beginning of the holidays.

During the drive to Bad Mergentheim I took stock in my mind of the years that had elapsed. What had we and what had the German automobile industry achieved since the low point it had reached in 1932? In the 1920s it had been considered chic to drive an American car, which were imported in large quantities into Germany. It was fashionable to own a Buick. It was also cheaper than a comparable Daimler model, since a Buick could be bought for RM 12,000. In this connection, an interesting episode occurs to me which my father told me about. On 29 September 1927, at a Daimler-Benz board meeting, the following was noted in the minutes:

'In response to the declaration that the German Automobile Club takes a dim view of the company's [Daimler-Benz's] non-participation in the German Grand Prix, it should be pointed out that many of the members of the German Automobile Club drive American cars, the manufacturers of which never take part in motor racing!'

As is common knowledge, the Nürburgring in the Eifel was opened in 1927. The Grand Prix race held on this circuit was won by a Mercedes-Benz driven by Otto Merz. At the time, however, the average citizen valued foreign products more highly than domestic ones. I can still remember very clearly the great difficulties experienced at the time by Daimler, and others, in selling their own cars. True, a Mercedes was not exactly cheap, but anything the Americans sent over was simply considered better.

At that time we were visited by Count Kolowrat, who at the beginning of the 1920s had been the inspiration behind Austro-Daimler's small car, the Sascha. One of the new things he showed us was a hand-operated windscreen wiper from America which wiped the windscreen both inside and out.

My father, who was still working then for Daimler, occasionally brought American cars home which I was allowed to drive; in this way I acquired a certain amount of first-hand experience. For example, I can still clearly remember a Willys Knight with a sleeve valve engine. At that time the Americans were indeed a whole stage more advanced than we were, particularly as far as production engineering was concerned, and their cars were good value for the price at which they were sold.

As a result of our study trips to America, we were fully aware of the difference in production engineering between Germany and the USA. We discovered, for example, that in Germany piston rods were manufactured by subcontractors with a much greater range of tolerances than was the case in the USA. Indeed, standards were so low that on delivery we had to sort the piston rods prior to assembly in order to obtain sets of the same weight. In America, on the other hand, a completely different method of production had been developed. In Germany, a piston rod, for example, was forged in one and the same die-block until it no longer glowed; as a result the die-block would gradually lose its shape, which meant that with each rod that was forged, the tolerance increased. In contrast, the Americans did not forge the workpiece in one single process, but rather in four stages and always at the same temperature. In simple terms, this meant that the Americans were not always hammering on the same die-block until the piston rod acquired the desired shape; rather, they proceeded in stages and took care to ensure that a constant temperature was maintained. The result was a piston rod with a lower tolerance and, no less importantly, the die-block lasted at least four times longer than with our method. When we requested that German forges should adopt the same procedure, the manufacturers just stood open-mouthed, but finally they said, 'Of course we can do it like that!'

Our intention was to develop a modern production system. The German motor industry did make considerable progress in its production engineering techniques, but unfortunately this positive development was halted prematurely by the outbreak of war.

The German motor industry had begun to experience an upturn from the moment that vehicle tax was abolished by the Third Reich, thus stimulating the market. As a consequence, sales increased and people began to drive much more, so that the loss of the vehicle tax was more than offset by increased revenue from petrol tax. (Incidentally, I believe this measure could usefully be implemented today.)

The general upward trend in the motor industry naturally inspired engineers and entrepreneurs to become involved in new ventures. Suddenly people had sufficient confidence to develop new types and new models. The progress made in production engineering was clearly visible. There were export subsidies for cars, particularly cheaper models, because the earning of foreign exchange was a top priority. At the time, it was not entirely obvious to me that this foreign currency was required primarily for the purposes of rearmament. We had nothing at all to do with the armaments industry at the time. We were busy with the Volkswagen, the people's tractor and sports models such as the T80. The industry was now tackling more expensive projects, which had not been possible to realize for reasons of cost, at a time when half the industry had been living in fear of bankruptcy. Engineers were prepared to take greater risks. It was just at that time that the changeover from the rigid axle to independent wheel suspension in all its possible variants was taking place. As far as technical development was concerned, there were a great number of initiatives being implemented which may well have already existed in embryo but which it had been impossible to realize because of the general economic situation.

The Silver Arrow racing cars were another example: the technical design was already in existence, but it could not be realized until state subsidies became available.

The racing cars were also the inspiration for certain developments in the mass produced cars. It could even be said that the

Auto Union racing car had some influence on the design of the Volkswagen. At any rate, the design of the Auto Union racing car, with its engine mounted on the driving axle, was pretty unusual. No less unusual at the time was the design of the Volkswagen, with its engine located behind the rear axle.

There were also parallels between the Auto Union racing car and the Volkswagen in the design of the front axle. The torsion-bar suspension on the VW's axle was a simplified and much cheaper version of the axle used on the racing car. This link between racing cars and series production persists even today. As this is being written, we are building an aero engine into which some of the experience acquired in the development of the Formula 1 engine for TAG is being incorporated or, having been used in series production, is now influencing the design of the aero engine. In the Formula 1 engine, we use a particular kind of piston cooling system in which some of the oil flow is diverted through the piston. This system was of course very expensive to develop for the TAG Formula 1 engine, but in the meantime our engineers have discovered a cheaper way of accomplishing the idea. Of course that is not exactly a disadvantage for the piston temperature in an aero engine, but probably of great benefit, and if it is beneficial for the aero engine, it will probably also be of benefit to the engine of the 911, which will once again complete the circle linking racing and series production.

9

Hitler goes mad

In March 1939 German troops marched into Czechoslovakia and the country became part of the German Reich. As a result, there were renewed expressions of outrage in the foreign press and much diplomatic activity among governments. Our reputation in the world had declined still further.

In America and elsewhere, the outrages committed against the German Jewish population and the racial laws had understandably given rise to bitter protests. Even during our trip to America in 1937 I had felt what was going on there. We travelled on the *Bremen* and in our class there was a Hungarian Jewish family with a large flock of children, four girls and a boy. Disparaging remarks were made about this family at the captain's table, and their presence on board a German ship was criticized. The captain of the *Bremen*, Commander Ahrens, said in reply to this, 'They are passengers who travel with us every year. In any case, they bring foreign currency with them, which we urgently need!'

This put an end to the conversation, although for me the subject was not closed. I found one of the young girls very attractive and one evening I asked her for a dance. My invitation was accepted. The next day, however, one of the passengers said to me, 'Herr Porsche, it would be wise not to do that again!'

The atmosphere was tense. Evil hung in the air. One felt that the future was uncertain. Although in material terms people were considerably better off than at the beginning of the 1930s, and nobody wanted war, it no longer seemed possible to stop Hitler in his territorial claims and his political extremism. When the German-Soviet pact was announced in August 1939, it was thought initially that it reflected a certain easing of tension, but this was a false conclusion, since from that moment on Hitler became more determined than ever to go through with his plans, starting with the invasion of Poland.

Despite this, we went ahead with the plans for our annual excursion, in which the whole company was to take part. Our planned destination was Chiemsee Lake, but we had no intention of going by coach; rather, every single vehicle we could get hold of, including the test cars, was made ready for the journey. Even at the end of July, there was already a petrol shortage due to the military build-up, so we took the necessary fuel with us in cans. My father took a room at the motel in Chiemsee, while I lodged at an inn in Prien where we all met for our evening meal. Everything was very well organized; there was a Bavarian country band and my father of course gave a speech.

The speech he gave that evening surprised me a great deal, since his words were very positive. Although he did not mention war as such, it could be inferred from his speech that such a thing as war was unthinkable. I had the impression that my father felt he had to calm his people down. He seemed to succeed in this, since there was much merriment that evening; people danced and everybody was very boisterous.

When I saw my father next morning for breakfast at the motel, he looked at me and said, 'Did you get any sleep?' Of course I had not even been to bed. After a good breakfast I drove my father to our house on the Wörthersee. We reached our destination as planned, and despite the lack of sleep I drove faultlessly. After my father had disappeared into the house I went to the beach, lay down in the grass and immediately fell asleep. I had not slept for more than 24 hours.

It was the last holiday that we were to spend in peacetime on the Wörthersee. It was brought to an end by the announcement on state radio that German troops had marched into Poland on 1 September 1939. On 3 September, my father's birthday, England and France declared war on Germany. My spontaneous reaction was to state, 'Now Hitler's gone mad!'

This remark gave rise to a sharp reprimand from my father. His straightforward character and his sense of decency made it impossible for him to imagine that a German government, with responsibility for the welfare of the people, would deliberately follow a policy that could only end in war. Of course the opportunities for work offered to him in the Third Reich had impressed him, but that was not the decisive factor. It was his uprightness that made it seem inconceivable to him that everything that had been achieved hitherto was to be put at risk by going to war. As an engineer, he was accustomed to thinking logically and clearly, and he could see no sense in what had now happened.

It was perfectly clear to me at that moment that the whole affair would end badly.

The outbreak of war put paid of course to the plans for the Berlin-Rome race, and so the three light-metal coupés that had been prepared for it could now be used for private purposes. One of the cars had in fact already been used extensively by my father, and a second had been reserved by Dr Lafferentz. This coupé was later wrecked in an accident. The third car was loaned occasionally to Herr Werlin.

It had been planned to make the first KdF cars available to cus-

A portrait of Professor Dr Ferdinand Porsche before the Second World War.

tomers at the beginning of 1940, but that could now be forgotten as we had other things to keep us busy than the development of cars for private use. Cross-country vehicles had not until now featured on our programme, although it is true that the light, easily manageable Volkswagen tempted us now and then to all sorts of fun, including mounting two bucket seats on its chassis and driving the vehicle cross-country. During these not infrequent races we were repeatedly impressed by the range of things that could be done with the Volkswagen.

Consequently the conversion from Volkswagen to cross-country vehicle was not so extraordinary, and with the outbreak of war was even to be expected.

The Military Ordnance Office was at that time responsible for the army's technical equipment, and it was here that we had to deliver our Volkswagen for cross-country trials. On the basis of the vehicle's technical design and its performance, we viewed the trials without any particular concern. That at least is what we thought, but we were very wrong. We very soon noticed that the Military Ordnance Office was not favourably disposed towards us, despite the fact that we had been recommended by Daimler-Benz and that there were several high-ranking officers in the Ordnance Office who had known my father during the First World War and were thus aware of his earlier work.

One of the ways in which the ill-feeling was expressed was that our VW bucket car, as the soldiers were later to call it, was driven much harder on test drives than its rival designs. The Military Ordnance Office was in the habit of putting its projects out to tender and then working on them in collaboration with companies of its own choice. For example, our vehicle had to cover the entire test track, including the most difficult obstacles, while the vehicles preferred by the Ordnance Office only had to cover part of the course, and of course, anything can be deliberately driven into the ground.

At that time my father had a number of projects to complete and was often away on business. During this period I was in charge of the design office, and was thus responsible for the development of the Volkswagen. Consequently I intervened in the cross-country trials and addressed the committee in the following terms: 'Gentlemen, if our car has to complete the entire course that you've laid out, then I expect you to make the same demands of its rivals!'

This request could not of course be refused, and in the trials that followed our VW actually turned in the best performance. But this did not mean that we had an order for production of the car in large volumes, and that in the final analysis was what mattered. It was Hitler himself who made the decision and ordered the production of the VW cross-country vehicle. I had presented

The first cross-country version of the Volkswagen without its body, shortly before the Second World War at the Porsche factory on Spitalwaldstrasse 2 in Stuttgart-Zuffenhausen.

the vehicle to Hitler myself and he had quite understandably shown a particular interest in it, since it was based on 'his' KdF car.

However, Hitler's decision was not necessary in order to prove that our design was the superior one. This judgement was made by the soldiers themselves who, on all fronts, gave preference whenever possible to the VW bucket car with its air-cooled engine. It was light, easy to maintain, robust and its four-man crew could manoeuvre it over the most difficult terrain without a tank or tractor being needed to pull it out of the mud, because of its low weight.

Incidentally, the cross-country vehicle made a significant contribution to the world-wide fame of the later Volkswagen. Enemy soldiers would sometimes capture one, and they soon became aware of its advantages. When the VW came on to the interna-

This is the final form of the cross-country version of the Volkswagen, better known as the Kübelwagen. In the Porsche programme the car was given the type number 82.

tional market after the war, soldiers remembered its earlier 'relative' with a certain degree of affection.

We were subsequently commissioned by the Ordnance Office to develop a version of the VW cross-country vehicle for use in Africa. The conditions prevailing there made it necessary to introduce some special technical features. Thus a suction filter had to be fitted in order to prevent desert sand from getting into the cylinders. We also fitted broader tyres with no tread and strengthened the front axle; in short, after trials in Africa, the car was prepared for use in the desert conditions of North Africa.

The planning of the North African campaign was being conducted in the strictest secrecy. Indeed, it was surrounded with such great secrecy that the departments responsible for supplies did not know precisely where the various *matériel* was to be sent.

Here the VW-Kübelwagen is shown with folding top. The car was widely used by the German army during the Second World War.

Porsche type 128 was an amphibian version of the VW-Kübelwagen, built for the German army. Here it is during a test, with myself behind the steering wheel.

101

As a result, the vehicles that had been specially adapted for use in North Africa were sent to Russia, while Rommel's Afrika Corps received the Russian version. However, the Russian version proved to be well suited to conditions in North Africa.

When we came to develop the amphibious car, we learnt at first hand how the narrow-mindedness of bureaucracies can sometimes produce results more akin to folly than good sense. The Ordnance Office handed over the vehicle to the Department of Engineering Equipment, which had a regulation that watercraft should carry red and green running lights. Now the amphibious car was indeed a watercraft when it was using its ability to cross a river. I asked the people at the department, 'Do you want the lamps to show the enemy which direction you're travelling in? And perhaps we should fit it out with an anchor?'

This amphibious car developed for the engineers had a VW engine bored out to 1,131 cc, like its successor.

One day, some officers of the Waffen-SS appeared in my office and said that we were to develop a motor cycle for them, with a VW engine and a driven sidecar wheel. I asked them, 'What do you want to do with this vehicle?' The answer was, 'To drive anywhere!' 'Right,' I replied. 'I'll make you a vehicle which will take you anywhere, but it won't be a motor cycle!'

My proposal was accepted and as a result we built a smaller version of the amphibious vehicle with broader tyres and four-wheel drive which was able to hold its own with the Panzer divisions even when the army was bogged down in the Russian mud. It was also the only cross-country vehicle that could really go anywhere. In all, 14,283 units of this type were produced, while about 60,000 units of the standard VW cross-country vehicle were made. We also produced a tracked vehicle based on the VW for winter use.

It might be useful at this point to use the type designations to give an overview of the development of our military cross-country vehicles in the order in which they went into production. The first VW bucket car bore the designation Type 62 in the Porsche company programme. This was the vehicle that was very thoroughly tested by the Military Ordnance Office. The Type 82 then went into mass production with just a few changes.

The amphibious vehicle developed for the army bore the designation Type 128. Its overall dimensions were somewhat larger than those of the Type 166 which we developed for the Waffen-SS. The Type 166, with its four-wheel drive, proved itself to all intents and purposes as the best cross-country vehicle for military use.

In between there were also special versions. Attempts were made, for example, to improve the wintertime capability of the bucket car. There was a half-track vehicle, designated the Type 155. We used various types of wheels with a widened tread or

skis on the front wheels, and for the VW bucket car there were even wheels which made it possible for it to be driven on tracks.

The Type 87 was derived from the saloon; it had greater ground clearance, four-wheel drive and special tyres for use in desert conditions, particularly North Africa. The Type 82E saloon also had greater clearance for travelling across country, but did not have four-wheel drive.

Above and below left Porsche type 166, the famous Schwimm-wagen, first developed at the demand of the SS. Altogether 14,283 units of this all-round amphibian were manufactured.

Rear view of the VW-
Schwimmwagen.
Clearly seen is the
propeller, which here is
in the raised position
for driving the car on
land.

However, it is not at all true that the Volkswagen had been developed with the aim of using it for military purposes. Nor was the Volkswagen factory intended to be used for the manufacture of armaments. This is abundantly clear from Hitler's answer when my father questioned him on the matter.

At the beginning of the war, there were already almost 300,000 owners of VW savings cards who were eagerly collecting their stamps and sticking them to the cards. The Volkswagen was conceived as a means of mass transport; it was designed with the aim of offering the man in the street a little bit of independence by making it possible for him to afford his own car. With the outbreak of the Second World War, this aim unfortunately passed completely out of sight. Nevertheless, it was to become a reality after the war, when democracy had been restored.

Incidentally, we also gave Hitler a VW amphibious vehicle, which I myself presented to him. In this connection, I have very clear memories of a visit to his headquarters in East Prussia near Rastenburg. The place was swarming with mosquitoes. After Hitler had inspected the vehicle, his aides were still standing together discussing the new machine. Suddenly, a mosquito landed on Field Marshal Keitel's cheek. Hitler saw it and, taking his glove that he was holding in his hand, he swatted the mosquito and killed it. However, it had already bitten the Field Marshal, leaving a small bloodstain on his cheek. Hitler said, 'Here is the first German general to spill his own blood!'

Since the vehicle had been designed for his troops, Heinrich Himmler, head of the SS, attended the presentation of the amphibious vehicle at the Führer's headquarters. The evening after the presentation, Himmler paid us a visit in our quarters and during our conversation asked, 'Herr Porsche, are you actually a member of the SS?' Truthfully, I answered, 'No, sir!' Indeed, I was not a member of any party organization. At this, Himmler beckoned to his adjutant and said to him, 'Please note that Herr Porsche has been appointed to the rank of SS Untersturmführer!' He shook my hand and left.

Shortly afterwards I received a letter from SS headquarters which contained the certificate of honour giving formal notice of my appointment to the rank of honorary SS Untersturmführer. Everyone who remembers the conditions that prevailed at that time will agree that it would have been extremely dangerous to refuse this 'honour'. However, it was later to cause me some trouble.

After the collapse of the Third Reich, I was 'interrogated' in Salzburg by American officers. One of them asked me whether I was a member of the SS or any other Nazi organization.

I looked the man straight in the face and said, 'You'll have to help me there, because I was made an honorary Untersturmführer, but I never gave my consent to it.' He replied, 'Well, were you or were you not in the SS?' I said, 'Allow me to ask you a simple question. If you were made an honorary citizen of Salzburg, would that make you an Austrian?' The American shook his head and let me go.

In December 1951 I was invited to go to America for the first time after the war. An American company was planning to build a small jeep and wanted to use components supplied by us. When I applied for my visa, I was asked the questions normally asked at that time: 'Were you a member of the SS or any other Nazi organization?' With a clear conscience I answered 'No.' I received my visa and flew to America.

On my return a memo was waiting for me. It read, 'Please telephone the US consulate in Stuttgart. Urgent!' I telephoned immediately and I was told, 'You did not inform us that you had been a member of the SS!' I replied, 'If you do not believe me, then you can check whether I was in the SS. It is true that I was appointed by Himmler to the rank of Untersturmführer, but you will not find anything in the documents that has my signature on it, or any personal records, nothing at all except what Himmler himself arranged!' A week later I received a telephone call from the consulate to tell me that everything was in order.

But I have anticipated events somewhat, so let us return to wartime.

Our contract with Daimler-Benz had come to an end in 1940 because work in the civilian area covered by the contract was now non-existent. The war and everything connected with it took priority. Nevertheless, Daimler-Benz suggested to the Ministry of Armament, which was then under the leadership of Dr Todt, that we should be hired as consultants. Dr Todt gave his approval and my father was appointed head of the Tank commission. That was probably also the reason why in the latter part of the war we were mainly employed in the design and development of armoured vehicles.

From the very beginning, my father got on very well with Dr Todt. They had similar views and Dr Todt respected my father as an expert in his own field. In addition, the difference in age between them was not as great as that between my father and Albert Speer, for example, who took over the Ministry of Armament after the death of Dr Todt. Although my father may have had a somewhat irascible temperament, he was a very approachable and talkative man with whom it was easy to speak.

On 12 September 1940 my father, who had already been given the honorary titles of Doctor of Technology and Doctor of Engineering, was awarded an honorary professorship by the Minister for Science and Education. This honour gave him a great deal of pleasure.

And in Ferry Porsche's family also there was a happy event: on 29 October 1940 our third son, Hans Peter, was born.

10

Tanks for the army

The war naturally shifted the focus of our activities to military work, in particular because of the position of responsibility that my father had assumed with the Tank Commission. In addition to the various orders for cross-country vehicles, our time was spent mainly on armoured vehicles.

We had received the first order for the development of a tank in December 1939, before my father became a member of the Tank Commission. The order was for a medium-weight tank of between 35 and 40 tons to be built on behalf of the Military Ordnance Office; if possible, it was to be powered by an air-cooled engine.

The tank was given the designation Porsche Type 100 and the name Leopard. It has nothing at all to do with the Leopard currently in service with the German Federal Armed Forces, but it was a very modern design. The Leopard had a mixed power system, like those used with success by my father before and during the First World War. Via two flange-mounted generators, two internal combustion engines supplied power to electric motors mounted behind each other in the middle of the vehicle. These electric motors drove the two front sprocket wheels via the corresponding special gear systems. As a result of this drive system, both the power transmission and the steering of the 35 ton vehicle were virtually stepless. For a tank of that period, this was undoubtedly a very advanced design.

We also intended to use an air-cooled diesel engine as a power source, because it is easier to run and more robust, even under difficult weather conditions, than a petrol engine. We designed an air-cooled V10 diesel engine with a cubic capacity of 10 litres which produced 210 hp at 2,500 rpm. Two of these diesel engines were to be used to power the tank by means of the system described above. Our proposal would have been a very sound one, as later events, particularly the Russian campaign, were to show. The conditions in Russia made tremendous demands on material and a diesel engine would have been more robust than the petrol engines that were used.

The engine was to be developed at the Nibelungen factory set up and operated by Steyr AG in St Valentin in Lower Austria.

Since a tank must have as small a frontal area as possible, in order to present the enemy with a difficult target, our tank was built very low. This was achieved with three roller carriages on each side, each with two rubber rollers and longitudinal torsion bars per track, which ran via bent levers on to the roller carriages.

The design work was completed in April 1941; the Russian campaign began on 22 June 1941. According to our contract with the Ordnance Office, the next stage was to be the building of two prototypes without turrets for test purposes. In July, Steyr delivered the first two sample engines. The engines were installed and the trials could begin. We obtained good results, but in the meantime the position had changed. At a meeting with Hitler at the end of May 1941, which my father had attended as representative of the Tank Commission, Hitler suddenly demanded a heavy tank.

'I have received information,' he said, 'which suggests that the English are sending a tank of that kind to the front!'

My father and the Henschel company were commissioned independently to develop a 40 ton tank with heavier guns and armour than all previous models. Work on the Leopard was halted forthwith and we started to design the Porsche Type 101, named the Tiger. Nevertheless, the design of the Tiger was in many ways a continuation of the work we had done on the Leopard, and the experience we had gained with that design served us well in our work on the heavier tank.

In July 1941, the German armoured regiments encountered the Russian T34 for the first time, which was clearly superior to the German designs being used. As a result of this, Hitler ordered that the development of the 40 ton tank be accelerated. Shortly afterwards, German troops captured some intact T34s. One of these was very soon made available to the Tank Commission and was thoroughly examined and tested at a training ground on Lüneburg Heath.

The T34 was equipped with a V12 water-cooled diesel engine which produced 500 hp. Our engineers put the engine on the braking platform in order to find out its actual output. After a while they came up to my father and said, 'The Russians aren't half exaggerating! The output is nothing like 500 hp, more like 350 at the most!'

My father went with them to the braking platform and took a close look at the engine. It did not take him long to see what had happened, 'Look, they've slowed down the engine. You can see the lead seal on the injection pump!'

The men were convinced and now knew why the engine was not producing its full output. 'Now I know why the Russian engines last longer than ours. They force their soldiers to drive with less power. As a result, the engines not only use less fuel, but are also not pushed to the limits of their capabilities, as our petrol engines are,' explained my father.

The simplicity of its design and its robustness made the T34 very impressive. It was designed in such a way that it could be produced without difficulty, and hence more quickly. Its running gear, which was basically designed in accordance with the patent held by the American engineer Christie, also employed our torsion bar suspension. We never received any licence fee from the Russians, and I doubt whether any such fees were ever paid to Christie.

My father had very quickly formed a clear opinion of the T34, because when he was asked what he would suggest as an answer to what was probably the best tank in existence, he said bluntly but clearly, 'Copy it!'

This was not at all a bad strategy, since it would have meant that an answer to the T34 could be found very quickly, while at the same time the German engineers would be at liberty to make improvements if any were required.

At the same time, my father remembered something that had happened while he was working at the Daimler Motor Company. At that time Daimler were developing two tanks which went under the code names Big Tractor I and II. Under the Treaty of Versailles, the Germans were forbidden to develop such machines, yet one of these tanks had also been tested at a training ground on Lüneburg Heath. When representatives of the Allied Commission announced their arrival for an inspection visit, the tank, together with the engineers, very quickly disappeared into the Soviet Union, where trials of armoured vehicles were being held in Kama in conjunction with the Red Army. It is likely that both sides benefited technically from these trials.

My father's suggestion that the T34 should simply be copied was not approved by the military authorities. The arrogance of the leadership and the doctrine of the 'master race' meant that it would have been intolerable to admit, even indirectly, that the Soviets had been working more effectively in this specialist area.

My father, whom Hitler considered as a sort of fatherly adviser in technical matters, occasionally made his presence felt at Hitler's headquarters by making astonishing proposals. He once suggested to Hitler, in the presence of the internationally renowned tank expert, Colonel General Guderian, that in future smaller soldiers should be used in the tank corps. 'The maximum height for a member of a tank crew should not exceed 1.65 m [5 ft 3 in],' said my father, and went on, 'There's absolutely no reason to use men of Guardsman size in a tank! In this way, we can not only save raw materials, but we can also build smaller tanks which will offer the enemy a smaller area to aim at!' We had always been proponents of lighter, quicker and more manoeuvrable tanks.

Hitler's reply was, 'There's something in that. And what's more, small men are more courageous than big ones, look at Napoleon and Prince Eugene — and Victor Emmanuel [King of Italy] is the exception that proves the rule!' But the matter never went any further.

On 8 February 1942, Dr Fritz Todt, the Armaments Minister, was killed in an aeroplane crash. My father very much regretted his death, not only because he liked him as a person, but also because they had understood each other in technical matters. His successor was Albert Speer, the 'Führer's architect'. Speer was certainly a talented young man, whose strength was construction, while he subsequently proved himself as an administrator.

A great deal has been written about my father's relationship with Speer. All I would like to say is that the good understanding that had existed between my father and Dr Todt gave way to a somewhat distant relationship. This was quite understandable, because the difference in age between my father and Speer was just too great. My father was a representative of the generation that had come to maturity before the First World War, while Speer was a young, dynamic manager who touched the dictator's weak spot, architecture, and who had what amounted to a father and son relationship with Hitler and could therefore count on his support.

I experienced often enough the reality of the relationship with Speer. One example from a meeting of the Tank Commission, at which I was also present, will illustrate this very well. We were proposing, with the aid of engineering drawings, that a five-man tank should be replaced by a small tank weighing less than 30 tons with a two-man crew. This was to be achieved by fitting an automatic cannon like those used on fighter aircraft and having the second man drive the tank. Speer, the trained architect, who had initially been responsible only for architecture in the new German Reich, said, 'If that weight's right, I'll eat my hat!', to which my father replied in a real Swabian manner (he had really settled down in Stuttgart!), 'And I'll eat the charlady if it's not right!'

The engineer had thought about this proposal a little and had come to the conclusion that what was possible in an aircraft, which is much more difficult to control than a tank, ought to be possible in an earthbound vehicle. But even Speer could not think in dimensions other than those of the military. A tank had to have a crew consisting of a commander, a gunner, a loader, a radio operator and a driver.

In the meantime, progress had been made with the development of the Tiger, although Hitler had demanded further considerable changes, such as, for example, stronger armour. On 20 April, Hitler's fifty-third birthday, the two prototypes, one produced by Henschel and one by us, were presented at Hitler's headquarters near Rastenburg. Hitler was impressed by our designs and ordered that both tanks should go into series production.

Shortly afterwards, the Ordnance Office started testing the two tanks at a military training ground between Mühlhausen and

The Porsche Tiger tank was later modified into the so-called Jagdpanzer (Porsche type 130) called Ferdinand. Here the Ferdinand is being test driven by minister Albert Speer and my father (with hat) is sitting next to him on the tank.

Eisenach in Thuringia called Berka am Hainich. Both tanks performed well in the trials, but in his official capacity as armaments minister, Speer tended to lean towards the Henschel version. This was a tank of conventional design with a water-cooled V12 Maybach engine, Type HL 210 P 45, which produced about 650 hp. Unlike our unit, this was a petrol engine.

During the deciding trial at Berka am Hainich, Henschel used a tank without a turret. We nicknamed the vehicle the 'sports car', because without the enormous weight of the turret, with its huge armoured dome and cannon, the tank could be driven over the terrain just like a sports car. Speer obviously enjoyed driving the vehicle across the countryside, whereas he did not once take the trouble to test the Porsche Tiger.

As the man in charge of armaments, perhaps he was afraid of putting the innovatory and advanced Porsche design into production instead of the conventional Henschel tank, since Hitler wanted to see production figures. However, Hitler had also decided to put both versions into series production, and Speer could not go against his order.

So what was innovatory about the Porsche Tiger? Basically, it was designed on the same principles as the Leopard, except that the power units were two V10 air-cooled diesel engines with a cubic capacity of 15 litres and an output of 320 hp at 2,400 rpm. The Porsche drive system, in which the two diesel engines drove a generator which in turn provided power for two rear-mounted electric motors, was a mixed system which made use of both internal combustion engines and electric motors. It was the electric motors which, through an appropriate gear system, drove the track wheels. This system made it possible to use a virtually unlimited number of different transmission systems. The electric motors used in the system were supplied by Siemens-Schuckert in Berlin.

Another possibility for the transmission system was a hydraulic gearbox with two torque convertors per engine designed by Voith Heidenheim. Two prototypes of this design were ordered in March from the Nibelungen plant established by Steyr in St Valentin for tank production.

Unfortunately, however, we did not have time to develop the new diesel engine to the production stage. There were problems with the oil circulation because oil was being lost through faulty seals. We estimated that another two years were needed until the air-cooled diesel engine could be put into production.

Even a 16-cylinder diesel engine in X formation proposed in the meantime did not alter the fact that new designs and new concepts required a certain amount of development time.

We had initially planned a conventional system with a mechanical gearbox and clutch as an alternative for the Tiger. However, we were not convinced that this was the right design solution for the Tiger, the weight of which had increased in the meantime to almost 60 tons. The conservative drive system employed by our rivals Henschel finally won the contract. The real reason for this decision was probably that the army could not warm to the completely new design that we were proposing. They believed that it would create too many problems when used at the front, which it would take too long to put right; and with the increasing pressure being felt on all fronts in the war, time was just what we did not have.

The estimates we had made in 1942 gave a good idea of the performance of which the Porsche Tiger with its diesel-electric power system was capable. It could climb gradients up to 1 in 3 with no difficulty at all, and despite a weight of around 60 tons its top speed was still about 22 mph (35 km/h). It was armed with an 8.8 cm cannon and two machine-guns.

The Porsche Tiger was now put to a different use, while the Henschel Tiger went into production immediately. Our design was turned into a so-called tank destroyer with the Porsche designation Type 130. This vehicle was a self-propelled gun mount with 200 mm of armour on the front, even thicker than that on the Tiger. However, the tank did not have the usual turret, but a casemate structure mounted behind the front armour with an 88 mm PAK 43/2 cannon. The PAK 43/2 was an anti-tank cannon derived from the 8.8 anti-aircraft gun, with a high V_0 (the initial velocity at which a bullet leaves the barrel) and great penetrating power.

The air-cooled Porsche diesel engines were not yet ready for production, and so we used two water-cooled V12 Maybach engines, Type HL 120 TRM, which produced 320 hp at 3,000 rpm. They powered the flange-mounted generators, while the electric motor was mounted in the rear and acted as a sort of underfloor engine on the rear two track wheels. As far as the Maybach engine is concerned, it should be pointed out that it was at the time the preferred German tank engine and was built in large batches in various versions with power outputs up to 700 hp. During the Second World War, about 140,000 Maybach tank engines were produced.

The driver and radio operator sat in the front of the tank, and a further four men were accommodated in the casemate. Their task was to remain in readiness, well camouflaged, until the enemy attacked, then bring their strong fire power to bear and knock out as many enemy tanks as possible.

The Ordnance Office named the tank destroyer Ferdinand after my father (Hitler later called the tank 'Elephant'). In all, 90 units of the 68 ton Ferdinand were built and used in both Russia and Italy. On the Russian front, Ferdinands knocked out about 700 tanks and a large number of guns of various kinds.

In describing the development of the Tiger, I mentioned an air-cooled, X16 diesel engine with a cylinder angle of 135° which was considered as a possible alternative to the Porsche 10-cylinder. My father had always been a proponent of air-cooled diesel engines as a power unit for tanks, since they have many advantages over petrol engines. They are not only less demanding with respect to fuel quality but are also less prone to breakdowns, both factors which could not be too highly valued in hard use at the front. Our design office drew up plans for a 16-cylinder engine in X or double V format with fan-driven air cooling and exhaust-driven turbocharging, the Brown-Boveri Buechi system, which had a cubic capacity of 36.8 litres. It was given the Porsche designation Type 220 and was produced in collaboration with Simmering-Graz-Pauker AG of Vienna.

Boost pressure, at 1.33 ata, was to be kept as high as possible, while the compression ratio, at 1:14.5, was to be kept relatively low in order to extend the operational life of the power unit. Its dimensions were to be such that it could be substituted for the widely-used Maybach petrol engines. Since the diesel engine ran more slowly than the Maybach (2,000 rpm and 3,000 rpm respectively), an appropriate transmission system had to be used. While the Maybach engine produced 600 to 700 hp, the Type 220 had a power output of between 780 and 800 hp.

The exhaust turbocharger was also new, and the design selected reached standards still prevalent today. This turbocharger increased output considerably, so that the 80 hp could be used to drive the cooling fan, which required 6,000 litres of air per second.

The engine had a Bosch direct fuel injection system and a crankshaft cast from manganese steel which ran in five lead and bronze bearings. The pistons were made of aluminium with five thrust collars and a deflector. The exhaust valves were filled with sodium for better cooling; this method had already been used before the war in the racing car engines and in the 600 series Daimler-Benz aero engines. Twin pumps, mounted behind each other, conveyed the lubricating oil via an oil cooler to the bearings. The very compact engine was 1,680 mm long, 2,500 mm wide and 1,150 mm high (65.52 x 97.5 x 44.85 in).

Of course this engine was well ahead of its time and production of it would have required the best raw materials. At that time, however, there was a shortage of high-grade raw materials, and the people in charge of distributing them were reluctant to sanction their use, in view of the constant deterioration in the situation at the fronts. Nevertheless, I still maintain that this air-cooled diesel engine would have been the best power unit for tanks. Moreover, it could have been used for many other purposes.

By the end of the war, only two engines of the Porsche Type 220 had been produced. It was planned to use them in a Tiger or Panther tank in trials at the Nibelungen factory, but these plans came to nothing. When the Russians occupied Austria in 1945, they probably captured the two engines and all the engineering drawings.

Looking back, I still believe that my father's suggestion of simply copying the Russian Type T34 would not have been a bad idea, given the multiplicity of types that prevailed at the time. Of course the optimal solution would have been not to start a war at all.

Hitler's yearning for the gigantic was to lead to another tank heavier than anything yet produced, although Soviet tanks of the heaviest class had occasionally been observed during the invasion of Russia. Thus Hitler had, probably unconsciously, been thinking of earlier examples when he divulged his thoughts to my father. The conversation took place in June 1942 in the Chancellory in Berlin. Speer was also present. Hitler instructed my father to build an overheavy tank fitted with one 12.5 cm and one 7.5 cm cannon in a turret, or alternatively one 18 cm cannon in a casemate. Obviously, my father first of all wanted Hitler to tell him the purpose for which this monster was to be used. Hitler explained his ideas to the assembled company:

'My idea is that a tank of this kind could be used in formation like a battleship, accompanied by smaller tanks travelling in front of or alongside it in order to protect it from mines or air attacks. Its firepower will be sufficient to break down any resistance. What do you think, Herr Porsche?'

My father was very much an engineer rather than a soldier, and he gave Hitler his honest opinion, which went something like this: 'I think it's a bad idea to use materials and labour that are urgently needed elsewhere for a project of this kind. I am not sufficiently acquainted with the military way of thinking to be able to say with any accuracy what advantages such a mammoth tank might have!'

Hitler, who valued my father's opinion in technical matters, listened quietly to his arguments, but did not seem willing to abandon his idea. He replied,

'I've got another task in mind for this land battleship. It looks as though we could do with a number of mobile bunkers to strengthen the Atlantic Wall, which has gaps in a few places. Let us assume that one of these concrete bunkers is destroyed during an enemy landing attempt; this steel monster could fill the breach very quickly and keep the enemy at bay with its enormous firepower until the bunker is operational again. The heavy tanks would always be available for this purpose!'

On this basis, Hitler's idea seemed to make more sense to my father. Once erected, a bunker was of course completely immobile. Moreover, we knew from conversations with Dr Todt that not all bunkers were stable enough to withstand all attacks, nor did they all have guns. A further argument in favour of Hitler's idea was that the guns that were in the bunkers could only fire towards the sea. A 'mobile bunker' in the shape of a heavy tank thus had much to commend it.

My father remarked that a tank of this kind would have to be particularly heavily armoured in order to be able to withstand a direct hit from a large-calibre shell. Hitler had already realized that, but he wanted to know what else my father had to say on the technical aspects of such a massive tank.

'The weight will create problems. Just in order to move such a monster, we will have to reduce considerably the weight per square centimetre of track. However, I believe we can solve this problem!' declared my father. Hitler rejoined, 'By widening the track?' 'Yes,' said my father, and went on, 'and we shall also have to lengthen it considerably.'

My father suggested a track width of about one metre, which subsequently proved to be correct. The tank would not have to be so wide that it could not be transported. Bridges and tunnels clearly imposed restrictions in this respect. Despite all the arguments to the contrary, including those of the army, Hitler decided to put his idea into practice, and the Ordnance Office awarded us the contract.

During the discussion with Hitler, it had become obvious to my father that Speer was very sceptical about Hitler's idea, and he expressed this opinion to my father. In his book *Memories*, published by Propyläen Verlag, Berlin, he wrote of the heavy tank:

'In order to please and pacify Hitler, a super-heavy tank was developed at the same time by Porsche; it weighed over a hundred tons and for that reason alone could have been built only in very small quantities. In order to mislead spies, this new monster was given the code name 'Maus' [mouse]. Porsche had embraced Hitler's enthusiasm for super-heavy vehicles such as this and from time to time he brought him news of similar developments in the enemy camp.'

Speer's remarks completely miss the point, because the development of heavy tanks had in fact been neglected by the Ordnance Office, as was shown at the beginning of the Russian campaign, and it was Hitler who ordered it. We never disputed the tactical significance and advantages of a medium-weight, fast tank, as our proposals to Speer made clear.

My father was of course much too much of an engineer to refuse a challenge of this sort from Hitler. Nor did he ever make any secret of the fact that he knew too little of military matters to be able to assess the military usefulness of the super-heavy tank. He had a small-scale model of the new tank built and proved once again that he thought himself capable of solving this problem.

Our suggestion that the Maus should be fitted with the X16 diesel engine that we had designed and were developing was rejected by Speer. He suggested a Daimler-Benz aero engine as an alternative. Here we were able to fall back on the experience we had gained in the design of the T80, which was also to have been powered by a Daimler-Benz aero engine.

Under the type designation 205, code name Maus, the Porsche design office developed the heaviest tank of the last war. It had a fighting weight of 189 tons, with the turret alone weighing 51.5 tons. Special wagons were built by the Simmering-Graz-Pauker company to transport the tank by rail. However, most bridges were not built to take such a weight, so the Maus had to be transported by river. It could operate at a depth of 8 m (8.8 yd).

We decided to use the electric power transmission for this project as well, although at this time the system had not been rejected

Porsche type 205, the famous Maus ('Mouse') giant tank. At 189 tons it was the biggest tank of the Second World War, and was powered by a Daimler-Benz V12 engine of 1,200 PS.

Rear view of the supertank 'Maus', designed by Porsche.

for use in the Tiger, on the grounds mentioned above. My father considered this system the best solution for a heavy vehicle of this kind.

Since only one engine was used, Siemens-Schuckert developed a double generator to replace the twin generators. The electrical control system was altered considerably, so that when steering the Maus the driver had the same feel as with a mechanical system. With the Porsche Tiger, he felt as though he was driving with a free wheel when the two levers which operated the steering were in neutral.

The first prototype was powered by a Daimler-Benz Type 509 engine. This was a V12 engine with overhead valves, water cooled, with four valves per cylinder and direct petrol injection. It was basically a DB603 aero engine, with lower compression so that fuel with a lower octane rating than aviation fuel could be used. The MB 509 produced 1,200 hp.

The running gear was initially intended to be based on the roller carriages with torsion bar suspension used on the Tiger, suitably increased in number. After the army had requested that a flame thrower with 1,000 litres (220 gallons) of fuel should be fitted, the weight of the Maus rose by almost 5 tons. This additional weight could not, however, be carried by the number of roller carriages that could be used. As a result, we collaborated with the Skoda company in Pilsen, which was responsible for manufacturing the running gear, in the development of a simple suspension system with truncated cone springs. The time available for the development of the tank was also a factor in this decision.

The turret, complete with guns, and the hull were supplied by Krupp in Essen, who were also involved in the development of similar large tanks. The tanks were assembled by Allkett in Berlin. The electrical drive system was supplied by Siemens, also in Berlin.

The first blueprints were finished on 4 June 1942, and at the beginning of January 1943 we showed Hitler the first wooden model of the Maus built to a scale of 1:10. He inspected the model with interest but said nothing.

At a meeting of the companies involved held in Berlin on 21 January and chaired by Speer, the remaining unanswered questions were clarified and the Maus project was given top priority. On 14 May 1943, a life-size mock-up was presented to Hitler; he remarked that the 12.8 cm cannon looked like 'a toy' in comparison with the bulk of the tank. As a result, Krupp had to design a 15 cm cannon, although the 7.5 cm cannon was dropped.

The changes that were required naturally delayed the programme, and the first test drive did not take place until December 1943. Nevertheless, this still seems to me to be a considerable achievement for a project of that scale.

In the meantime, the relationship between my father and the Minister for Armaments and War Production, as Speer had called himself since autumn 1943, had apparently become more tense. Speer demanded that my father be replaced by a younger man. My father was then 68 years old and still felt himself very capable. His achievements were also recognized by Hitler, who on 20 April, his birthday, awarded him the Distinguished Service Cross, First Class with swords.

I remember very clearly the day, 23 December 1943, a Friday, that the first prototype of the Maus was driven under its own steam out of the Allkett assembly shop in Berlin. However, the turret was still only a mock-up, since Krupp had not been able to deliver on time because of the heavy air raids in the Ruhr area.

The Maus could only be driven with Speer's express permission, but our people were very anxious to ascertain how the monster handled, particularly since the army, especially the Ordnance Office and its experts from the Institutes of Technology, were of the opinion that this tank, now increased in weight to 189 tons, would be scarcely manoeuvrable and particularly difficult to turn. Two days before Christmas, our engineer Walter Schmidt finally managed to convince the guards to look the other way when he took the Maus for a test drive.

The upper platform of the giant tank towered 2 m (2.2 yd) above the body and it made a really fantastic impression as it crawled between the wall of a house and a fence with a gap of only a few centimetres to spare and then carried out turning manoeuvres when it reached an open space. The turning circle was about 8m (8.6 yd). Schmidt was visibly impressed by this performance and telegraphed the news to my father, who was spending Christmas with his family at our estate in Zell am See in Austria. However, my father did not consider the 8 m turning circle to be a success. He telephoned Otto Zadnik, the engineer responsible for the electrical system who was ill in bed with 'flu in Vienna. There was nothing for it: Herr Zadnik had to go to Berlin on the first day of Christmas and test the electrical system. He found a switching fault in the system which he rectified, and when the Maus was next taken out on a test run it was able to turn on the spot. Only then was my father satisfied.

In January this first prototype was taken to Böblingen, where the real trials began on 9 March 1944 on the training area there; from the beginning of June, the trials were conducted with the fully-equipped turret.

These trials lasted until October, when the tank was taken to Kummersdorf near Berlin, the Ordnance Office's test area. The test revealed astonishingly few weaknesses in the Maus, and none of them caused us any serious problems. The engineers involved in the trials and neutral observers testified that the Maus was in no way inferior to the Tiger as far as manoeuvrability was concerned. In the judgement of the drivers, who were all in agreement, the tank was as easy to drive as a child's toy, since everything was controlled electrically. My father drove the Maus on several occasions and he was thoroughly satisfied with the performance of the vehicle, which had a top speed of 12.5 mph (20 km/h).

In March 1944 the second prototype was taken to Böblingen near Stuttgart, where the Daimler-Benz MB 517 power unit was to be fitted. The MB 517 was basically a supercharged Type 507. It was a vertical V12 diesel engine, in which the cylinders were arranged at an angle of 60° to each other, had a cubic capacity of 44,500 cc, was water-cooled, and had a Bosch fuel injection system. When the diesel engine had been fitted, the tank went back to Kummersdorf without any further trials.

I must admit today that I had been sceptical about my father's claim that it would be possible to design a tank in such a way that it could achieve any desired turning circle. Thus I was just as impressed as the no less sceptical Colonel General Guderian when the Maus proved itself able to turn on the spot. However, when we demonstrated this once on a cobbled square at the barracks in Böblingen, new cobblestones had to be laid afterwards.

It is said that at the end of the war the two prototypes of the Maus were blown up in Kummersdorf. I have not been able to this very day to confirm this, so I tend rather to believe that the Allies captured the two tanks and took them away.

As we now know, Speer had forbidden the building of further units, yet after the war British officers found some individual components for the Maus at the Krupps factory, which indicate that a small batch of 10 tanks had been planned after all.

This chapter on tank development has certainly turned out to be fairly extensive, but this should not be taken as an indication

119

that I was particularly enthusiastic about working in this area. From a technical point of view, it presented us with a real challenge and it demonstrates the high engineering standards that we had already attained by that time. That was where my main interest lay.

Of course there were other things that we particularly liked to work on. These included, for example, the trials of the various versions of the bucket car. They took us to regions where no bombs had yet fallen and where the world was still in order. While testing the bucket cars, we set ourselves tasks which were anything but easy or a matter of simple routine. Thus we drove the amphibious vehicle up the Kitzbüheler Horn, a mountain north-east of Kitzbühel, the summit of which reaches the considerable height of something over 6,000 ft (1,800 m). That was an astonishing achievement for a car, to say nothing of the driver. At the summit, we simply ran out of space and were unable to turn the car round under its own steam. Four of us had to lift it up and point it in the right direction for the descent. It was one of the main advantages of the VW cross-country vehicle that its crew could usually manage to get it out of almost any difficulty.

In June 1987, incidentally, I was at Zell am See when the German Amphibious Car Club held its annual meeting. There were more than 100 owners of the Porsche Type 166 who were as enthusiastic about their cars as only collectors of vintage cars can be. They were not allowed to conduct their 'swimming exercises' in the lake, so they went to another nearby stretch of water and carried out their extensive programme with great enthusiasm.

We also carried out our trials on the amphibious vehicle in the Kärntner Alps, and at that time, in 1943, there was hardly a mountain pasture that we did not climb, often to the great surprise of the dairymaids. There were hardly any men there, since they had all been conscripted.

It was also in 1943, on 10 May, that our fourth son was born. We christened him Wolfgang Heinz, but he was known to us all as Wolfi.

──── 11 ────

Goering is proved wrong

In 1941, when my father became chairman of the Tank Commission, he handed over the management of the Volkswagen factory to my brother-in-law, Dr Anton Piëch. In addition to the cross-country vehicles that we had developed, all kinds of armaments were being produced there, including some for the Luftwaffe. The conversion of the factory into an armament plant had not been at all easy, since it had been designed entirely for the production of the civilian KdF car. Consequently, the machinery was suited to the manufacture of military products to only a limited extent. Nevertheless, some of the components used for the cross-country vehicle were identical to those in the saloon, and we were still producing saloons alongside the bucket car. Later on, we also produced parts for the Junkers Ju88 and the V1 flying bomb.

As the war in the skies became more and more intense, with night raids by the British on the cities and daytime raids by the US Air Force on the factories, the Wolfsburg factory was not spared. Because it was a self-contained industrial complex, it stood out very clearly on aerial photographs, so for this reason factories that had been specifically designed and built as armament plants were divided into smaller units distributed over a larger area, usually surrounded by woods. Since they were all well camouflaged, they were much more difficult to make out than Wolfsburg, which was very vulnerable to attack. However, it is further proof of the fact that prior to 1939 my father had not the slightest idea that there would be a war.

Thus it was no surprise that the VW factory was heavily hit in the very first attack. In all, the Allies launched four attacks against Wolfsburg in 1944, and because of the severe damage they caused, production facilities had to be evacuated as much as possible, and some were even accommodated in underground workshops.

Nor was Stuttgart, with its high concentration of industrial buildings, spared the bombing, and indeed the city suffered some of the heaviest raids. The anti-aircraft command post had been set up next to our house in the Feuerbacher Weg, which made things twice as dangerous for us. The air raids on Stuttgart began in 1943, and during one of the first attacks a bomb landed in an open space not far from our house. Our house remained standing, but the roof was completely blown off by the blast of the exploding bomb.

When we returned from the air-raid shelter which had been built into the hill in the Parlerstraße, there was a fiery glow in the valley: Stuttgart was burning. Our house is situated above the city centre near the Killesberg, so we had a view over the whole city.

While on the subject of the air raids on Stuttgart, my father telephoned me one day and asked, 'Have you actually put the archives into the cellar yet?' 'No,' I replied, 'we haven't got round to it yet.' My father replied, 'You're mad if you don't put all the archives into the cellar immediately, or at the latest within two days; something might happen!' The archives to which he was referring were the company archives that were stored in the upper storey of the Zuffenhausen factory.

I immediately gave the order for the archives to be taken to the cellar. When the Zuffenhausen district suffered its first air raid, our factory sustained some damage and a single bomb hit the building where the archives were stored, penetrating right into the cellar. The archives were completely destroyed.

When my father returned, I greeted him with this news and said, 'You see, we shouldn't have been in such a rush; now everything's gone up in smoke!'

I remembered an aphorism that Goering had delivered in his loud-mouthed way at the beginning of the war: 'I'll eat my hat if a single enemy bomb falls on the territory of the German Reich!' I am even certain that he meant it seriously; and now it was rather more than just one bomb that was falling on Germany.

I have unpleasant memories of Goering, since from the outset he had wanted to exert his influence on the Volkswagen plant and incorporate it into his enormous chain of factories, some of which were known as Hermann Goering Factories. Above all, however, he wanted to lay claim to it as an armament plant for his Luftwaffe. Ley objected vigorously to this. By chance, I witnessed a conversation between Ley and Goering about cheap labour from the East. They were not agreed as to how workers from this part of Europe should be paid. At one point, Goering said, 'Well at least one thing is clear: we shall never pay a worker from the Ukraine as much as we pay a German worker!'

It became clear to me in that period at the beginning of the war that the idea of a Europe united on a basis of equality was absolutely out of the question. I had unpleasant memories in another connection. At that time, the famous sheet-metal cartel was in existence; it had been of concern to us because of the price of the Volkswagen. The price per kilogram of sheet steel was about 40 pfennigs, although the actual cost price was only about 20 pfennigs. Consequently, Ley planned to incorporate a sheet-rolling mill in Czechoslovakia into his organization in order to obtain cheap sheet metal for the KdF car. Goering, who would not tolerate any incursion into his territory, put an end to the plan.

Nor would Goering allow the war to disturb his usual lifestyle. In the autumn of, I think, 1942, I was driving at hunting time over the Tauern mountains when I saw Goering travelling towards me in his supercharged Mercedes, wearing a hat with an enormous tuft of chamois hair on it. He had been to Mauterndorf on the southern side of the Tauern mountains where he had a large hunting area at his disposal.

But back to Stuttgart. At any rate Goering had not been able to prevent a bomb falling on German territory: at that time, rather a lot of bombs were falling all over it. Not only did the house next to ours, which belonged to the Wolf family, house the headquarters of the Stuttgart anti-aircraft forces, but in the vicinity there were also several gun positions with heavy 8.8 and 10.5 cm anti-aircraft guns. In order to avoid the danger to which we were exposed, I decided to send my wife and children to the safety of Zell am See.

One day my eldest son, Ferdinand Alexander, known as Butzi to the family, asked me, 'Papi, were you in the Hitler Youth?' 'No,' I replied, 'I couldn't have been, because the Hitler Youth didn't exist when I was your age!'

However, this answer did not seem to satisfy Butzi, and he pursued his questioning. 'But why aren't you in the army? All my friends' fathers are soldiers!'

'Well, Butzi,' I replied, 'your grandfather needs me here. He has a lot of technical problems to solve for Germany, and I have to help him.'

'Why?' asked Butzi.

'Just imagine, ' I replied, 'if we were all soldiers, who would design and build the tanks and all the other weapons? Who would supply the army with them?' My eldest son's logic was at that time orientated more towards practicalities, but he said quite spontaneously and with a gleam in his eyes, 'Daddy, when I'm grown up, will I be able to do that work?'

'I hope that won't be necessary,' I replied. How wrong I was!

With each day that passed, the situation became increasingly menacing. The first thousand bomber raids came, with terrible consequences for the cities and their inhabitants. Hamburg was the first German city to be devastated by a tremendous firestorm, triggered off by the massive use of incendiary bombs and phosphorous canisters. Speer was exerting pressure to have our company evacuated to areas that were suffering less from the heavy bombing, and one day the military authorities in charge of armaments ordered us to leave Stuttgart and evacuate our operation to the Protectorate of Bohemia and Moravia, the remaining part of Czechoslovakia that had been occupied by Germany.

Neither I nor my father had any intention of allowing ourselves to be evacuated to Czechoslovakia, where we would certainly not have received a friendly welcome, to say nothing of what would have awaited us after the fall of the Third Reich, as former Czech citizens who now held German passports.

Consequently, I contacted the military authorities responsible for the Salzburg area and enquired whether they could suggest any suitable sites to which we could evacuate our Stuttgart operation. The authorities in Salzburg made some suggestions, one of which was the Luftwaffe flying school at the Zell am See aerodrome, the other being a sawmill at Gmünd in Kärnten. Zell am See was the perfect place, because our estate bordered on the aerodrome. So I drove down and looked around the proposed site. The flying school at Zell am See trained pilots for cargo-carrying gliders. The hangars were suitable both for conversion into small workshops and for the storage of materials, while the work force could be accommodated in the residential quarters at the flying school.

The site at Gmünd required a great deal of building work, and we erected several sheds and cast baseplates for our machines. However, the decisive factor was that Gmünd could be considered relatively safe from air raids.

The evacuation began at the end of 1943 and lasted until well into 1944. My organization of the removal was based on an old Jewish saying: 'Divide your possessions into three, then you will always have something to start again with!'

In accordance with this method, our operation was divided into three parts: the headquarters remained in Stuttgart, production went into Gmünd, while the flying school at Zell am See became our storage depot. Since I was in charge of the head office, I naturally remained in Stuttgart.

The transfer of operations meant of course that I had to travel a great deal between Stuttgart, Gmünd and Zell am See. In the main, we had chosen people of Austrian origin for the 'evacuation' to their native country, leaving Germans in Stuttgart.

At that time, incidentally, we were developing a drive motor from the VW engine which was to be supercharged with a Roots blower. In this way, we increased the output of the engine, which had been bored out to 1.1 litres, to 45 hp. I reserved one of these engines for myself and fitted it in a VW convertible that I usually used when I was commuting between Stuttgart and Austria. The only pleasurable thing about these journeys was that my family was living at Zell am See. The drive itself was always very risky, and the risk increased as the American and British air raids became more frequent; they had begun to use not only bombers but also fighter escorts, mainly Mustangs and Thunderbolts. However, since the German Luftwaffe was permanently overstretched and exhausted because of the numerous theatres of war in which they had to operate, the Americans used to pursue and attack lone vehicles and even farmers in their fields, just for the fun of it. I was also at risk from such activities, but I did have a method of getting to safety at the right time. I knew the frequency on which the air surveillance people broadcast details of the situation in the air; consequently, I used to drive with my radio tuned to that frequency. When I heard the announcement, 'Attention — low-flying aircraft in the Munich-Rosenheim area', I would quickly turn off the motorway and take cover under a bridge or anywhere that provided shelter, where I would remain until the danger passed.

In the later stages of the war, it was no longer possible to protect airfields, and German fighters, particularly the new Messerschmitt Me 262 jet fighter, used stretches of the motorways for take-off and landing. As a result, I was forced to make long detours, so that it took much longer than previously to get from Stuttgart to Gmünd or Zell am See.

Eventually I too moved to Austria, but commuted constantly between Gmünd and Zell am See. From Gmünd I would usually drive north over the Katschberg and the Tauern, then turn off in a westerly direction in Flachau and drive to Zell am See by way of Wagrain, St Johann and Lend.

One day, shortly before Christmas 1944, I was driving along this route for the last time during the war when a chimney sweep waved to me from the side of the road, near Wagrain. I stopped and he said, 'Can you take me to St Johann?' 'But of course,' I replied. I am not superstitious, but it is supposed to be lucky to meet a chimney sweep, particularly if one touches him; and luck was just what we wanted at that time, in large quantities. Indeed he did bring me luck, because a few months later the war was over.

Around the time I met the chimney sweep, a young man wearing civilian clothes and riding a motor cycle appeared in Zell am See. He introduced himself as a special commissioner who had been sent to assist companies that had been evacuated to Austria. He showed me identity cards from the Todt organization and the military authorities in Salzburg. In this respect at least he was excellently provided for, and he said, 'So, if you need anything, wagons, lorries, special allocations, just let me know.' I laughed at him sarcastically and replied, 'What's the point of you coming to help us, the war's been over for a long time!' He did not know what to say to that. Our people from the flying school repaired his motor cycle, because he had been pushing it when he arrived. He thanked me profusely and disappeared.

Now I must jump ahead of events. When the Americans arrived in Zell am See, they had a Volkswagen bearing the number of the Gauleiter of the Tyrol. The car stopped at our house and the same young man who had claimed to be a member of the Todt organization got out, greeted me and said, 'Now that I know your position, I would like to ask you again: can I help you?'

I must have looked pretty perplexed at this, but suddenly I heard a laugh and it emerged that the young man had been nothing other than an American spy. With the chaos that prevailed then, his job cannot have been too difficult.

Thus the war was over, and everybody heaved a sigh of relief. Our district was occupied by the Americans.

12

We are proved wrong

The American advance proceeded much more rapidly than planned. As a result, a unit arrived in Zell am See that had not actually been destined for that area at all. The troops had for the most part been recruited from former inmates of Sing Sing prison, who had apparently been promised remission if they volunteered for service at the front. They were pretty tough characters who were not in the habit of treating their former enemy with kid gloves. It must be said, however, that their officers conducted themselves very decently and tried to restrain their troops as much as they were able to.

Before the surrender our entire family had gathered together at the estate in Zell am See. Father had come from Vienna, my brother-in-law Dr Anton Piëch from Wolfsburg and I myself from Stuttgart. My wife and children had gone to Zell earlier, in order to escape the air raids on Stuttgart. The Americans were billeted in the flying school and our people were simply thrown out into the open air.

Gmünd was occupied by the British; communications had been cut off and all we knew was that our Herr Rabe was there.

Our estate is on a mountain slope a little above the Zeller See. A narrow road leads up to it from the valley. At that time there was of course very little traffic, so that we immediately noticed when a vehicle came near. One day we heard a car approaching and immediately we rushed inquisitively out of the house, my mother in the lead. It was a jeep with a driver and two officers. My mother went up to them and was apparently so strongly affected by the uniform that instead of greeting them with the usual 'Grüss Gott' welcomed them with the words 'Heil Hitler' and a raised hand. The men got out, seemingly unmoved, indeed amused, by this greeting. They introduced themselves. One of them was an English lieutenant colonel called G.C. Reeves. He knew my father as the designer of the Auto Union racing car, since he had himself done some motor racing. He also knew about the Volkswagen and some of our other products.

The other man was Major Torre Franzen, an American and a former development engineer with Chrysler who had met my father during his first visit to the USA in 1936. After the introductions had been made and old memories revived, the tension very rapidly disappeared. However, communication was not so simple. I am no linguist, as is well known, but I was the only one who was able to communicate a little with the two men in English; the other members of the family had to accept me as interpreter. Our visitors had come from Stuttgart, where they had been told where we were living.

Our factory at Stuttgart-Zuffenhausen had been taken over first by the French and then by the Americans. Directly after the end of the war, Zuffenhausen was used as a transit camp for Russian prisoners of war awaiting repatriation. Later, the Americans used it as a workshop for repairing lorries.

After this short introductory report, and after both men had greeted my father as 'an old acquaintance', the conversation developed into a sort of interrogation, though without any tension.

'Where do you keep your technical drawings and equipment? We must have a look at everything!' began the interrogation.

They had not known of the existence of our factory in Gmünd until they had arrived in Stuttgart. Astonishingly, their secret service had known nothing about it. We enlightened them and gave them the information they sought. Then they asked, 'Have you already been visited by the French or Russian officers?' Quite truthfully, we replied that we had not. Their answer, which sounded almost like an order, was to say, 'If these people do turn up here, you are not obliged to give them any information at all. Is that clear?' 'Yes,' I replied, 'that is absolutely clear!'

However, I did ask the two men to consider that both Soviet and French officers would certainly be completely unimpressed if we forbade them access to us. They took my point, and they ordered the American commander at Zell am See to billet a guard at our house to prevent any strangers from gaining access to us.

The visit of the two Allied officers was my first contact with non-German soldiers, and the difference was very marked. The officers took up residence on our estate. Their luggage was in a small trailer behind the jeep, and when they arrived, the American driver got out and lit a cigarette. He did not even consider carrying the officers' luggage into the house, but just asked quite casually what further duties there might be for him. Such a scene would have been unthinkable in the German Wehrmacht.

Mr Reeves and Mr Franzen then drove with us into the British zone to Gmünd. There they put all the documents into safekeeping and also put a guard on them. Our Herr Rabe was put in charge of the works there.

In the meantime, at the flying school at Zell am See the Americans had discovered one of the Berlin-Rome cars that was stored there and were racing it on the airfield. It was such a beautiful hot summer that the soldiers eventually used metal cutters to remove the coupé's roof, turning it into a 'roadster'. They had great fun with it, but they did not think of filling up with oil and one day it ran dry, and the dream came to an end. The wreck ended up on a dungheap.

This first contact with the occupying power had actually been quite civilized, as had the interrogation, so that we were relieved that the burden of the war had been lifted from us. We took stock and tried to start work again. We succeeded in getting a damaged tractor going again by fitting it with a wood-gas producer. At that time there was no petrol or diesel to be had, and the food supply situation was also pretty bad. As 'newcomers' we could obtain only what was on the ration cards. Since there were more than 30 of us, the little extra food from the estate improved matters only slightly; sometimes we only had potatoes for breakfast. However, millions of our fellow countrymen were far worse off. But even our relatively favourable situation did not last for long.

At the end of July 1945, when my father was staying in Gmünd, a German in the service of the English forces turned up at the estate. He had spent the last years of the war in a concentration camp, for criminal not political reasons. After being freed, he had insinuated his way into favour with the English, who eventually appointed him chief of police in Wolfsburg. It transpired that two bodies had been discovered in the hut that my father used to live in during his visits to Wolfsburg, which was sufficient reason for the German policeman to accuse us of murder. He left no stone unturned in his efforts to pin the crimes on us, although we had not been in Wolfsburg at all in the past three months. So because he had not been able to 'detain' any of us or our engineers in Wolfsburg, he had come to Zell am See with the help of the English in order to arrest the 'guilty parties'. If the whole affair had not been so serious, we could have dismissed it as a sort of practical joke, but the poacher had now turned gamekeeper, and when his investigations produced no conclusive evidence he went to the chief of the American military police in Zell am See and denounced us as criminals suspected of murder in Germany. This was of course a pack of lies, and since we all had clear consciences we did not worry any more about the matter. However, we had completely misjudged the situation, particularly the fact that informers were having a field day at that time. At any rate, the military police turned up at the estate and arrested all the male members of the Porsche family; only the women and children were allowed to remain on the estate. Our test engineer was lucky; when the Americans arrived, he was lying under the tractor covered in oil and they took him for an estate worker. It was not only members of the family who were taken away, but also Erwin Komenda, one of our most able engineers, and several other Porsche employees.

We were detained first of all at the fire station in Zell am See. The next day, we were taken to the Landel in Salzburg, the district court consisting of the court buildings with a jail attached to it. The prison was packed with high-ranking German officers and party functionaries, as well as completely innocent people who were party members in name only and had been picked up indiscriminately on the streets. American GIs out on patrol used to imprison people who seemed suspicious to them and who they considered to be Nazis.

Fortunately, a workroom was cleared for us to use as a recreation room. However, extra mattresses had to be put into our cell in order to accommodate all 32 of us, so that we literally felt like sardines in a tin. Moreover, the cell was completely filthy and bug-ridden. Since the Americans are very touchy about bugs, they gave us the disinfectant we requested and we all helped to make our new accommodation more fit for human habitation. We also started to hunt down the bugs and had soon killed several hundred. After a few days we were able to sleep relatively undisturbed. However, we were of course anxious about our future, particularly since nobody seemed bothered about us or took us for questioning. After six weeks, the guard ordered me to follow him and I was at last taken to an American officer who interrogated me.

'Were you in the Wehrmacht?' was his first question.

'No,' I replied, 'I have never served in the army. I presume that's the answer you want?' The officer did not react at all; he was studying my papers which he had in front of him and then continued his questioning.

'But you were a member of the party?'

'No,' I replied.

'Were you a member of the SS?'

'No!'

'But you were in the Storm Troopers?'

'No, I had nothing to do with them either!' My interrogator apparently seemed uncertain as to how to continue; he raised his eyebrows and said,

'Were you at the front in any capacity?'

'I'm sorry, but I never went to the front!' With this, he appeared to have reached the end of the standard interrogation procedure, and he simply asked a few more personal questions: date of birth, parents, marital status. When he had taken down this information, he asked,

'What did you do then during the war? You look pretty healthy.'

'I am an engineer — Porsche of Stuttgart.'

This should have been a cue for this representative of the US army to ask questions about tanks, VW bucket cars and so on. He did nothing of the sort, and the interrogation ended with a few general questions. I was then transferred to the Glasenbach internment camp near Salzburg where I remained until my release seven weeks later.

But what had happened to my father, who was in Gmünd at the time of our arrest? Well, he had been interned there by the British. At the investigation of a British officer, very probably obeying orders from a higher authority, he was transferred at the beginning of August to the Kransberg internment camp near Bad Nauheim. The British charitably allowed him to drive there in his own car, chauffeured by Herr Goldinger.

In his book *Memoirs*, published by the Propyläen Verlag of Berlin, Albert Speer, the former Minister for Armaments and War Production (as he was known by the end of the war) describes how he was transferred to Kransberg:

> 'We turned off the autobahn near Nauheim; soon after that we drove up a steep road and found ourselves in the courtyard of Schloss Kransberg. In the winter of 1939, I had fitted out this large castle, which was three miles away from Hitler's control room, for use as Goering's headquarters. A two-storey wing had been built on in order to accommodate Goering's large retinue of servants, and it was here that we prisoners were housed. We had actually been taken to the castle in order to answer questions on the technical aspects of the German war effort. A large number of technical experts arrived, virtually the entire management of my ministry, almost all the office heads, the managers in charge of munitions, tank, automobile, ship, aircraft and textile production, important figures in the chemicals industry and designers such as Professor Porsche. Only seldom, however, did any inquisitive people stray anywhere near us.'

Speer in fact used his influence on my father's behalf and strenuously defended him from any accusations that he had been involved in political activity. He had had a very high opinion of my father as a technical expert, even though they had not always been in agreement. Incidentally the activities at Kransberg were codenamed Operation Dustbin by the Allies.

The basic purpose of the Kransberg camp was to separate the wheat from the chaff, in other words to ascertain who would have to stand trial for their alleged war crimes at the Nuremberg Court. After intensive questioning, my father was cleared of any suspicion of complicity in war crimes, and given a certificate which stated that no charges were to be brought against him and that he was free to resume his design and engineering work for the Allies in Austria.

During his internment at Schloss Kransberg, on 3 September 1945 my father celebrated his seventieth birthday. Speer was one of the many people who offered him their congratulations.

My father then returned to Austria, where he learnt that his son and his colleagues were being held in an internment camp, while he had been absolved of any guilt and was a free man. He immediately got in touch with the British authorities in Klagenfurt and requested them to examine our files at the American High Command in Vienna and assess the accusations contained in them. He did not know that we had been arrested, having been denounced by a convicted criminal, in connection with the two unidentified bodies in Wolfsburg. Incidentally, none of us had ever been interrogated about this matter. Afterwards, nobody was able to explain how the two bodies had come to be in my father's house. However, anyone who experienced the chaos that reigned at the end of the war will understand that anything was possible and that it could easily have been pure chance.

My father eventually succeeded in convincing the British of our innocence and he secured our release from the American military government in Vienna. Early in the morning on 1 November 1945 the camp commandant informed us that we would be leaving the camp. We were taken by lorry to the next village, where we were officially set free. We drove back to Zell am See in the hope that we would now be able to begin a new, freer existence. We were to be proved hopelessly wrong.

13

A guest of the French

At the end of the war Austria, like Germany, was divided into four occupation zones. Salzburg and Upper Austria were occupied by the Americans, the Tyrol and Vorarlberg by the French, Kärnten and Styria by the British and Lower Austria and Burgenland by the Soviet Union. Without travel documents issued by the appropriate occupying power it was not possible to travel from one zone to another. This was particularly difficult in the Russian and French zones; the Americans and British did not always make such rigorous checks.

At that time there was still much talk of the so-called Morgenthau plan. Morgenthau was the Secretary of the Treasury in President Roosevelt's administration and an advocate of a harsh peace settlement for Germany. Among other things, his plan provided for the decommissioning of all industrial plants, the closure of the mines and the conversion of a highly industrialized country into an agrarian state. In those days, if one expressed a desire, in conversation with American officers, to make motor cars again, they were quite likely to reply, 'If you were a craftsman your future would be guaranteed, but you can kiss goodbye to any hopes of ever building automobiles again!'

Nevertheless, we had already started to involve ourselves with motor cars again, albeit on a very modest scale. Firstly, there were small repairs to be done to captured VW bucket cars. We did this largely in return for food, which had become very scarce. The Morgenthau plan was then shelved. However, the future still held little joy for us.

It was the beginning of November when we had our first visit in Zell am See from a French officer. He was Lieutenant Henri LeComte, who had gone first to our Zuffenhausen factory and discovered that we were living in Austria. One of our engineers, Herr Jung, had said he would be willing to accompany him to Zell am See. His offer was accepted. Carrying special travel documents issued by the French authorities, the two had set off by car for Austria. LeComte claimed to be working on behalf of Marcel Paul, the French Minister for Industry. In 1945, the French Communist Party was participating in government and Paul was a member of the party. He wanted to obtain the Volkswagen factory as part of Germany's reparations payments to France. Of course the agreement of the Americans and, more particularly, of the British, in whose zone the factory was, had to be obtained. The minister appeared to be making good progress in that respect, but he was also astute enough to realize that he would need our help, particularly my father's, to build up the production plant again.

LeComte was a very shrewd man and excelled at presenting his minister's plans in as good a light as possible. He also impressed my father, who was certainly unclear as to the scope of this plan. In any event, he asked me to go with LeComte and Herr Jung to Baden-Baden, the headquarters of the French military authorities in the occupation zone, in order to start the necessary negotiations. Equipped with French travel documents which LeComte had apparently prepared in advance, we travelled together to Baden-Baden. I attempted to open negotiations with Major Trevoux and Major Maiffre, but they refused to get involved in lengthy discussions, but rather explained to me briefly and concisely that without my father there could be no discussions. So we drove back to Zell am See, where we arrived on 8 November. I told my father about the French stipulations. He said he would go to Baden-Baden, a decision which was to have very serious consequences for him, but which also clearly shows that my father was much too honest a character to suspect that this might have been a trap.

We set off for Baden-Baden on 16 November, a date that I will never forget. We were accompanied by my brother-in-law, Dr Piëch, and my cousin Herbert Kaes. When we arrived in Baden-Baden, we were greeted immediately by the two French officers in the Hotel Müller. We were told that France was planning to establish a state-owned automobile factory which was to include half of the VW factory and the necessary machinery as part of the reparations settlement. We would be expected to supervise the transfer to the French location, which was still to be named, and help in the commissioning of the new plant. Trevoux presented us with a contract that had already been drawn up, which my father and I were required to sign immediately.

In principle, the proposal was of some interest to my father, but we asked for time to consider the proposal and returned to Zell am See. 'It looks as though the French are pretty serious about this business!' said my father one day casually in conversation. However, I was somewhat sceptical about the whole proposal.

We returned to Baden-Baden, where the French accommodated us in the Villa Bella Vista. Discussions continued in the Hotel Müller, but Trevoux's place was taken by a Colonel Lamis, who confined himself to asking a few irrelevant questions. No concrete result was achieved and after the brief conversation we were sent back to our quarters. Colonel Maiffre, incidentally, was still in Baden-Baden, but was apparently no longer involved in our affairs.

My father gradually became more and more impatient and decided to go back to Zell am See the next day. That was on 15 December 1945. There were no indications that we were facing a serious situation. That same evening, Maiffre and LeComte were dining with us when two Frenchmen in civilian clothes suddenly appeared and told us that we were under arrest. LeComte acted surprised and said, 'The whole thing is a misunderstanding, believe me! Please remain calm and don't get excited, we'll have the matter cleared up by Monday!'

Saturday 15 December: the warrant for our arrest had been signed by Pierre Henri Teitgen, the French Minister of Justice.

The next morning, 16 December, the day we had actually intended to go home, we were taken to the Baden-Baden prison, which fortunately was in a much better state than the Landel in Salzburg. Our fellow sufferers there included Herr Steigenberger, the owner of the hotel chain of the same name, now dead, the mayor of a small village in the south of the Black Forest and a Herr von Schewen, a former officer who had once been manager of the Baden-Baden casino.

Fortunately, my cousin Herbert Kaes had escaped arrest since he had not joined us for dinner, choosing instead to go to the cinema. With the aid of a distant relative who lived in Baden-Baden, he made sure we received extra rations.

What was the reason for our sudden arrest, which absolutely contradicted the plans drawn by Paul, the Minister for Industry? In France, representatives of the French automobile industry had caught wind of Monsieur Paul's plans. They had been able to get hold of the documents, with all their valuable technical data, that my father had brought with him from Zell am See and given to the French officers, who were to hand them over to Monsieur Paul. These people refused to surrender the documents, apparently with the intention of preventing my father from working for Paul because of their opposition to the industry minister's Volkswagen project.

It is obvious with the benefit of hindsight that the French automobile manufacturers were objecting to the production of a French version of the Volkswagen, which would have been a serious rival to their own models.

Lieutenant LeComte proved unable to sort the matter out: instead, we underwent several interrogations, during which we were repeatedly asked to give details of our commercial links with the French motor industry during the war. These interrogations angered my father, since he had nothing to hide, but he very soon recognized that they might very well result in Peugeot being accused of collaboration with the Germans and the sabotaging of Paul's plans.

There had indeed been close links between Peugeot and the Volkswagen plant during the war. My father had paid several visits to Montbéliard, near the Swiss border, where VW parts were produced, and expressed very positive views about the factory.

There was obviously a great deal of scheming going on; my father's view was that the French could not agree among themselves, with some of them wanting the Volkswagen factory while others wanted to prevent its construction in France and hoped to achieve their aim by taking us out of circulation.

This assessment of the situation was proved correct when Jean-Pierre Peugeot, owner of the Peugeot company, was accused of collaboration.

The central point in Peugeot's argument was a comparison of his cars with the Volkswagen, in which the Peugeot naturally came off better in all respects, maintaining that my father had obliged French people to work against their will in Wolfsburg and had even treated them as forced labour. Moreover, he was alleged to have had several Peugeot managers taken under duress to Germany and to have had machinery from French factories dismantled and taken away for use at the Volkswagen plant.

My father was accused of being a 'war criminal', on the grounds that, after a few incidents of sabotage at Peugeot factories, some French people had been arrested by the Gestapo at my father's instigation. There was alleged to be evidence that a few Peugeot managers had been thrown into prison during the German occupation.

This was all contained in the charge brought against my father which we would have dismissed as ridiculous if the situation had not been so serious. In reality, my father had intervened on behalf of the Peugeot managers and had complained bitterly to the Gestapo that co-operation would be impossible if the Peugeot management were locked up in jail. The managers were subsequently released. However, when shortly afterwards there were further acts of sabotage at Peugeot, several managers were thrown back into prison. My father intervened again, but this time the strength of the available evidence meant his efforts were in vain. One of the managers died during his imprisonment.

The same accusations were made against my brother-in-law, Dr Piëch, and myself. However, there was enough evidence to prove that I had never been a member of the management of Volkswagen GmbH and had had nothing at all to do with Peugeot. Consequently, I was released from Baden-Baden prison in March 1946, but remained in internment. I was accommodated in the Hotel Sommerberg in Bad Rippoldsau, together with my cousin Herbert Kaes. Initially we were very relieved, but were very worried about my father, whose gall-bladder was giving him trouble again. He was admitted to hospital in Baden-Baden, where as a result of the hardship he had suffered in jail and his advanced age, he was found to be suffering from intestinal colic. Fortunately there were no complications, but he was still being detained by the Sûreté, the French police.

At the Hotel Sommerberg we met up again with Lieutenant LeComte, in his capacity as 'Monsieur Paul's special representative for production matters'; obviously the French minister had not given up his Volkswagen project. When I was allowed to visit my father in hospital in Baden-Baden, accompanied by LeComte, the Frenchman suggested to my father that all the drawings for the VW should be brought from Gmünd, so that they would be available for use at any time for the French VW project. My father raised no objections, but hoped in this way to be released more quickly. His secretary, Ghislaine Kaes, was instructed in writing to go with LeComte to fetch the drawings. Kaes, who was a British citizen, nevertheless informed the English liaison officer in Baden-Baden of the plan; he passed the information on to headquarters in Bad Oeynhausen. As was to be expected, however, Herr Rabe, my father's authorized representative in Gmünd, would not surrender the drawings. LeComte was ordered by the British to leave their zone forthwith, and so returned empty-handed to Bad Rippoldsau.

I was expected to start work immediately on designing the car. In the meantime, however, my father had been discharged from hospital and was back in prison once more. I refused to start work on the drawings as long as my father and brother-in-law remained in prison. I also demanded that I be released from internment and be allowed to return to my family. The French realized I was in earnest, with the result that nothing at all happened for several weeks. The whole affair was dragged out until May 1946. LeComte was still hoping to find a way to an acceptable solution, since Monsieur Paul was still interested in the VW project. In the end it looked as though everything was taking a turn for the better. It was agreed that my father would work with Renault on a French version of the VW.

On 2 May 1946 he was taken with Dr Piëch to Sûreté headquarters in Baden-Baden; the next day they were taken, still prisoners, to Paris. Instead of the decent accommodation that LeComte had agreed to, they were housed in the servants' quarters in Renault's villa. LeComte soon made himself scarce, and in his place there appeared a group of Renault engineers led by Monsieur Lefaucheux, the managing director, and including the chief engineer, Edmond Serre, and Messrs Fernand, Picard, Guettier, Metzmaimer and Super. They asked my father to look over the drawings for the new 4CV model and subsequently to test it. He drew up a test report and proposed some changes to the suspension, the weight distribution and the size of the tyres. In addition, he worked in the Renault assembly shop on the preparations for the series production of the 4CV.

My father repeatedly asked the French to release him, since if he was really going to build a new car and a new factory, he would have to be allowed to do that in freedom. Yet all his requests were in vain. Indeed the opposite was the case, for on 17 February 1947, almost two years after the end of the war, he was taken with my brother-in-law to the police jail in Meudon in the department of Seine-et-Oise not far from Paris. The next day he was taken, heavily guarded, to the Gare de Lyon and thence to Dijon. My father and Dr Piëch were handcuffed throughout the entire journey, as if they were dangerous criminals. In the prison they were placed in separate cells. My father had this to say in later years: 'It was a terrible time. The cell was unheated, even in the depths of winter. I felt completely isolated and abandoned by all my friends!'

While my father was in prison in Dijon, changes in the French cabinet resulted in the Communist Marcel Paul losing his seat. On the other hand, Teitgen, the Minister of Justice, who was probably largely to blame for our misfortunes, had seen his own power grow. This of course had a negative effect on my father and left him completely dejected. Moreover, he was in very poor physical shape, but although he was ill he was refused medical treatment in Dijon and was interrogated further. It was not until 24 February 1947 that he was allowed to consult a doctor, who immediately certified him unfit for imprisonment. He was then transferred to the prison hospital. With medical treatment he made a slow recovery, but his spirits remained very low since he had not the slightest idea what was to become of him.

Three months passed before he was interviewed again by the examining magistrate, Raymond. This time the interview was conducted in the presence of two witnesses, both from Peugeot, Monsieur Materne, a director of the company, and Monsieur Falaise, whose precise role at Peugeot I can unfortunately no longer remember. Both made astonishing statements and confirmed that my father had ensured that no Peugeot workers were forced to go to work in Germany. They also confirmed that my father had successfully refused to accept interference at Peugeot by German committees of inspection. In the meantime a former Gestapo official by the name of Hulf had been questioned; he had named the departments which had sent French workers to Germany as forced labour. From this it emerged that my father had had absolutely nothing at all to do with it. After these investigations and the completely new legal situation arising from them, my father and Dr Piëch were released on bail of one million francs. We were able to raise this large sum only because we had, with the support of good friends, received a large and interesting commission from Italy, of which more later.

On 1 August 1947 my father and brother-in-law were released from prison. They were permitted to travel to Austria but not for the time being to leave the French zone, so they took up residence at the Hotel Klausner in Kitzbühel. A year later, the 'Porsche affair' was brought to an end by the due process of law; the French absolved my father of all guilt and declared the charges null and void.

After endless delays, I had been allowed to leave Bad Rippold-sau in July 1946. In the meantime it had been established that there was absolutely no legal basis for my arrest and imprisonment in Baden-Baden. There was a complete absence of appropriate documentation and my personal papers had simply disappeared, which made the whole affair seem even more peculiar. Without papers one became a non-person, and nobody needed to bother with a non-person. LeComte had to go to Paris three times in order to arrange for the issue of the discharge papers. On his first two trips he was told that my discharge papers were already on their way to Baden-Baden, but they never arrived. On the third visit LeComte was cunning enough to have the papers issued to him personally at the Ministry of Justice in Paris and to hand them over in person to the relevant authorities in Baden-Baden. After all this I was free at last. I wasted no time and set off immediately in my own car to Innsbruck, accompanied by Monsieur Castel-lani, an official from the Sûreté. At the High Command for the French occupation zone in Innsbruck it was confirmed in the presence of Castellani that I was permitted to leave the French zone. I said farewell to my 'escort' and drove home to Zell am See in the American zone.

At this point my father and brother-in-law were still languish-ing in the servants' quarters in the Renault villa in Paris. As I have already mentioned, 13 long months would pass before they too were able to return to Austria.

———————— **14** ————————

A Grand Prix car for Italy

During our enforced absence, my sister Louise had kept the company alive with remarkable courage. As soon as I returned I got down to work, but this was not so easy as a German citizen in what was now a foreign country. The annexation of Austria, enforced in March 1938, had been revoked, which meant that we had become a foreign firm under British supervision, since our headquarters in Gmünd were in the British zone. Our chief designer, Herr Rabe, had been appointed manager of the company.

When I arrived at the former Karnerau sawmill outside Gmünd, where the factory had been evacuated, the union's district representative turned up and informed me that I was no longer the managing director of the Porsche company. 'Fine,' I replied. 'Then you are no longer entitled to use my name in connection with the company!'

The fellow had not considered my release from this point of view. My reaction had taken him by surprise and he obviously had no idea how to respond to it. Eventually he relented sufficiently to accept me as owner of the company and the person who could take decisions in my father's absence.

Karl Rabe had been part of our company since time immemorial and had become a friend of the family. He had given my sister a great deal of support during our imprisonment and subsequent internment.

The company was continuing to repair VW bucket cars. We were also repairing other manufacturers' vehicles and making parts for agricultural vehicles, but were not yet involved in automobile design. In any event, towards the end of 1946 we were already employing more than 200 people in Gmünd. In that same year my sister and I had set up our 'Austrian' company in Salzburg under the name of Porsche Konstruktionen GesmbH.

Gradually old friends began to get in touch with us again. Things were looking up; all we lacked was my father and brother-in-law. An old acquaintance had contacted my sister; he was Carlo Abarth, who had married Dr Piëch's secretary. Carlo, who in pre-war Austria, when he was known as Karl Abarth, had been a well-known dirt-track racing driver, had retreated to Yugoslavia before the Nazis seized power. My brother-in-law had helped him to get away. When I returned in July 1946 he started to correspond with me. Another old acquaintance, the engineer Rodolfo Hruska, had already got in touch with Herr Rabe in Gmünd in February 1946 as he was on his way back to Merano from Mannheim accompanied by an American officer. One fine day both of them came to see me in Zell am See and made us an interesting proposal. Rodolfo Hruska had worked for us before the war. He had left Austria for Germany in 1937 and we had subsequently taken him on. Among other things, he was the intermediary between our design office in Zuffenhausen and the VW factory to be built in Wolfsburg. Hruska had also collaborated on the tractor and worked at the Nibelungen plant. In April 1945 Hruska had travelled on business to Northern Italy. In Brescia, the starting and finishing point for the famous Mille Miglia, he was supposed to enter into negotiations with the commercial vehicle manufacturer OM about the production of automobile parts. He was unable to return to Stuttgart because the Americans had already reached the city, and so stayed with friends in Merano. Both Abarth and Hruska experienced the greatest difficulties in coming to us in Austria because it had not been easy to obtain authorization for the journey. However, after American jurisdiction was extended over both Merano and Zell am See, permission was finally granted.

Both men were interested in representing us in Italy. Although we had not at this point started designing cars again and could not therefore grant any licences, they stuck to their offer. I saw no reason to deny them their wish and a contract was duly drawn up and signed. The Italian partner was a certain Piero Dusio, a wealthy Turin businessman who was already involved in several companies. He had done some motor racing himself and was considered an automobile enthusiast. The arrangement was that Dusio would seek orders for our company; it was not long, however, before he himself placed an order with us.

There is a very interesting story behind this order which can be traced back to Tazio Nuvolari, the famous Italian racing driver. Nuvolari had been a very successful driver before the war, particularly for Alfa Romeo. He recorded one of his most impressive victories in 1935, when, in the face of stiff competition from Mercedes-Benz and Auto Union, he drove an Alfa Romeo car to victory in the German Grand Prix on the North Loop at the old Nürburgring. For the 1938 and 1939 seasons Nuvolari was under contract to Auto Union as the driver of the Type D 12-cylinder racing car. Nuvolari was now looking for a competitive Formula 1 racing car. A friend of his worked as chief driver at OM and had been his co-driver in the Mille Miglia. This friend suggested that Nuvolari should get in touch with Hruska, who was staying in Merano. Hruska had worked in the past for Porsche and Porsche had designed the first Auto Union racing car. So Nuvolari turned up one day at Hruska's house in Merano and during the ensuing conversation it was suggested that the Porsche design office, which had now resumed work, should be commissioned to design a Grand Prix car. The only problem was how to raise finance for the project.

At that time racing drivers and motoring journalists who had been active before the war were beginning to make contact with each other again. People with common interests were meeting again. Hruska and Abarth had connections with this circle which included, among others, Brivio and Corrado Millanta. Before the war, Millanta, who spoke perfect German, had been a representative for German aviation companies in Italy and had made a name for himself as a motoring journalist, especially after the war; with his Leica, he also took very good photographs of motor racing events. A number of excellent articles by Millanta can be found in the early issues of *Das Auto* magazine, known later as *Auto, Motor und Sport* and *Motor Revue*. This group of dedicated motor racing enthusiasts soon concluded that Dusio would be a suitable backer for Nuvolari's Grand Prix car project and began preliminary discussions with Dusio, who also knew Nuvolari well.

After the war, Dusio had built a 1.1 litre single-seater racing car based on Fiat parts which enabled many drivers to start racing again. Dusio's company, which was also developing a light sports car, was called Cisitalia and the cars built by the company bore the same name. Dusio was very enthusiastic about the proposal that he should develop a Grand Prix car with the assistance of the Porsche company and declared himself willing to make the necessary funds available. The collaboration did not stop with the racing car; Dusio drew up a whole programme of automobile designs that we were to put into effect.

Eventually a contract was drawn up in Kitzbühel in collaboration with Rodolfo Hruska and Carlo Abarth, acting on behalf of Dusio. According to this contract, we were to supply the following designs: a small tractor, Porsche Type 323, a Grand Prix car, Porsche Type 360, a sports car, Porsche Type 370, and a water turbine. Given the shortage of fuel at that time, Dusio hoped the turbine would be commercially very successful.

A further meeting took place with Dusio in Austria, with Millanta acting as interpreter and adviser, and on 2 February we signed a contract with Dusio. With the fee that Piero Dusio paid us we were in a position to stand bail for my father and brother-in-law. However, the transfer of the required sum from Italy to France proved somewhat problematic. With the aid of the well-known French motor journalist Charles Faroux, and the racing driver Louis Chiron, who was based in Monte Carlo, we eventually managed to transfer the money to France.

All we had to do now was obtain the approval of the British authorities in Klagenfurt for the Dusio commission. I went to see the British officer in charge of such matters and said to him, 'I have a commission here for the Porsche company, but in order to fulfil this contract we need some of the liberality that is extended to Austrian companies. If this is not forthcoming, we shall have to move our operation to Italy!'

The British occupying forces were very concerned to set the Austrian economy in motion again, since without a functioning economy the occupying authorities would have had to bear the additional burden of responsibility for the material well-being of the country. In other words, a functioning economy was essential if a reasonable standard of living was to be achieved. My application was sent to Allied Headquarters in Vienna. The authorities there came to an interesting decision: on account of the origin of the founders of the Porsche company, it was in fact half Austrian. Consequently it was decreed that the part of the company located in Austria should be regarded as Austrian and not German. The other part of the company, our factory in Stuttgart-Zuffenhausen, was located in the American zone in Germany. That meant that we could at least continue working at the Karnerau factory in Gmünd without any further conditions.

The commission from Piero Dusio was of great significance for us. It meant that we once again had a future in the automobile industry. The Grand Prix car, which we also called Cisitalia after Dusio's racing designs, was to have a supercharged 1.5 litre engine, in accordance with the Grand Prix formula valid at the time. We had to follow the formula laid down, but otherwise we had a free hand. We planned a mid-engined car with a 12-cylinder boxer engine and four-wheel drive. It was to be a very advanced design and we were of course able to draw on our wealth of experience with the Auto-Union-P racing car.

Although we were to design the Cisitalia, it was going to be built by Dusio's team from the drawings that we produced. The problems that we had to overcome while designing the car are probably best illustrated by the fact that each drawing had to be submitted to the British for approval. We were not trusted as we might perhaps have been able to design something that went against the requirements laid down by the Allies. However, it was intended that we should supervise the construction of the prototype in Turin.

The Cisitalia was way ahead of its time. Its 1.5 litre engine, a flat twelve with two overhead camshafts for each row of cylinders, could be supercharged with either a Zoller or a Roots blower. In both cases, the fuel was mixed in a Weber double down-draught carburettor. The engine cubic capacity was 1,498 cc, designed to produce 350 hp at an engine speed of 10,500 rpm. Another inno-

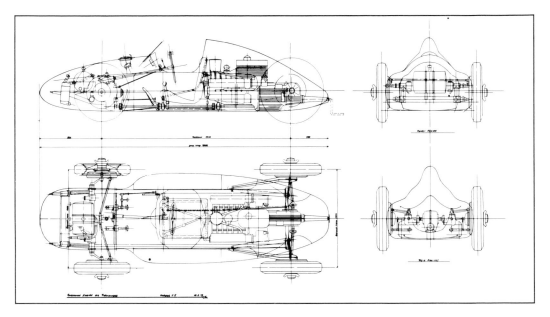

Above This photo shows very clearly the design of the Porsche type 360 Grand Prix racing car, the Cisitalia, with the engine in front of the rear axle and four-wheel drive.

vation was the switchable four-wheel drive. The gearbox was fitted behind the rear axle in order to ensure that the weight distribution was suited to the car's lightweight construction and to improve handling. The gearbox had five forward gears and synchronized mesh. The synchromesh system was based on the servo ring designed by Leopold Schmid, an Austrian engineer who had been working for us since 1941. The development of this ring synchronization system to the series production stage was a costly business, but it led in the end to the production of a gearbox that was to be used by many important companies.

We started work on the Type 360 in January 1946 with a small team under the direction of Karl Rabe. However, we were lacking an engineer skilled enough to send to Turin to supervise the construction of the prototypes. Finally, I remembered a former colleague of my father, Professor Eberan von Eberhorst, who had worked with us on the 16-cylinder Auto union racing car and had later played a major part in the design and manufacture of the twelve-cylinder Auto Union racing car, in accordance with the formulas laid down for 1938 and 1939. I had learnt that Eberan von Eberhorst had been living in Germany in the Soviet occupation zone and had fled from there to Bavaria. I traced him and wrote asking him whether he would like to work for us and supervise the construction of the racing car in Turin. The experience that he had gained with the two Auto Union racing cars made him the ideal man for us. He accepted the offer with great pleasure and came first of all to Gmünd, where he acquainted himself with the Cisitalia project.

Our contract with Dusio also included a sports car, designated

Porsche Type 370. Dusio's aim was to extend his sports car range with a larger model. He had hitherto been building a sports car of his own design based on Fiat 1.1 litre engines. The car that we were to design was to be a four-seater with an air-cooled six-cylinder engine mounted in the rear. Since the car was to be a very compact design, it was planned to fit the five-speed gearbox with a torque converter under the engine. With its pressed steel chassis the car would weigh about 600 kg (1,323 lb). Unfortunately the Type 370 was not built because in the meantime Dusio had had considerable success with his own sports car in, among other races, the Mille Miglia.

In 1947 Herr Rabe and I went to Turin in order to see what progress had been made in building the Grand Prix car. This was

Opposite below, above and below The Porsche Cisitalia, designed by myself and my staff in Austria after the Second World War.

Famous Italian racing
driver Tazio Nuvolari
(with cap) inspecting
the Cisitalia Grand Prix
car with Piero Dusion
on his right.

a wearisome business, because it took almost nine months to
obtain the required authorization for this trip abroad. This made
me think of the ease with which one could travel in Europe before
the First World War. Many things had changed for the worse. On
the journey back from Turin I became increasingly convinced of
the viability of an idea that we had had before the war, namely
the construction of a sports car based on Volkswagen components.
Our visit to Dusio had rekindled my enthusiasm for the idea, since
we could very easily do with Volkswagen components what he
was doing with Fiat parts.

Project number three for Dusio was the small tractor, designated
Porsche Type 323. Our outline proposals included two different
models, one with a single cylinder engine and the other with a
two-cylinder unit. However, Dusio did not build either of these
vehicles and they never got beyond the design stage. Since we

This is the special
gearbox for the Cisitalia
racing car with new
advanced synchronizing
rings, based on a
patent of Leopold
Schmid.

146

were already involved with tractors, we took the opportunity to resume work on the long-delayed Type 113 tractor. We were able in this instance to fall back on the wealth of experience acquired during the development of the 'people's tractor'. We designed a tractor powered by an air-cooled two-cylinder diesel engine which underwent thorough trials. OM, the Italian commercial vehicle company, expressed an interest in it, but in the end in 1949 we sold the vehicle to the Allgaier company in Uhingen near Göppingen (Baden-Württemberg). Since we are discussing the tractor project, let me anticipate events somewhat and state that between 1949 and 1957 Allgaier produced 25,000 of these tractors with engines of between 17 and 44 hp. Allgaier then sold their tractor business to the Mannesmann group. This latter company then built a factory in Friedrichshafen (the Porsche-Dieselschlepper GmbH) to produce the tractor. Large quantities of the

Myself with my chief engineer Senator Karl Rabe during the design phase of the Cisitalia.

147

Mannesmann-Porsche tractor were exported. That was in 1963 and 1964, but then the tractor market went into recession and the Porsche Dieselschlepper GmbH was eventually closed down and the factory was sold to the Motoren und Turbinen-Union of Friedrichshafen (MTU). At that time both Daimler-Benz AG and MAN had a 50 per cent stake in MTU. In 1985 Daimler-Benz took full control of MTU.

But back to 1947. The Formula 1 rules applied to cars with engines of up to 1.5 litres with supercharger and up to 4.5 litres without supercharger. Dusio had decided in favour of a supercharger. This formula was initially valid until 1948 and was subsequently extended until 1951. During that time, however, normally aspirated engines came into fashion; Ferrari, for example, were developing a 4.5 litre V12 engine. This was of course a good enough reason for Dusio to consider developing such an engine for the Cisitalia, in order to be ready for all eventualities. Unfortunately, this engine never went beyond the drawing board. At that time, Dusio had just launched a series of his own sports car. It was customary then for suppliers to require payment in advance. In the immediate post-war period capital was in short supply and it was not unusual for small companies to get into debt. For Dusio, however, this led to the commitment of considerable amounts of money which he could recover only when his sports cars were up for sale. However, when the production of his sports car was relatively well advanced, he had to decide either to finish the sports car series or to build the Grand Prix car, since there was not enough finance available for both projects. Eventually he decided in favour of the sports car. The Grand Prix car was built, but the project could not be continued.

At the end of 1951 Alfa Romeo with its Alfetta withdrew from Grand Prix racing, and from 1952 Formula 2 cars contested the World Championship because of the lack of Formula 1 cars.

In 1947, in addition to the important contract with Dusio and the repair of VW bucket cars, we were also making components for agricultural vehicles and machinery. The production facilities were housed in the large workshop at the Gmünd sawmill, which was heated to an acceptable temperature in winter by iron stoves. The place certainly did not look like a modern factory, but our main concern was to be back in business again. The people in our design office were naturally thinking about additional products that we could manufacture. Josef Mickl, our graduate engineer who at that time was in charge of the calculations department, hit upon the idea of making life easier for farmers, particularly in the Austrian mountains, by mechanizing more of the farmer's activities. It should be remembered that because of the war virtually no progress had been made in that direction for eight years. So we made cable winches for working on steep mountain slopes and, among other things, small power plants which used the water power that existed in the mountains to generate electricity. A programme of this kind was worthwhile because farmers received subsidies from public funds in order to purchase such machinery. It was not difficult to foresee that this state of affairs was unlikely to continue for long, and that it would then be a question of whether farmers could still afford to buy our products. This meant that we had to start thinking about new products, particularly those more connected with the automobile industry. Incidentally, one of our small power plants can still be seen at the estate in Zell am See.

As I have already described, my father was released in August after 20 months in prison and had to live in Kitzbühel. Nevertheless, he was given leave to visit us. He came to Gmünd and inspected what we had been doing during his absence, particularly the Cisitalia. He scrutinized the technical drawings for the racing car without saying a word. I was of course impatient to hear his verdict. Finally I asked, 'So what do you think of our work then?'

He replied, 'I'd have gone about it in the same way as you!' and laid his hand on my shoulder. I hardly need to say that I was very proud of this judgement from my father, who was always so critical in matters of engineering.

15

A sports car of our own

In 1945 the Volkswagen factory in Wolfsburg was little more than a heap of rubble. The Americans had initially occupied both the town and the factory, but after four weeks everything had been handed over to the British in whose zone the factory was situated. It was English army officers who had the ruins cleared up to a certain extent; the factory had not only been heavily bombed but had also been ransacked. However, by the end of 1945, the 6,000-strong work force had produced 917 cars. This pleased us greatly, because we had never abandoned the plans that we had formulated in the period before the war for building our own car.

We began work on implementing this plan at about the same time that we received the commission from Dusio. The basis for our development work was the Porsche Type 60 K10, the sports car that had been built for the Berlin-Rome race. The new car was known as the Type 356 and was to be a sports car. It had a tubular chassis which we had designed ourselves and welded together from steel tubes. The power unit was a 1,131 cc Volkswagen engine fitted in front of the rear axle, while the gearbox was flange-mounted behind the axle. The front-wheel suspension, as well as the steering and gearbox, were also original Volkswagen components, as was the entire running gear with its 85 in (216 cm) wheelbase, the 40 hp, four-cylinder, air-cooled engine and the non-synchronized, four-speed gearbox, slightly modified to give better handling and higher performance.

The aerodynamic lines of the elegant open two-seater with its aluminium body were developed on the basis of the experience we had gained with the Berlin-Rome car. The body had in fact been designed by Erwin Komenda shortly before the war. The type 356 was not designed as a pure racing car, but rather as a more comfortable sports car. The body was hand-formed by Friedrich Weber, an excellent craftsman and a master of his trade, who had arrived in Gmünd at the beginning of April 1948. It took him only two months to make the body, which for a first prototype was a considerable achievement. All the sheet-metal work for the subsequent vehicles was completed by hand within a week. The finished car had a dry weight of about 1,300 lb (590 kg).

Friedrich Weber had started his apprenticeship with Austro

Daimler in 1922, at the time when my father was the member of the board responsible for technical development. My father had advised Weber at the time to train as a coachbuilder because they were always in demand.

The Porsche 356, the first Porsche of all, was completed on 8 June 1948. With its compact design, low weight and short wheelbase it exceeded even our expectations. The Katschberg mountain pass, practically on our front doorstep, made an ideal test track on which to give the car a thorough examination. The 356 climbed like a mountain goat and achieved 80 mph (129 km/h) without any effort at all. A month later, my cousin Herbert Kaes, who collaborated with our company on technical matters, drove the first Porsche to victory in its class in a road race in Innsbruck.

One day, when Professor Eberan von Eberhorst was visiting us from Turin, we were out testing the 356 on the Katschberg. I took Eberan with me as co-driver. He was very impressed with the car's performance, particularly its acceleration, and predicted great success for the car. 'It is essential that we raise sufficient capital to put it into production!' he said. We eventually found a financier in the person of Herr R. von Senger, who, with his associate Herr Bernhard Blank, ran, among other things, an advertising agency in Zürich. Initially it was Herr von Senger himself who made the necessary funds availabe. Herr Blank became involved later and took over some of the financing before AMAG eventually became our agents in Switzerland.

In addition to the mid-engined open two-seater, we were already working on cabriolet and coupé versions. These models were sig-

This is Porsche number one. In the final year of the war the firm was forced to move from Stuttgart to Gmünd in Carinthia, Austria. There, after the war, I developed the project of a sports car based on Volkswagen parts, the type 356. When my father returned from prison in France, the first car, a Roadster, was completed. This photograph shows me with my father beside the new car in Gmünd.

Porsche type 356 number one, the first car to take the Porsche name.

nificantly different from the Type 356-1, whose tubular frame not only took up a great deal of space but would also have been rather expensive to produce in small batches. Moreover, the car had to be more comfortable and provide more luggage space. For the new Type 356-2 and its successors we returned to the basic VW design, which meant that the engine was located again behind the rear axle, while the chassis was a box-girder design made of sheet steel which was so light that it could be lifted by two men. It was attached to the self-supporting body in a novel fashion. There was great interest in Switzerland in the first car to bear the Porsche name. We were at last in a position to realize our pre-war plan of building our own sports car based on VW components. The problem was that in 1948 we only had a few VW parts left from

Porsche 356 number two was a coupé with light metal body. It was on this concept that the very successful 356 line was built.

the time when we were developing the VW, and there were no VW parts to be found in Austria. Nor was it possible in post-war Austria to obtain sheet aluminium for the bodywork.

As early as 1945, however, AMAG, the VW agency, had already been set up in Switzerland. Consequently, we entered into a contract with Herr von Senger for the supply of VW parts from AMAG and sheet aluminium from Switzerland. Authorization for the import of these materials had to be obtained from the government in Vienna. It was granted to us, on the condition that we sold all the vehicles we manufactured abroad, since Austria urgently needed foreign currency.

We signed a further contract with Herr Senger for the import of our cars into Switzerland. The first delivery comprised five cars, the open two-seater and four coupés. However, it was anything but simple to produce a small batch of the new coupé. Its greater weight (1,560 lb (707.5 kg), compared with the open-top's 1,300 lb (590 kg)) made it necessary to fit a new brake system, which we purchased direct from the manufacturers, Lockheed in Britain. As you will doubtless remember, the original VW engine produced 23.5 hp; for the bucket car the cubic capacity was increased to 1,131 cc and the output to 25 hp. In view of the 40 hp produced by the VW engine in the open-top and coupés, we had to design a new cylinder head and make other slight modifications.

A whole range of problems cropped up in the production process, which was repeatedly delayed by the need to apply so often for the official authorization. Another difficulty was that the nearest railhead was almost 13 miles (21 km) away. Sometimes we were only able to obtain expensive parts, such as special spark plugs, in Germany; we would bring them over the border in our trouser pockets! It was altogether a hazardous business, which our young people today, accustomed as they are to a smoothly organized, sometimes computer-controlled production process, can scarcely imagine. If you talk to them about it, they look at you in amazement, as if they were uncertain whether to believe you or not.

A great deal of improvization was also required at the Volkswagen factory. It should be pointed out that special machinery and tools had simply been removed. Moreover, some of the management had no connection with the motor industry; the first general manager after the war had been a divorce lawyer in Berlin. This situation lasted until 1 January 1948, when Heinz Nordhoff, an expert of the highest class, took over the position of general manager. I had known Nordhoff during the war, when he was in charge of the Opel factory in Brandenburg, which was at the time the largest truck factory in Europe. Before Nordhoff took over, I had been to Wolfsburg several times; after all, our pre-war contract with VW still stood, but nobody there had felt themselves able to draw up any contracts for future co-operation or the supply of parts.

In the summer of 1948 I had a preliminary discussion with Nordhoff, and we very quickly agreed that the relationship betwen the VW factory and the Porsche company needed clarification.

Even today, I am still amazed, given all the problems we encountered, that we succeeded in producing 46 cars. At the same time as we were making the coupé, we were also producing the cabriolet. The bodywork for six of these cabriolets was designed by the Swiss company Beutler in Düren near Bern. At the 19th International Automobile Show in Geneva, which opened on 17 March 1949, Porsche cars were exhibited for the first time.

In the meantime, our collaboration with Herr von Senger had ceased. He had lost interest and his associate, Bernhard Blank, took over his commitments. Herr Blank, who also ran a garage in Zürich, had made the arrangements to exhibit our cars at the Geneva show. It was also in Geneva that AMAG made contact with us and expressed their interest in our cars. We eventually reached an agreement with AMAG, whereby they replaced Bernhard Blank as our general importer for the whole of Switzerland.

We were already engaged in something akin to market research. My brother-in-law, Dr Piëch, and our financial expert, Herr Kern, went to Belgium, the Netherlands and Sweden, in order to gauge the sales opportunities in those countries. They found a great deal of interest, but the post-war economic situation meant that free trade was impossible because of a lack of foreign exchange. The import of foreign cars was not very high on the list of priorities.

The purchase of materials was not our only worry in Gmünd; the mechanical equipment was also a matter of concern. Since

Myself (right) discussing design matters on a 356 engine with my father.

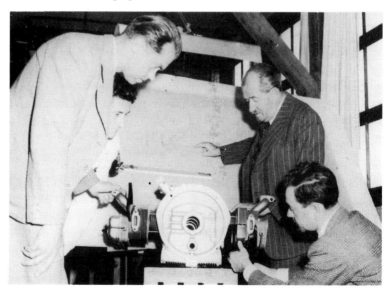

the move from Zuffenhausen to Gmünd, we had lost a great deal of our machinery. Some machines had simply been expropriated, while others had been stolen at the end of the war, together with some valuable tools. As a consequence, the cars that we built were mainly hand-made, but they were of excellent quality which was recognized throughout the world.

My father was satisfied with our work. He was well aware of the conditions under which we had to work, and he took a great interest in our activities. He was still mentally active, but his long and arduous imprisonment had drained him of the energy and ability to commit himself to a matter with the inexhaustible vitality that had been so characteristic of him in days gone by. He was no longer the man he had been, and it was obvious to me that I could no longer count on his active collaboration. I was out on my own.

At that time we were also holding talks with the Austrian government, Steyr-Daimler-Puch AG in Vienna and a group of industrialists in Styria about possible future collaboration on large-scale projects. However, the talks produced no concrete results. The most financially sound group taking part in these discussions was the Creditanstalt (credit bank), which after the war was virtually a state concern. At that time, German property was seized by the state and automatically became state property. As has already been mentioned, we were a German concern, and although we remained the owners of the company all our bank accounts were seized. This obviously meant that we did not have the necessary working capital. Naturally the Austrian government was extremely concerned to retain our company for Austria, and for this reason we received a visit from the general manager of Steyr-Daimler-Puch. It became clear to me very early in our discussions that there were no real prospects of co-operation. The company was managed by the same men with whom my father had had to struggle in the past and who had finally forced him to leave the company and accept the offer from Daimler. In brief, the prospects for our company in Austria were such that those in possession of the necessary financial resources were unwilling to work with us, while those who would have liked to collaborate with us had as little capital as we had. However, the finance provided by Herr von Senger and Herr Blank for the small-scale production of sports cars was insufficient to develop the car as we wished. Thus it seemed to be that the only realistic route for us to take was to enter discussions with Herr Nordhoff in an attempt to clarify the relationship between VW and Porsche.

In the meantime, there had been a noteworthy development in the West zone of Germany. On 20 June 1948, the virtually worthless Reichsmark had been replaced by the new Deutschmark and each German citizen was given 40 Marks. At the same time the

The last portrait of my father Professor Ferdinand Porsche after his release from 22 months in prison in France.

controlled economy was abolished and the free market economy introduced, thus laying the foundations for economic recovery.

On 16 September 1948 I met Heinz Nordhoff in Bad Reichenhall. I have always been a good negotiator, since I always make reasonable demands and do not attempt to pull any tricks. With the minimum of discussion, we negotiated a new contract between Volkswagen AG and Porsche. The next day we went to the lawyers with a clear idea of what we wanted, and on the same day, 17 September 1948, the contract was signed. The main provisions of the agreement were that the Volkswagen factory would supply the parts we required for our sports car programme and that we would be able to sell the cars manufactured by Porsche through the VW distribution network and have them serviced by the factory's service organization. In this way, the important issues of distribution and customer service were resolved. In addition, we were to act as design consultants to VW. Since Nordhoff was unable to give me any guarantee about the scope of future development contracts, I said, 'In that case, I want a licence fee for the VW that we designed!' As a result, it was written into the contract that we would receive a licence fee of 5 DM for each Beetle produced, and in addition became the general agent for Volkswagen in Austria. We regarded this contract as satisfactory. Undoubtedly Nordhoff's aim was to tie us to VW, since without this agreement we would have been able to develop a car similar to the VW for a rival company. The VW was now our intellectual property.

At the beginning of 1949 we set up an office in Salzburg from which the import, distribution and customer service for the Volkswagen in Austria would be directed. On 14 May 1949, a new company, Porsche Salzburg, was established to take over these functions; Dr Piëch and his wife, my sister Louise, were largely instrumental in getting the new company off the ground and they became the directors of the company. Sadly my brother-in-law died three years later of heart trouble.

At Gmünd, work continued. The main problem was to guarantee our future and to improve our financial situation, since we were literally living from hand to mouth. The rate of production that we were achieving meant that we were only just breaking even. Between 8 June 1948 and 20 March 1951, a total of 46 Porsches were built at Gmünd; after that, production at Gmünd came to a halt. We had realized long before this that our future in the motor industry did not lie in Gmünd, where the conditions were simply too unfavourable. We had to try to re-establish ourselves in Stuttgart.

My old school friend from Cannstatt days, Albert Prinzing, had paid me a visit at Zell am See before the end of the war. We already knew what the outcome of the war would be and began to think

about what one could do after the defeat. In our view we had
to find some way of utilizing the skills and experience that existed
within the Porsche company. Before the war, Albert Prinzing had
been one of the youngest professors in Germany and had lectured
in economics at the University of Berlin. During the war, he had
been, among other things, an official advisor to the cultural attaché
at the Germany embassy in Rome and acted as an intermediary
for Benito Mussolini. He was imprisoned for several years after
the war and was not released until 1948. On his return to his home
town of Stuttgart, he began to look after our interests.

Our factory in Stuttgart-Zuffenhausen was still being used by
the Americans to house a vehicle fleet. So we set up an office in
our old house on the Feuerbacher Weg, the house that my father
had built in 1923 when he was working for the Daimler Motoren
Gesellschaft. In addition to Albert Prinzing, our team in Stuttgart comprised engineer Hans Klauser, who had come to us in
1936 as a young man, Karl Kirn, our administrator in Stuttgart,
and a secretary. Since I still had to take care of our affairs in
Gmünd, I was very grateful that Albert Prinzing was running the
new Stuttgart company.

Our engineers set to work in our garage on modifications to the
Type 356 that we were planning to build in Stuttgart.

I contacted Dr Arnulf Klett, the new Lord Mayor of Stuttgart,
and asked for his help in our attempts to reclaim our old factory
in Stuttgart-Zuffenhausen from the Americans. That was unfortunately not possible, but we still needed premises where we could
begin producing cars. In the end, we managed to rent a hut near
our occupied factory, where we housed our design and sales
departments. We also had to rent 5,000 sq ft (464 sq m) of the Reutter coachbuilding works, with whom we had collaborated before
the war, for final assembly.

In September 1949 we were able to start work. It was during
this period that my secretary, Helene Werkmeister, joined the company; she was to work for me until her retirement. On 3 September, my father's 74th birthday, she sent him a telegram signed by
myself, Professor Prinzing, Karl Kirn, who was responsible for
the financial affairs of our new company, and Hans Klauser, the
manager of our Stuttgart operation.

Our collaboration with Reutter could be regarded as a sort of
quid pro quo for the space they made available to us, and it mani-
fested itself in an initial order for 500 bodies, placed in November
1949. The Reutter coachworks were to build bodies for the Type
356 in accordance with the design produced by Erwin Komenda
and his team. We had to abandon the aluminium bodies used for
the 356 series built in Gmünd and use sheet steel for the outer
skin. Although aluminium would have been easier than sheet steel
to work by hand and the tools required would not have been any

more expensive, the workers at Reutter did not have enough experience of welding aluminium. There was no problem at all in welding sheet steel. Reutter produced the first series of 356 bodies in its workshop at 82a Augustenstraße in West Stuttgart. At virtually the same time an order for a small cabriolet series went to the Gläser company which had previously had its headquarters in Dresden and which had started up again in Ullersricht near Weiden.

Reutter completed the first body at the beginning of 1950. My father and Erwin Komenda went with me to the Augustenstraße to take delivery of it. When we arrived, my father inspected the body closely, walking round it without saying a word and finally sitting down on a stool right in front of the body. There was general astonishment; the Reutter people perhaps thought that my father was tired, when he said suddenly, 'The body will have to go back to the workshop. It's not right, it's not symmetrical!' The body was measured and indeed it was discovered that it had shifted 20 mm (0.78 in) to the right away from the central axis.

We had planned a first run of 500 cars; this was a very modest target, but with only 200,000 DM of capital available to us it was just not possible to plan a larger run. The Type 356 was offered for sale in 1950 at a price of 9,950 DM (£2,100 in the UK), which was a very low price for a hand-built car of that quality.

In the spring of 1950, a meeting of dealers and importers from the rest of Europe was held in Wolfsburg at the VW factory. This was a good opportunity for us to exhibit our product, so my friend Prinzing went to Wolfsburg with a coupé and a cabriolet with bodywork by the Swiss company Beutler. Interest among the dealers was high, and Prinzing came back with 37 firm orders, 20 from Germany and 17 from other European countries. Who would have thought, after this modest but nonetheless promising start, that we would eventually produce 78,000 Type 356s? The deposits paid by the VW dealers for the cars they had ordered amounted to exactly 200,000 DM, the sum required to finance the first production run.

The first Porsche Type 356 coupé was completed on Maundy Thursday 1950, and became my own private car. It was little different in appearance from the cars we had produced in Gmünd. However, subsequent experience had led to some changes under the 'skin'. The first series was fitted with a Lockheed brake system which we had obtained from England. Alfred Teves GmbH (Ate), Lockheed's German licensee, did not produce this brake system, and we were not allowed to use original English components. In the meantime, VW had introduced a hydraulic brake system which we used for the 356. In order to improve heat dissipation, we later fitted cooling fins to the brake drums. By 1951 Ate were ready to supply us with twin-leading-shoe Lockheed brakes.

One of the first 356
coupés to be sold is
shown here in Egypt.

The engines in the cars produced in Stuttgart were already fitted with the new aluminium cylinder heads with exhaust valves set at an angle. These heads were cast by the Karl Schmidt company in Neckarsulm. We then bored out the engine and used aluminium cylinders, chrome plated on their working surfaces, which had been developed by the Stuttgart company Mahle. This gave the engine a cubic capacity of 1,300 cc; at the same time, the aluminium cylinders reduced the weight by more than 2 lb (0.9 kg) per cylinder compared with the steel cylinders used previously.

Our next target was a 1,500 cc engine. We had bored the 1,100 engine out as far as possible, so it was only logical to lengthen stroke to get 1,500 cc. However, we were restricted by the crankshaft. As a result, we changed over to a Hirth crankshaft with roller bearings which made it possible to increase the cubic capacity to 1,500 cc. The disadvantages of the Hirth crankshaft were firstly that it was very expensive and secondly that the company could not supply it in sufficient quantities, so we were forced to replace it with a die-forged crankshaft with plain bearings.

When we had decided on the VW engine as the drive unit for the Porsche, we knew that it would present a problem if we increased its performance. For a sports car, however, that was absolutely essential. The reason for the limited development capability of the VW engine lay in the lack of space between crankshaft and camshaft; moreover, the distance between the cylinders was too small to achieve a cubic capacity in excess of 1,500 cc and the tappet-driven valves did not allow any significant increase in engine speed. Consequently, as early as 1950, our Dr Ernst Fuhrmann began to design a high-performance engine. It later went

159

into production under the designation Carrera. Dr Fuhrmann, who had worked for us in Gmünd and then moved with us to Stuttgart when we established ourselves there again, was to design a four-cylinder engine with four overhead camshafts, two per cylinder head. A number of sketches were drawn and various means of driving the valves investigated. We looked at chain drives, spur-gear drives and bevel-gear drives. In the end we opted for a bevel-gear drive similar to the one that we had already used in the Cisitalia engine. The short-stroke engine had a cubic capacity of 1,498 cc, but was designed in such a way that the capacity could be increased to 2 litres. It was a good five years before this engine went into series production.

I have firm ideas about the styling of a car, and these ideas were very much the basis for the Type 356. I prefer a shape which gives the driver a feeling of stability and direct contact with the road. Grand Prix cars, for example, which make great demands on drivers, have independent wheels, which means that they are able to take bends on exactly the right line. I experienced this for myself when I drove racing cars or put test cars through their paces before the body had been built on. It is also an advantage when parking if the driver can see the wheels. It was for this reason that the front of the bonnet on the 356 sloped away steeply, giving the driver as direct a view of the road as possible. This also enabled the driver to gauge the exact position of the front wheels, as with a racing car. I still remember the problems experienced by Fangio in 1954 when he drove the fully-streamlined Mercedes in the British Grand Prix at the twisty Silverstone track and was unable to see the wheels. I know of earlier sports cars whose designers had apparently made the same discovery as I had. These cars, for example the Tornax and the Adler Trumpf Junior, had small mudguards on the front wheels which moved in the same direction as the steering wheel. This would have been the ideal solution, but it was not acceptable because of the higher unsprung masses that occur with independent wheel suspension.

In 1950 we set up a new company in Stuttgart because our original company, Dr. Ing. h.c. F. Porsche GmbH, which had subsequently been converted into a limited partnership, was still under the control of the Allies. Our former partner Adolf Rosenberger was responsible for this state of affairs: he had sued us for compensation. So we established a second company in addition to Dr. Ing. h.c. F. Porsche KG in order to be able to work unimpeded. The new company was called Dr. Ing. F. Porsche GmbH. However, this second company was very soon wound up when it was no longer required, and the limited partnership became Dr. Ing. h.c. F. Porsche GmbH and Co. KG. The managing directors were myself and Professor Alfred Prinzing. As far as our problem with Rosenberger was concerned, he had left the company of his own free will during the Third Reich. His stake in the company was taken over in 1933 by Hans von Veyder-Malberg, who paid Rosenberger in Austrian schillings, a currency which at that time was still freely convertible. In addition, we also gave Rosenberger a contract as overseas representative for our design services. However bad things might have been for Rosenberger at that time, we did everything we could under the circumstances to treat him fairly and decently. Things at that time were far from easy for us as well. However, we were able to reach a compromise that was acceptable to both sides. Rosenberger received a financial settlement from us, together with a Volkswagen car.

On 3 September 1950 my father celebrated his 75th birthday. There was an impressive ceremony at Schloß Solitude in the west of Stuttgart, where a whole host of Porsche drivers from all over Europe used their cars to form a guard of honour. The guests included Rudolf Caracciola and his wife, who arrived in a Mercedes, in memory of the time that my father had been technical director there. Rudolf Caracciola had won many races in cars designed by my father.

In October, in a Porsche manufactured in Stuttgart, my father and Ghislaine Kaes, his secretary, went to the Paris Motor Show, which at that time was still held in the Grand Palais. There he met an American of Austrian descent by the name of Maximilian Hoffman who was making strenuous efforts to have German cars imported into America again. We reached an agreement with 'Maxie Hoffman', as he was known to everyone in the motor business, and he imported Porsche cars into the United States with great success. By the time he died, Hoffman had imported virtually every make of German car into the United States, including Mercedes, BMW and Volkswagen.

In October my father also received a visit from the well-known French motoring journalist Charles Faroux, who had done so much to support the Le Mans 24-Hours Race. Faroux had not only helped to transfer the bail money for my father and brother-in-law, but had also provided food parcels for my father throughout his imprisonment. Faroux now wanted to see my father to see how his health was after his detention in France.

In November I went with my father to Wolfsburg to see Dr Nordhoff and visit the Volkswagen factory. This visit made a deep impression on the old man; one got the impression that he was proud of his life's work. He inspected everything closely and seemed very satisfied that the factory that he had built before the war was now producing the 'civilian' Volkswagen for ordinary customers as he had originally intended. This journey certainly inspired my father, particularly in view of the great injustice that had been done to him during his imprisonment. It was his last trip. The night after our return on 19 November he suffered a

161

stroke from which he never recovered. He had to spend the last three months of his life in bed. He was a very impatient invalid; as an engineer, he viewed the human body with the logic of his trade. If a machine could be repaired, doctors also had to be able to restore a human being to health. He celebrated Christmas and New Year with us, but after the holiday his position deteriorated. He had to be taken to the Marien Hospital, where he died on 30 January 1951.

Father's death left a large, painful void. His full life, with all its diverse achievements, had left a deep impression on all those who knew him. Although he was often impatient, particularly with those he called 'wafflers', nobody could ever deny his brilliance and great modesty.

The requiem mass was read by Abbot Johannes of the Benedictine monastery of Neresheim in Württemberg. He had been prison chaplain in Dijon during my father's imprisonment and had had many lengthy discussions with him. Out of this developed a friendship. Father Johannes Kraus also visited my father several times during his illness in Stuttgart and had done much to console him.

My father's funeral took place on 4 February 1951 in Stuttgart; it was attended by Dr Nordhoff, the Lord Mayor of Stuttgart, Dr Klett, and the Minister of Transport, Dr Seebohm, representing the Federal Government, as well as many friends and business associates from all over the world. From Stuttgart, a large convoy of vehicles wound its way to Zell am See, where on 5 February father was laid to rest in the chapel on the estate.

16

Demonstration in Le Mans

When he visited us in October 1950, Charles Faroux had suggested to my father that a Porsche car should be entered for the Le Mans 24-Hours Race. The Frenchman Auguste Veuillet, our importer and general representative in France, was also thinking along similar lines. He had discussed his plans for Le Mans with my father; my father's response was to take his slide rule out of his pocket and after making a few calculations he said, 'That may well be possible, as far as performance is concerned!'

In March 1951 Veuillet invited French motoring journalists to Monthléry in order to demonstrate the performance of the Porsche. Monthléry is a fast track near Paris at which the Grand Prix of the French Automobile Club had already been held. During these test runs at Monthléry an average lap speed of 90 mph (144.8 km/h) was achieved. The journalists were impressed. Eventually Faroux issued an official invitation for us to enter two Porsches in the Le Mans 24-Hours Race.

Porsche customers had already achieved some sporting successes with their cars. By way of an example, I shall mention the Austrian Otto Mathé, who scored some notable victories in his Porsche, despite the fact that he had only one arm. In 1950, for example, he drove an aluminium-bodied coupé from the Gmünd series to victory in its class in the International Alpine Contest.

At that time, in 1951, Le Mans was a long-distance race which received a great deal of attention in the world press. Taking part in the race could be an invaluable advertisement for us, although failure would of course have a negative effect. I had an important decision to make, and after mature consideration I decided that we should take part. We thought it advisable to work with someone who had already driven in the race. There were several German racing drivers who had taken part before the war, one of whom was Paul von Guilleaume. Before the war he had been a member of the Adler works team and had driven at Le Mans in 1937 and 1938. I discussed our plans with Herr von Guilleaume and eventually hired him as our team boss with responsibility for the entire organization of our entry. Our works manager, Hans Klauser, and engineer Wilhelm Hild were responsible for technical matters. The preparations could begin.

Above The famous light metal coupé, the so-called Gmünd-Coupé with which Porsche started racing in 1951. This 356, with 1488 cc engine of 70 PS and a weight of 640 kg (290 lb), reached a top speed of over 160 km/h (99 mph).

Right Start of the Le Mans 24 Hours Race in 1951. Car number 46 is the light metal 356 of Veuillet/Mouche, who won in the 751-1100 cc class, and finished twentieth overall.

We decided to use the Gmünd aluminium-bodied coupés that weighed about 1,400 lb (635 kg). By fitting a new camshaft, we increased engine output to 49 hp; however, we reduced this to 46 hp in order to increase engine stability. We intended to use three coupés. The aluminium-bodied coupé from the Gmünd series had a better coefficient of drag than the cars built in Stuttgart and had a top speed of 100 mph (160.9 km/h). Before it went to Le Mans, we celebrated the production of the five-hundredth Porsche on 21 March. We had achieved this figure more quickly than we had imagined, and sales were also very encouraging. This meant that

we were able to produce the one-thousandth Porsche on 28 August the same year.

However, back to Le Mans, where the race was held in June. From the technical point of view our preparations were going well, but in other respects there were few grounds for optimism, because even before the starting flag was raised three cars had been demolished. While out on a course inspection, Herr von Guilleaume had to swerve to avoid a cyclist and ended up in a ditch. One of our mechanics had an accident during a test run on the Bruchsal-Karlsruhe autobahn, while the third car was so badly damaged during night training that it was impossible to repair it before the race. Rudolf Sauerwein, who was driving this last car, had come off the road near Maison Blanche during a cloudburst and was taken to hospital with a broken leg. (He had also driven at Le Mans before the war.)

After the first two accidents we had prepared a replacement car and repaired the least damaged car. After Rudolf Sauerwein's accident we only had one car left which was driven by Auguste Veuillet, with Edmond Mouche as his co-driver. Both of them had driven in the race the previous year for Delage. If I were superstitious, I would certainly have been far from happy about our entry in the race. I must admit that I was indeed nervous virtually throughout the 24 hours of the race, which I spent with my team in the pits. Twenty-four hours without sleep is a long time, but in fact I was on my feet much longer than that because the race did not start until 4 o'clock in the afternoon. However, the whole event is so enthralling that one forgets one's tiredness. In the end, things turned out even better than we had hoped: not only did Veuillet and Mouche finish the race, but they also won their class and were placed twentieth overall with an average speed of 74 mph (119 km/h) for the 1,777.665 miles of the course. They also completed several laps at an average speed of 87 mph (139.9 km/h). At the same time, victory in the 1.1 litre class ensured us a place in the next year's race.

This success also made us internationally known and people began to follow our development closely, particularly in the specialist publications. However, Le Mans was so important for us that we took part in the race every year with success, and in 1970 we were overall winners for the first time. The victorious team that year was made up of the British driver Attwood and the German Hans Herrman in a 4.5 litre Porsche.

In 1951 we set up our headquarters in the small town of Téloché near Mulsanne and there we have remained for each race until the present day. Veuillet had recommended a workshop suitable for our purposes in Mulsanne, and we found lodgings for the drivers and the technical team not very far away. We were the first German team to take part in the Le Mans race since the war, and indeed the first German team to compete in any race in France since 1945. If the tubular-framed roadster is excluded, the successful car was the tenth unit built at Gmünd. It is now owned by the Hamburg VW and Porsche dealer von Raffay who has put it on display in his automobile museum. A year later, in 1952, Veuillet and Mouche again won their class at Le Mans, while the overall victors were Lang and Rieß in a Mercedes-Benz 300 SL.

Le Mans had given us valuable information about the capabilities of our car. The information was evaluated and used to develop our vehicles still further. Our participation in the race naturally required additional finance, and we had to assess whether the expenditure was justified. Our success in Le Mans had brought us a great deal of international publicity. We now had to decide whether motor racing was a more effective form of achieving publicity than placing advertisements. We calculated that our expenditure on motor racing was about the same as we would have had to spend on advertisements. There was no doubt, however, that the press reports that followed our motor racing successes reached the section of the public likely to consider buying one of our cars. A Porsche is not only a sports car, but it also offers a great deal of motoring pleasure. Thus it was clear to us right from the beginning that we had to carry on with the motor racing.

Racing makes great demands on cars, so there is always a challenge for the engineer. The engineers who worked on our racing programme did not have a normal working day, but had to

Prince Metternich (right) with his Porsche 356 during the Carrera Panamerican Mexico in 1952, where he finished eighth overall against the much stronger competition of Mercedes and Ferrari.

be prepared to give significantly more than is expected from an average employee. Our people were always prepared to feel challenged on a personal level if success in a race or rally was at stake.

For the Le Mans race we had used the 1.1 litre engine, but in August 1951 Paul von Guilleaume and Count von der Mühle used the bored-out 1,488 cc engine in the no less arduous long-distance Liège-Rome-Liège race; they won their class and even took third place in the overall classification. In the autumn of the same year we had devised something special for the opening of the extremely important Paris Salon in the Grand Palais. We were planning to make some speed-record attempts at the Monthléry track, for which we prepared an aluminium-bodied coupé from the Gmünd series. The wheel housings were encased and further improvements were made to the bodywork, in order to reduce wind resistance and thus achieve a higher final speed. The 1.5 litre engine was fitted with larger carburettors and a new camshaft and output was increased to 72 hp. We provided the car and technical support, while it was driven by a team of five drivers, Petermax Müller, Walter Glöckler, Huschke von Hanstein, Hermann Ramelow and Richard von Frankenberg. Our aluminium-bodied coupé set not only 11 new international records for cars of up to 1,500 cc, but also a new world record for 72 hours with an average speed of 95.2 mph (153.2 km/h). This last record, an extremely important one, was achieved on the opening day of the Paris Salon. We took the record-breaking car, covered in oil and fly-specks, to the Grand Palais and displayed it on our stand. As the doors opened to the public, the car was standing there, exerting a magnet-like attraction. The 1.5 litre engine was put into normal series production, although with its output reduced to 60 hp.

From this point on, our company became increasingly involved in motor racing. It was then, and still is today, the best advertisement for our product. In this respect we differ from the Volkswagen company, whose cars are mass-produced and sold to a wide range of people. Volkswagen of course operates in a different market sector, in which expensive advertising and other measures are required. In addition to our own motor racing activities, a large proportion of our customers were also involved in motor sport, so that over the years we built up a list of successes that is probably unique.

Our growing involvement in motor racing and the need to publicize our activities on an international level led me to believe that we needed to find somebody who could not only act as manager of the racing team but also take charge of public relations. The person I found was Baron Fritz Huschke von Hanstein, who had been actively involved in motor racing before the war and had also raced modified Volkswagens and Porsches after the war. This was a new departure for Huschke von Hanstein, but he tackled it with great gusto and to my complete satisfaction. The Baron, a veritable polyglot, is still today a popular representative of our company in many countries. Despite the fact that he has officially retired, he is still very much active on our behalf.

Since the sales of our cars were progressing so well and our old factory had not yet been vacated, we were obliged to seek alternative solutions to the problem of our lack of space. We tried to obtain a site for a new building adjoining the Reutter workshop. It was still agricultural land and there was some difficulty in acquiring the site, but with the help of the city authorities we eventually managed to purchase it and set to work planning the new premises. The architect Rolf Gutbrod, a lecturer in planning and design at the Institute of Technology in Stuttgart, was commissioned to design the building. However, when the cost estimate was submitted, it exceeded the financial resources then available to us. We had to postpone the project, particularly since the banks were showing little faith in the automobile industry.

Another solution was also ruled out for lack of capital. It originated from France in the form of an offer from Emile Mathis, who was prepared to lease a part of his factory together with the necessary machinery. Mathis was one of the longest established French motor manufacturers. His company, which was located in Alsace and had its headquarters in Strasbourg, built cars which bore the name Hermes. One of his former designers was a certain Ettore Bugatti, who had worked for Mathis between 1904 and 1907. We had had business connections with this French company before the war, when he acquired the licence for our wheel suspension system with torsion bars.

Towards the end of 1951 we completed the prototype for a new Volkswagen which we had designed. However, since the Beetle was a runaway success, it remained in production for the time being.

It was also in the autumn of 1951 that we met Herr Rolf Waldmann in Switzerland and entered into a commercial relationship with him. Herr Waldmann introduced us to a group of Indian industrialists, whose spokesman was an Indian called J.R.D. Tata. He was a member of one of the biggest industrial families in India which had its headquarters in Bombay. Like all the sons of influential Indian families he had been educated at English schools and universities. The Tata family had built a locomotive factory near Bombay in collaboration with Krauss-Maffei. They now wanted to build a truck factory in partnership with a European company. Discussions were already taking place with the Leyland Motor Co and Daimler-Benz. Since the new factory was also to be used to manufacture military vehicles for the Indian army, the Indian government would not authorize co-operation with a foreign partner unless this latter had experience in the design and manufacture of tanks. At that time, however, German companies were still banned from operating in this area. In the end we suggested a solution that made it possible for Daimler-Benz to collaborate with Tata in the new venture. Nobody could prevent us from going into partnership with a Swiss businessman, namely Herr Waldmann, in order to set up a company in Switzerland that would develop a modern tank of about 32 tons. Porsche had experience in this area and we were able within a very short time to submit proposals for a tank of this class. We informed Daimler-Benz of our intentions, and three years later — in 1954 — the Indian government in Delhi granted permission for collaboration with the German company. On 1 April 1954 a so-called Technical Aid Agreement was signed, whereby the Tata Engineering and Locomotive Company (Telco), with the assistance of Daimler-Benz, was to build a commercial vehicle assembly plant in Jamshedpur. Daimler-Benz acquired a 12.5 per cent stake in Telco.

I got to know Mr Tata personally in Davos; he was a great skiing enthusiast and spent several weeks there each winter with his wife. My wife had also accompanied me to Davos, together with my friend Prinzing and Herr Waldmann. We took this opportunity to discuss his new project with Mr Tata. He told us during our talks that he had been very satisfied with his collaboration with Krauss-Maffei and wanted to co-operate with a German partner on the new venture. He told us quite frankly that his government would prefer a British partner because the British were not subject to any restrictions as far as military projects were concerned. After the talks in Davos and the establishment of the company in Switzerland we drew up detailed proposals with engineering drawings for a tank which Prinzing and Waldmann presented to the Indian government during a visit to New Delhi. They succeeded in gaining the approval of the Indian government for our proposal. The amusing thing about the whole affair was that the plans had been drawn up by Porsche Engineering, but the cover of the file bore a Mercedes star.

Daimler-Benz were later to pay us back for our assistance with the Indian project. When it was decided that West Germany should rearm, Daimler-Benz recommended us to the Ministry of Defence in connection with the development of a new tank. Quite apart from the so-called Cold War, it had not taken our former enemies very long to realize that it was good for general prosperity if money did not have to be spent on armaments. In the end, this realization and the political situation made it necessary for the Federal Republic of Germany to raise an army, which would of course need modern tanks. Senior people at Daimler-Benz said to officials in Bonn, 'Porsche have already designed a tank!'

However, before we got to the stage of developing a tank for the German Army, we became involved in the tendering for a bucket car for the new German armed forces. To this end we developed the so-called Jagdwagen which was powered by our aircooled, 1.6 litre, four-cylinder engine with an output of 50 hp at an engine speed of 4,250 rpm. It was amphibious, which meant that it could cross streams, and had a switchable four-wheel-drive system. The department in charge of the tendering was the Federal Department of Defence Engineering and Procurement which, like the former Ordnance Office, also tested the vehicles put forward for selection.

In view of the great experience we had acquired during the war with the bucket car and amphibious vehicles, we reckoned we had every chance of winning the order. Consequently, we built a prototype at our own cost and without any order. When the day of the final selection meeting arrived, which I did not attend, one member of the government committee arrived too late. The three rival vehicles were on display in the courtyard of the building in which the meeting was taking place. The late arrival stopped to inspect the three vehicles and asked a sergeant who happened to be standing there, 'Which car is the best one?' The sergeant pointed to our vehicle and said, 'That one, the Porsche, but during the trials we were always ordered to use the Porsche when one of the other ones got stuck in the mud and we had to pull it out. This meant that it was more heavily used than the others. We were also ordered to keep the Porsche's engine running when we were in barracks, so that the petrol consumption would go up, because they want that one.' He pointed to the DKW jeep which was powered by a two-stroke engine.

This member of the government committee, whose name I shall not reveal, came to me later and told me what he had heard and said, 'Herr Porsche, you may use this information if you wish.

Porsche type 597, built for a competition to select a cross-country vehicle (Kübelwagen) for the new German army. This amphibious car had a horizontally opposed, air-cooled four-cylinder engine of 1582 cc and 50 PS. With a top speed 100 km/h (62 mph), the car became the Jagdwagen.

But of course you will have to give the sergeant I quoted a job!'

After the decision had been taken, a final discussion took place to which the tenderers were summoned individually. First it was the turn of Auto Union, the winner, and then finally Porsche. The committee explained to me that, despite the many good qualities of our vehicle, it was not yet ready for series production. There had been some damage, for example a shock absorber mounting had broken and the silencer had developed a fault. I could only reply, 'Gentlemen, I cannot understand why these minor problems should lead you to such a conclusion, particularly since I have been informed that on the other vehicle engines, gearboxes and axles sometimes had to be replaced several times because they were not working at all!'

The committee's answers were evasive, and the contract went in the end to Auto Union with their DKW cross-country vehicle. As I learnt later, the company desperately needed the order for their Ingoldstadt factory, and one of the main shareholders made it known to officials in Bonn that there would have to be mass redundancies if the company was not given the contract. The whole story did not exactly have a happy ending for us. I sent our financial director to Bonn to discuss the question of compensation for the prototype we had delivered. We were asking for 1.8 million Marks, the real cost of producing the vehicle, but our representative was told, 'We will offer you 1.2 million Marks, and if you don't accept that, you won't get anything at all!'

From this point on I made up my mind never to lift a finger in this section again unless there was a firm order on the table. This was a decision I was to stick to in the future.

The Porsche Engineering Centre at Weissach carried out the development and engineering work for the Leopard tank, one of the most successful post-war armoured vehicle designs.

171

After this initial experience with the German Army, now integrated into NATO, we began to collaborate with Bonn in the area of tank development. We were involved right from the start in the development of the Leopard. When the product requirements specification was made available to us, we realized that it had been formulated in such drastic terms that it could hardly be complied with. I wondered whether they had ever built a tank before.

The Leopard bore little resemblance to the design we had produced for the Indian project on the basis of our experience in the Second World War: the Germany Army wanted something very different. The German tank was to be more heavily armoured than the Indian tank, but at the same time it also had to be significantly lighter. It was virtually impossible to reconcile these two requirements, which is why I described the product requirements specification as drastic. In the end, the German tank turned out to be heavier than our 32 ton design for India.

In 1957 France, Italy and the Federal Republic of Germany had agreed to build a standard tank for their NATO forces, specially adapted to the requirements of these countries. The first Leopard was the result of the joint tank design developed in Germany; the basic concept originated from us. France then quit the group and built its own tank, the AMX 30.

In the meantime the Americans had also begun to show an interest in the Leopard project, and they collaborated in the next phase, the development of the Leopard II. At this stage, all those involved, including us, submitted further proposals. This stage of development is of particular interest, because our proposal was chosen as the basis for the joint project. This decision led to the Americans vetoing our participation in the Leopard II project. They justified their position by saying that our company was part Austrian, that Austria was not a member of NATO and that from a strictly military point of view we were not acceptable. That was of course just a pretext: Porsche is a German company and I myself hold a German passport. The real reason was quite different. The Americans probably said to each other, 'If the Porsche Leopard is developed, we shall sell fewer of our own tanks in future!'

Indeed it emerged later that the Leopard II had no competition and that only German legislation prevented the major export success that would certainly have ensued.

Of course the ideal solution would have been to build a single standard tank for all those countries that were members of NATO. However, since this could not be achieved because of nationalistic feelings in the individual countries, the production of the necessary spare parts for the various models and the consequent supply problems now require a great deal of expenditure.

However, right up to the present day, we have played a leading role in the development of the Leopard. In this connection I am

often asked whether we should be involved at all in the armaments industry. My answer is always 'Yes', because we never know
how the political situation might develop. Our armed forces have
been built up in order to provide the country with the capability
to defend itself. If they are to achieve this aim, we must provide
them with the best available weapons. However, we cannot supply the best if we withdraw from technical development.

17

Development work for Volkswagen

Our collaboration with Volkswagen, which had developed during the war, was formalized in a new agreement signed in 1948. In the past, a few of our people had worked permanently on urgent tasks at the Volkswagen plant. Some of them were employed by Volkswagen after the war, while others returned to us.

After the signing of the agreement in 1948, our design office, which at that time was still in Gmünd, began once again to receive a constant stream of commissions from VW, and at the end of 1949 the design office was transferred back to Stuttgart. Some of the projects that we had already started in Gmünd were continued in Wolfsburg at the VW plant itself, and 10 or 12 of our people went to work there temporarily.

In the course of our many years of collaboration with VW, we have worked on a large number of developments and also delivered completed prototypes, from which I would like to single out a few examples.

In those days Herr Nordhoff was even thinking of developing even closer links with us, in a way which did not, however, fit in with my own ideas. It was in 1954 that the former Auto Union racing manager, Dr Feuereisen, visited me in Stuttgart. He had taken up the position of sales director at VW and came as Nordhoff's representative. Nordhoff and his people were considering converting the outwork in Braunschweig into a research and development centre for VW. The so-called outwork had been built before the Wolfsburg factory and carried out preparatory work for the main factory. Various devices and gadgets were made there, and assembly and detailed work was carried out. Later on, tools for Wolfsburg were also made there. Feuereisen informed me on behalf of Nordhoff that the plan was for me to direct the new development centre. However, a pre-condition for the offer was that I should give up my Stuttgart business but of course that was completely out of the question. Quite apart from that, I had my own ideas about a position of this kind in a large company. I needed free space in order to be able to work. My activities as an entrepreneur meant more to me than a position on the board of a large company, where plotting and scheming are an integral part of the job.

However, this episode did not in any way change our co-operation with VW. As early as 1949, we had investigated for VW the possibility of designing a car which had a shorter wheelbase than the Beetle, of variable length, and with a self-supporting body. At that time small cars accounted for a not inconsiderable share of the automobile market. This was of course only a study that was used to investigate the practical aspects of the then current trend towards small cars. This study (the Type 402) had been started in Gmünd.

Also in Gmünd, we had started investigating electrically driven cars. A Volkswagen was converted for this purpose, with the petrol engine being replaced by an electric motor. The batteries were housed in the boot at the front and underneath the rear seat. This of course meant that there was no space for luggage, but this was only an experiment. The original feature of this vehicle was that the electric motor also provided power for the braking system, and each time the brakes were applied the batteries were charged. The car had an operating range of 62 miles (100 km) and a top speed of 37.5 mph (60.3 km/h). However, when the so-called 'economic miracle' arrived, there was no longer any interest in cars without petrol engines and the issue did not come to the fore again until the oil crisis of the 1970s.

Another interesting project followed in 1952, a VW with a shorter wheelbase and a self-supporting body (Type 534). The car was presented to Nordhoff in the autumn of 1953 but did not go into production; instead it was used in development work on the self-supporting body design. Its body had certain similarities with the Porsche 356, particularly the front section. However, it proved impossible to find any practical application for the car in the current series.

At the end of 1952 VW had decided to build a new bodyshell for the VW. Between 1953 and 1954 we developed two models with different bodyshells. One was a further development of the Beetle bodyshell, while the other had a notchback. Both prototypes, together with the relevant technical documentation, were handed over to VW in April 1954. Neither model went into production.

At this time the Beetle was enjoying increasing popularity with customers, which was reflected in rising sales figures. Exports were also increasing and new markets were being opened up. Consequently, any change to the existing programme had to be considered very carefully. On the other hand, models in production were constantly being improved.

Among the engines that we investigated and sometimes also developed to prototype stage between 1954 and 1956 was the Type 619. This was an air-cooled, two-stroke diesel engine with a cubic capacity of 600 cc which produced 20 hp at an engine speed of 3,000 rpm. Two designs were submitted, a two-cylinder in-line engine with a conventional fan and a two-cylinder horizontally opposed unit. We finally decided in favour of the latter design, of which three units were to be built. The two-stroke engine with loop scavenging had direct fuel injection via a Bosch pump. However, the theoretical output could not be achieved without creating smoke. One engine was delivered and further trials were halted for the time being. Tests were also carried out on V6 engines with a cubic capacity of either 1.2 or 1.5 litres.

In 1955 we started work on a very interesting project for VW, the Porsche Type 672. The aim of this was to investigate the various possibilities for a small car with an under-floor engine and various axle designs. The engine was located in the rear under the boot.

In the course of this project, tests were carried out with V6 under-floor engines with cubic capacities of 1.2 and 1.5 litres in which the cylinders were fitted at an angle of 120° to each other in a V shape open at the bottom. In the end, however, we opted for an air-cooled flat six with a cubic capacity of 1.2 or 1.5 litres (Type 673) which, at an engine speed of 4,500 rpm, produced 43 and 54 hp respectively.

It was to be of importance in later VW developments. Between 1955 and 1959, for example, we worked on the design and construction of a small car with various engines (Type 675) derived from the Porsche Types 672 and 673. Two models were produced, both with self-supporting bodies and a swing-axle with a low pivot point at the rear and coil springs. Car 1 was powered by a three-cylinder in-line engine, air-cooled and rear-mounted as an under-floor unit, while car 2 also had an air-cooled under-floor engine mounted in the rear but this unit was a flat four.

The idea for this small car had originated from the VW agent in Italy and it was intended to be a competitor for the smallest Fiat. It took this opportunity to demonstrate to Nordhoff the running qualities of a three-cylinder engine compared to a two-cylinder. The three-cylinder version ran much more smoothly than the two-cylinder and Nordhoff was visibly impressed. We conducted this demonstration with our six-cylinder engine, simply shutting down three of the cylinders.

This small car never went into production either, apparently because the Italian market was not reckoned profitable enough to justify building a smaller vehicle than the Beetle especially for sale there. In fact, larger cars were beginning to find favour.

In March 1958 we were commissioned to build two bodyshells similar in dimensions to that of the Beetle. For this project, VW made available to us two Beetle chassis with the pedals moved 80 mm (3.15 in) towards the front. This car was to be fitted with our Type 724 under-floor engine, an air-cooled flat four producing 40 hp. Our competitors in this instance were the Italian coach-

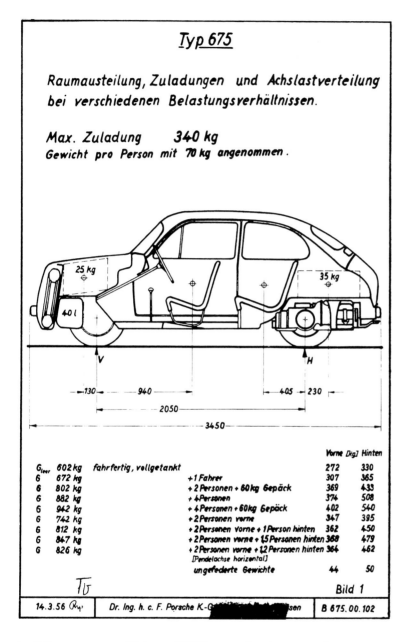

Typ 675

Raumausteilung, Zuladungen und Achslastverteilung bei verschiedenen Belastungsverhältnissen.

Max. Zuladung 340 kg
Gewicht pro Person mit 70 kg angenommen.

25 kg   35 kg

40 l

V   H

130   940   405   230
2050
3450

				Vorne [kg] Hinten	
G_{leer}	602 kg	fahrfertig, vollgetankt		272	330
6	672 kg		+1 Fahrer	307	365
6	802 kg		+2 Personen + 60 kg Gepäck	369	433
6	882 kg		+4 Personen	374	508
6	942 kg		+4 Personen + 60 kg Gepäck	402	540
6	742 kg		+2 Personen vorne	347	395
6	812 kg		+2 Personen vorne + 1 Person hinten	362	450
6	847 kg		+2 Personen vorne + 1,5 Personen hinten	368	479
6	826 kg		+2 Personen vorne + 1,2 Personen hinten	364	462
			[Pendelachse horizontal]		
			ungefederte Gewichte	44	50

Tö

14.3.56   Dr. Ing. h. c. F. Porsche K-G. ~~~~~~~~~~~~sen

Bild 1

B 675. 00. 102

Porsche developed several new cars for Volkswagen. This is the type Porsche 675, design for a small VW.

building company Ghia and VW's own development department. We produced a car with a fastback (Type 726/1) and a second with a notchback (726/2); there was a third variant with a shorter wheelbase (Type 728), which was more appropriate for a small car.

It was obvious at the presentation of the prototypes at Wolfsburg that ours were easily the most elegant. However, Nordhoff found it very difficult to come to a definite decision. He did not wish to offend anyone, so he said, 'All three of you should go away

The air-cooled, three-cylinder engine of 597 cc and 18.3 PS for the Porsche 675, developed for Volkswagen. The engine was an underfloor design leaving more space for the passenger compartment.

and produce a joint effort that looks like the Porsche prototype!'

The result was the VW Type 3 with a higher waistline than our version which made it possible, among other things, to place the headlights in a higher position. This was done with an eye on the American market where there was a regulation to this effect. When the Chevrolet Corvair designed by Arkus-Duntov appeared a few years later it had a very low waistline which took no account of the existing headlamp regulations. I had always been of the opinion that you have to take risks in life. The compromise proposal requested by Nordhoff turned our very advanced design into a car like any other. That is always the way if you believe that you must stick unswervingly to the rules.

The Type 728 was more or less developed out of the Type 675; it was a lighter vehicle than the Beetle, with a smaller engine, a self-supporting body and various body shapes. During its development between 1958 and 1961, an increasing level of comfort was demanded, which meant that the wheelbase had to be lengthened.

The styling of one of the bodyshells was much influenced by my son Ferdinand Alexander (Butzi). It had a boxy shape with a low waistline and a great deal of glass; it was a complete departure from the traditional Volkswagen shape and looked very attractive. It was powered by an under-floor engine and had a large tailgate. When Nordhoff saw this prototype, he said, 'If we build that, the Beetle's dead', to which I replied, 'I thought we were supposed to be making a replacement for the Beetle.'

Of course it was not an easy decision for Nordhoff and his people to replace the immensely successful Beetle with a completely new model. The tools were already written off and it would have been impossible to sell the new car at the same price as the Beetle which, to use a VW slogan, 'ran and ran and ran'!

Nevertheless, the time was gradually approaching when a decision on a successor to the Beetle would have to be taken. Nord-hoff and his production manager came to Stuttgart and we discussed all the possibilities and variants. Both front and rear-wheel drive were considered and a wide range of different options was thrown into the discussions. In the end a decision was made in favour of the variant with the under-floor engine, which ran best and at the same time was the only variant of which it could be said that it would have assured VW of its own unmistakable model line, a lineage that had its origin in the Beetle.

Prototypes were then ordered and trials conducted, including some in Africa. Things had already reached a very advanced stage and millions of Marks had been invested. Then, on 12 April 1968, Professor Nordhoff died suddenly and everything came to a halt.

VW then took over Auto Union from Daimler-Benz and NSU and formed Audi AG. Ludwig Kraus came from Daimler-Benz to Ingolstadt; he made a name for himself there for his innovations, which included a unit construction system which he also eventually implemented at the VW plant. In the meantime Leiding had replaced Dr Lotz as chairman of the board. It should be added that in 1968, when Beetle number 15,000,000 rolled off the production line, this Porsche-designed model took over from Ford's Model T as the most successful car ever made.

Of the projects that we worked on with VW, mention should also be made of the Type 700, which was a series of outline proposals for a so-called large capacity car, a forerunner of the vehicles now known as 'people carriers' or mini-buses. We worked on it between 1956 and 1957 and models were made on a scale of 1:7.5. This was many years before the Japanese and European manufacturers such as Renault began to market vehicles of this kind like the Espace.

We asked ourselves at the time what it was that customers did not like about mini-buses of this kind and concluded that they looked too much like buses and that women found it awkward to climb into them. And what was it that appealed to customers? Well of course they liked the space, particularly when going on holiday. They also liked sitting high up and being able to see things while travelling. In the final analysis, however, customers want a car not a bus. Our studies were based on the VW1200 and we used the engine, gearbox and axles from that vehicle. The result was a vehicle far in advance of its time; it was styled like a car, was comfortable inside and was easy to get into. It could carry five or six people. However, VW stuck to VW Type 2, which is built like a mini-bus and looks like one.

As is well-known, the VW in its basic form was fitted with a non-synchromesh gearbox. Under no circumstances, however, could this remain the standard, and as early as 1948 we were testing synchromesh gearboxes for VW, development work which

Right and below right
Porsche type 534,
another development
for Volkswagen, carried
out in 1952.

Below The Porsche
type 534 (left),
compared with the
Volkswagen Beetle then
in production.

Porsche type 728, developed for Volkswagen following the type 675 in the years 1957 to 1961. There were three different engines of 26.31 and 32.5 PS.

lasted until 1951. We were working on the basis of the gearbox for the Cisitalia racing car, that is on the principle of small servo rings and a system of progressive gear shifting similar to those on motor cycles. This gear shifting system had to be converted for use as a gearbox with the normal H layout. At the same time we were also working on a variant with large servo rings which was still, however, at the development stage and therefore not yet ready for series production. However, Volkswagen decided in favour of the speed-blocking synchromesh system developed by the American company Borg-Warner and put it into series production. Of course VW had to pay licence fees for it.

In 1955 and 1956 we developed another two gearboxes with Porsche synchromesh for VW (Types 671 and 677). They were tested in a car made available to us by VW and delivered after-

Porsche type 728 with an experimental, very advanced and elegant body designed by Butzi Porsche.

Rear view of the Butzi-
designed Porsche 728.

A spacious and very
comfortable five- or six-
seater limousine,
designed by Porsche for
Volkswagen in 1956
long before such cars
became popular.

wards to the Wolfsburg factory. However, neither of these variants was put into series production. VW had given preference to
Borg-Warner because, they said, our gearbox was not sufficiently
tried and tested. However, our system was subsequently used by
a number of important clients, including Alfa Romeo, BMW, Fiat
and even Ferrari. When Daimler-Benz entered the motor racing
arena again in 1954, the W196 Grand Prix car was fitted with a
five-speed gearbox in which the four higher gears were fitted with
the Porsche servo ring. This gearbox was also fitted to the W196S,

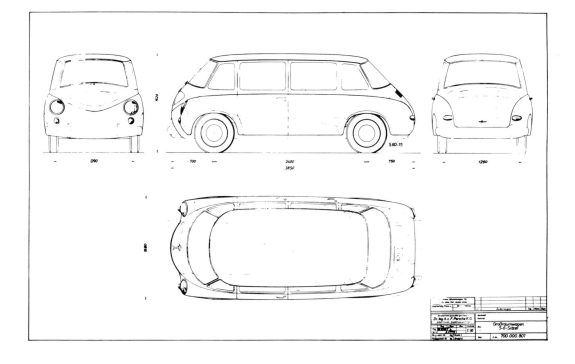

the 300 SLR sports car. Juan Manuel Fangio won the world championship in 1954 and 1955 in the W196. The 300 SLR was driven to victory by Stirling Moss and Denis Jenkinson in the demanding Mille Miglia of 1955, and in the same year it also won the Targa Florio and the Tourist Trophy. As far as we were concerned, this meant that the synchromesh system that we had developed was capable of withstanding the most arduous of conditions. In accordance with an agreement with Daimler-Benz we did not use these successes for advertising purposes.

The new synchromesh gearbox (Type 519) went into production as early as 1951. It was manufactured by the Getrag company in Ludwigsburg near Stuttgart, but we assembled it ourselves, for one very simple reason. At that time turnover tax had to be paid on every component produced and supplied, so if Getrag had obtained the individual components from the various suppliers and assembled them, turnover tax would have had to be paid several times, making the final product unnecessarily more expensive. We were able to get round this by assembling the gearbox ourselves.

If I were to summarize what we achieved in our development work for Volkswagen, I would say that our efforts not only helped to improve the Beetle, but also led to proposals for models that could have gone into production as worthy successors to the Beetle. The reason why this did not happen lies in the difficulty of making the right commercial decisions which can sometimes have consequences that could not have been predicted at the time. The Types Ro80 and K70 which VW took over from NSU are good examples of this.

Nevertheless, we did enter into close collaboration with VW on one more occasion when we decided to produce a sports car that was cheaper than the 911. Our studies showed that it had to be

When Daimler-Benz returned to Grand Prix racing in 1954, Porsche provided the synchronizing ring for the gearbox of the famous Silver Arrow. Shown here is World Champion Juan Manuel Fangio in the Mercedes-Benz W196 during the Belgian Grand Prix.

Porsche type 726/II saloon developed for Volkswagen in 1958.

a mid-engined design; at that time, mid-engined cars were making great strides forward, and not only in motor racing. Volkswagen had come to the same conclusion and so we decided on a joint development project. I need hardly point out that we had had a great deal of experience with mid-engined cars. In this way, the Porsche Type 914 was developed as a mid-engined two-seater with a hardtop. The 914 engine was a 1,679 cc fuel-injected, overhead-valve, flat four, unchanged from its 911 application, which produced 60 hp. The 914-4 (4 for four cylinders) was supplemented later by the 914-6 (6 for six cylinders), which was powered by the 2.0 litre 110 hp flat six from the 1969 model 911T. The price difference between the 914-6 and the 911 was relatively slight.

The Porsche 914 built in co-operation with Volkswagen. The basic type with a four-cylinder engine was followed by the 914-6 with a six-cylinder engine.

In April 1969 we set up the Porsche-VW-Vertriebsgesellschaft

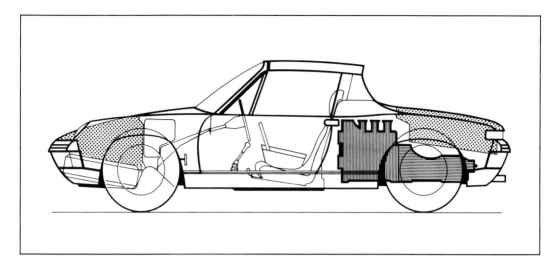

GmbH (abbreviated to VG) in Stuttgart with a working capital of 5 million DM. Both partners had a 50 per cent stake in VG, which was responsible for the distribution of the 914-4 and 914-6 as well as the 911.

Design characteristics of the 914, with the engine in front of the rear suspension.

In an interview which I gave in late 1969 to the French journalist Edouard Seidler, I made the following comments about the founding of VG. 'With the exception of France and Great Britain, Porsche cars are distributed everywhere through the VW organization. The establishment of a joint sales organization is nothing more than the confirmation of an existing state of affairs!'

Rumours had been spreading in connection with the founding of the joint distribution company, to the effect that VW and Porsche were about to merge. That was rubbish of course.

The body for the 914 was made by Karmann in Osnabrück. However, while the 914-4 was assembled by Karmann, the 914-6 was assembled by us in Zuffenhausen. Both types were presented to the public for the first time at the Frankfurt Motor Show in the autumn of 1969. The four-cylinder model was available immediately, while its six-cylinder stablemate was to be available the following February.

When the then general manager of VW, Kurz Lotz, left the company and his successor, Rudolf Leiding, took over a company that was in the red, he decided in favour of Ludwig Kraus's model range with water-cooled, front-mounted engines. As a result, production of the 914 came to a halt. Leiding took over from Lotz on 1 October 1971 and soon afterwards work started on the 924, to which I shall return later. This complete change of policy by VW naturally called into question the existence of the joint distribution company, the breakup of which had already been recommended by members of the VW supervisory board. Finally, on 8 May 1974, an agreement to that effect was signed. We acquired

VW's stake and moved our sales department into the VG building in Ludwigsburg.

In the same year, the 100,000th 914 rolled off the production line. When production came to a halt in the spring of 1976, a total of 118,976 units had been built. With the breakup of the joint distribution company, the existing development contracts also came to an end. Nevertheless, we maintained fairly close links with VW. At the time I was considering how we could add a second string to the Porsche bow, and I reflected on the benefits to be gained from joint development projects with VW. Consequently, in 1974, we investigated the possibility of converting the VW Passat to four-wheel drive. I considered how our programme would look in about five years' time. A four-wheel drive Passat would certainly have been far ahead of its time, as shown by the success currently being enjoyed by various four-wheel drive vehicles.

As long as the Porsche family had the final word in the company — it withdrew in 1972 — we did not necessarily take any wrong turnings. In 1971, for example, we were making sketches for a possible parallel development to the 911, a comfortable, four-wheel drive off-road car of the Range Rover type. It was to be based on the 911 and produced in conjunction with that model. In this way, costs could have been kept as low as possible. My designers' initial proposals were a little too extreme. My intention was to produce a four-wheel drive passenger car, which had variable ground clearance but which could also be used on public roads. I am very aware of the conflicts which arise among designers of four-wheel drive cars. It depends on which department is responsible for the design, the truck division or the car division. If we take the example of Daimler-Benz, where the G-Wagen originates, we can see that the Range Rover is not a G-Wagen and the G-Wagen is not a Range Rover. The truck division will design a vehicle in the manner to which it is accustomed and in accordance with its own engineering philosophy, and the same is true of those who design cars. Moreover, the designers of lorries and other commercial vehicles take into account the military applications of off-road vehicles because they also have experience in that area. The passenger car division, on the other hand, will design a vehicle that the average motorist will recognize as a normal car. In the case of our off-road vehicle, we also designed a variant with a 911 engine mounted the other way round.

In the case of the Passat, with its front-mounted engine and front-wheel drive, the conversion to four-wheel drive would have been a relatively simple process, since it would only have involved fitting a live rear axle. Dr Fuhrmann, who at that time was a member of the board of Porsche AG, discussed with VW the possibility of supplying us with Passats for conversion. According to Dr Fuhrmann, however, VW were not prepared to meet our request.

Some time later, at a dinner at VW, I found myself sitting next to Herr W.P. Schmidt of Volkswagen, who would have been responsible for the delivery of the Passats; in the course of the evening I said to him, 'It's really a pity you didn't allow us to make a Passat with four-wheel drive!'

Herr Schmidt replied, in a surprised voice, 'I beg your pardon?'

'According to Dr Fuhrmann,' I replied, 'it was you who said there was no question of making a four-wheel drive car.'

'Herr Porsche,' said Herr Schmidt, 'Dr Fuhrmann never discussed the matter with me!'

It was clear to me that my people did not want to build the car. It did not make any difference whether Fuhrmann had spoken to Fiala or Schmidt, in any event the four-wheel drive Passat would have been years ahead of the Japanese. However, Dr Fuhrmann wanted to produce his 928 at all costs, but more of that later.

18

Commissions from America

In the autumn of 1951 I received an invitation from an American engineering concern, the Mid-American Research Corporation in Kansas City, which was involved in a tender for a lightweight jeep for airborne troops. A Porsche engine was to be used in this project, which was codenamed 'Mighty Mite'. The company wanted to have discussions with us in order to clarify a few issues, such as whether the Porsche engine could be manufactured in the USA.

Fourteen years after my first visit to the USA, I now had a second opportunity to visit this interesting country. After the Second World War, America had become a sort of paradise in the eyes of many Germans, a country where everything was available at a time when Europe was still suffering very badly from the aftermath of the war. Since the people in the USA were expecting me within two weeks, I had no alternative but to travel by air. This was by no means an easy decision for me to take, however surprising it might seem today, because I had never flown before, either in a commercial aircraft or in a sports plane. Well, I thought to myself, you can't do anything about it, the fates have decreed that you will fly to America.

The flight turned out to be quite an adventure, not because of the speed with which we reached our destination but because of the way in which the plane hopped from place to place. We flew in a Boeing 377, which was dubbed the 'Stratocruiser' by Pan American. It had two decks, a normal passenger deck and a smaller one underneath it which was reached by a spiral staircase. The smaller deck could accommodate 14 passengers and in Pan American aircraft it was fitted out as a luxury bar. It was a very cosy place from which one had an uninterrupted view through the cabin windows.

So, somewhat nervously, I took off from Frankfurt and settled myself down for a long flight. However, the flight came to an abrupt halt in Brussels and we were taken to have dinner in the city. What had happened? Well, London Airport was closed because of fog, so we stopped off in Brussels in order to wait for the fog to clear. Our flight continued on its way the same day, but we landed at an alternative airport in London; we were not allowed to get out because it was a military air base. Our next stop was Shannon, on the West coast of Ireland. From there, we flew to Reykjavik, the capital of Iceland. The next stopover was at Gander in Newfoundland, where we could not even get breakfast. Finally we landed safe and sound in New York.

I naturally did not miss the opportunity, while in New York, of paying a visit to Max Hoffman's showrooms on Park Avenue and they did not fail to impress me. In the meantime, the people at the Mid-American Research Corp had arrived in New York from Kansas City to discuss the possibilities for future collaboration.

However, the talks did not produce any positive results because in the end another company won the order from the US Army. I was home by Christmas.

This was not the end of the story of the jeep for American airborne troops, because in the spring of 1952 I had a visit in Stuttgart from Wendell S. Fletcher. The Fletcher Aviation Company in Pasadena, California, which was owned by the Fletcher brothers, was also involved in the tender for the US army. Their vehicle was an aluminium design in which not only was the engine a Porsche but all the other components as well. Once again, there were talks about future collaboration and the granting of licences, but in the event, Fletcher did not win the order from the US Army, which put an end to the matter.

Ready for my first flight. This was when I first flew to the USA in a Stratocruiser after the Second World War.

In the meantime another American company, Gyrodyne, which had its headquarters on Long Island, had made contact with us. They were going to build a helicopter for the US Navy which had contrarotating rotors and did not therefore require any torque equalization at the rear. Gyrodyne wanted to use one of our air-cooled engines for this project. We used the Type 616 engine as the basis for an aero engine with dual ignition (Type 702), a 1.6 litre, four-cylinder engine which produced 72 hp at 4,500 rpm and had a dry weight of 158.4 lb (71.8 kg). The one-seater helicopter weighed 550 lb (250 kg), had a cruising speed of 60 mph (96.5 km/h) and could fly at a maximum altitude of 12,285 ft (3,744 m). It could fly for two hours on one tankful of fuel, which it consumed at a rate of 20 litres (4.4 gallons) per hour of flying. Work on this project continued from 1956 to 1961, during which time we built six prototypes. After it had been tested we received an order for 50 engines. The last ten were delivered in March 1961 and on 9 June 1961 this easy-to-fly, one-man helicopter, known as the Rotorcycle, was put through its paces at the Stuttgart-Echterdingen airport.

However, before work could begin on this project, we had to have discussions with Gyrodyne in the USA. Thus in August 1952 I embarked on my second post-war visit to the USA. Max Hoffman, who had been on holiday in Austria, had been in Stuttgart on his way back and discussed my trip with me. Once he was back in New York, he organized our programme which included, among other things, talks with the Studebaker company in South Bend, Indiana. We had already been commissioned by Studebaker to put forward proposals for a car with better performance than the 1952 Studebaker Champion and which was also lighter and easier to produce.

This time I did not travel alone but with my wife and Herr Rabe. We wanted to enjoy ourselves a little more this time and so we decided to go by sea. On 27 August 1952, in Cherbourg, we embarked on the *Queen Elizabeth*. On 29 August, when we were already at sea, we received a message via the ship's telegraph that my brother-in-law, Dr Anton Piëch, had died of a heart attack at the relatively young age of 58.

On the evening before our departure for Cherbourg Dr Piëch had called on us in Stuttgart on his way back from Wolfsburg to Austria. As he was wishing us farewell, he said, 'I don't know what it is, but I don't feel at all well', to which my wife replied, 'Toni, go and see the doctor — we need you!' We thought again about this conversation when, on the high seas, we received the news of his death. Unfortunately it was completely impossible for us to attend his funeral. We were much too far away from land for a helicopter and by the time we reached New York he had long been buried. So we were able to say goodbye to him only in our thoughts.

When we arrived in New York, we drove straight to South Bend. Max Hoffman, through whom we had established our links with Studebaker, drove us in his Cadillac Cabriolet. At a certain speed, the Cadillac's hood began to rattle noisily. At first we regarded this irritation as an unwelcome warning against exceeding the speed limit, but finally it became so annoying that I took a biscuit tin from our rations and stretched the hood more tightly. This improved matters considerably, although Hoffman then stopped obeying the speed limit.

At Studebaker we were greeted by Mr H.S. Vance, the president, the chief engineer Jack Churchill and the head of the sales department, Richard Hutchinson. The subject of our talks was the car that we at Porsche were to design for Studebaker. The Americans asked me, 'Mr Porsche, what does it look like, this car that you are proposing we should build?' I had of course brought all the necessary documentation with me, and I showed them the design. It was a compact saloon with an air-cooled, six-cylinder engine mounted at the rear which in its styling was not dissimilar to the Chevrolet Corvair, although this car, and other similar compact saloons, did not of course appear until several years later, so that our proposals were far ahead of their time. However, the people at Studebaker were unable to endorse our opinion. They looked at the drawings and said, 'That's not actually what we had in mind, because we did not want to depart from our normal styling!'

We could have submitted a design that was even more advanced than the one I had brought with me, but the reason why we had not adopted this course lay in Studebaker's limited production facilities. Our factory in Stuttgart was very much adapted to working with aluminium, which is an important basis for the construction of air-cooled engines. Studebaker, on the other hand, had its own foundry for cast iron but not for aluminium.

Moreover, it looked as though there would be problems with the final assembly of the vehicle, since the Studebaker plant was only designed to handle conventional cars, not rear-engined cars with self-supporting bodyshells. The cars produced by Studebaker had a chassis on to which the bodyshell, which reached only as far as the 'Spritzwand' (bulkhead), was then mounted. The bodyshell that we were proposing was not suitable for the production techniques in use in South Bend, since it could not be any longer than the bodies produced at Studebaker. The conveyor belt was laid out in accordance with the length of the Studebaker bodies and could not be converted. However, we solved the problem by designing the front part of our car in such a way that it could be bolted on to the main body at a later date.

After Studebaker had examined our proposals, we were commissioned to build two prototypes but with a conventional layout, that is, with a front-mounted engine. This was not a problem for us, since in other respects our proposed design was maintained. Studebaker wanted the two prototypes to be fitted with different engines, one with an air-cooled and the other with a water-cooled unit, and so it was that the Porsche Type 542 was developed with two different power units. In both cases, the engine was a 120° V6 unit with a bore of 90 mm and a stroke of 80 mm, which gave a cubic capacity of 3,054 cc. The air-cooled version produced 98 hp at 3,700 rpm, and the water-cooled version 106 hp at 3,500 rpm. Even the self-supporting body design was retained, and it was even discovered that bolting the front of the car to the main body was advantageous in terms of isolation.

Our design for Studebaker looked very elegant. It had either a fastback or a notchback, and the clean lines of both variants were pleasantly different from the American baroque style of that period. Even the coefficient of drag cannot have been bad.

When we were in the middle of our work on the project, the Studebaker management contacted us and informed us that they had had their marketing department conduct a survey on their own proposal and our design. Seventy-five per cent of those questioned preferred our design, but Studebaker said they had no more money to start a new project. It was well known that Studebaker were getting into financial difficulties and in the end they were forced to merge with Packard. The consequence was that Studebaker had to take over the Packard programme and were

Above and below
Porsche type 542
prototype designed and
built for the American
Studebaker company
with two alternative
engines: one air-cooled
and another water-
cooled, but both 120°
V6 cylinder of 3054 cc
capacity. The air-cooled
version developed 98
PS, the water-cooled
version 106 PS.

no longer in a position to put our designs into production. Had our car come along earlier and been produced to a higher standard than was usual at the time at Studebaker then it might have been possible to save the company.

This was confirmation of our view that good styling alone is not enough to keep a company alive, and that quality is also of great importance, and that is what I repeatedly tell my son Ferdinand (Butzi): 'You must always be very careful about who you do design work with, because even the most beautiful watch is useless if it doesn't work!'

The new model that Studebaker had produced themselves had been styled by Raymond Loewy, and the influence of our 356 was clearly reflected in the sharp slope of the front section. At that time, Studebaker was making references to the shape of our 356

Front view of the Porsche designed for Studebaker, to some extent similar to all Porsche's post-war designs.

in its advertising. Unlike in Germany, comparative advertising is allowed in the USA. However, as noted above, build quality did not match the excellent styling. Our V6 design for Studebaker, which we supplied from 25 October 1952 until well into 1954, was an early example of the so-called 'compact cars' which suddenly became fashionable during the oil crisis.

Our two years of collaboration with Studebaker also led to an exchange of engineers. I myself had to make many visits to the USA and I took the opportunity of going to Detroit to see an old friend of mine, Zora Arkus-Duntov. He had been born in Russia, had studied before the war at the Institute of Technology in Berlin and had married a Berlin girl. Together with his brother Yura he had gone to the USA and finally ended up in the Chevrolet Division of General Motors. He played a significant part in the development of the Chevrolet Corvette and was reckoned to be an engine specialist. He had driven for us in races and in 1954 drove the 1.1 litre Porsche with the four-cam engine to victory in its class at Le Mans. His team mate was the Frenchman Olivier. He repeated this success in a Porsche in 1955, driving with the Frenchman Veuillet.

Arkus-Duntov arranged for me to visit the General Motors Research and Development Center, where I was introduced to Bill Mitchell who was then a world-famous designer. He had become well known throughout the world not only through his position as chief designer at GM, but also through his provocative comments on the styling of Mercedes-Benz vehicles. These comments were probably largely an attempt to attract publicity. My visit made me realize the great difference between the mentality of the designer and that of the engineer. In Mitchell's office I saw a number of car models, most of which were design studies. He pointed to one of these models and said, 'In order to get a more elegant front section, I need a lower engine, so I've made a few changes to the engine. For example, I've made the carburettor lower.' As Mitchell was speaking, I noticed that Arkus-Duntov was growing impatient; finally he interrupted Mitchell and said, 'You're talking rubbish, you can't make such an engine, Bill!'

It must have been very difficult to reconcile these conflicting opinions. In my view, it was right to suggest that a third party be brought in, someone able to mediate between the two conflicting concepts and develop a realistic design. He would have to be a specialist who knew something of both design and engineering.

The problem of automobile styling can best be illustrated by a conversation that I once had with the chief engineer of an American automobile company. (Incidentally, this applies to all American automobile companies and shows very clearly that the costing department exerts a very powerful influence in these companies.) The chief engineer in question said, 'I have designed a completely new automobile. It has better road-holding, more powerful brakes and other changes which give it a character more like a Mercedes, for example. When I submitted this design to the people in the costing department, they were hardly enthusiastic. They wanted to retain the old front axle at all costs, indeed they wanted to use as many components as possible from the current production model. They said this would cut the cost by a few dollars. In the end this is what was decided, and the result was the old car with a new body!'

This story clearly illustrates the power wielded by costing departments in the American automobile industry. During my conversation with the chief engineer in Detroit, we discussed engine layout and considered the relative merits of front-wheel and rear-wheel drive and air-cooled or water-cooled engines. The chief engineer's reply was perplexing, because he said, 'As far as I'm concerned, there is only one important question, namely, how many cars can I sell?'

At Porsche we had a different philosophy, since I alone was responsible for making final decisions for or against a new design. It did not make any difference whether it was a new engine for series production or for racing, or work commissioned by Volkswagen. At that time I was still to be found every day in the design office or the test department. I loved this work, but the larger the company became the less time I had for it.

In the meantime we had built a new production facility, since our old factory had still not been handed over by the Americans. We were assisted in this by a strange coincidence. A few cases of cholera occurred in Stuttgart: there was no epidemic, but caution was advised, and as a result the Stuttgart city authorities

wanted to establish an isolation hospital. In Bad Cannstatt there was an army camp with suitable facilities, but the Americans also had a hospital there, and given their fear of infectious diseases, it was hardly surprising that the authorities' plan came to nothing. However, the Americans had a counterproposal and said, 'You can have the Porsche works in Zuffenhausen; we'll give it up for that!'

However, just as the city administration started work on converting our old factory into a hospital for cholera victims, the disease faded away. What was to happen now? It was only the plan to open a hospital for cholera victims that was preventing the Americans from occupying our factory again. Eventually, however, they gave up all claim to it.

We received the news of the derequisition of the buildings in which we had worked between 1938 and 1945 on 1 December 1955, 25 years after the foundation of the company. It happened at the same time as the factory designed by the architect Gutbrod became ready for occupation. At that time we had a work force of 616 people. We now had sufficient space for future expansion.

In the meantime, another factory had been built in Friedrichshafen on Lake Constance; this was the Porsche-Diesel-Motorenbau GmbH, where diesel-powered tractors and small diesel units for industrial applications were to be produced. A year later, the first tractors, powered by an air-cooled diesel engine, were offered

World Champion racing driver Juan Manuel Fangio driving the new tractor of the Porsche-Diesel-Motorenbau GmbH at Friedrichshafen. In the centre is Professor Prinzing.

On 15 March 1954 Porsche celebrated its 5,000th vehicle, a 356 which I drove from the factory.

for sale. At that time a photograph appeared in the specialist press showing Juan Manuel Fangio, the World Champion racing driver, at the wheel of one of our tractors. In 1957, the Argentinian won his fifth World Championship in a Maserati, a record which to date has never been broken.

However, our main interests lay, as ever, in sports cars.

19

The 911 is born

The introduction of the new servo-assisted synchromesh transmission, first exhibited in public in 1952 at the Paris Salon, was a considerable advance for the 356. In the years that followed, it earned us almost ten million Marks in licence fees and was the subject of 70 patents granted to us. Every small improvement and refinement made to transmission was patented, however small it was. The idea of the servo rings came from an earlier patent awarded to Leopold Schmid, although in a different connection, and from the beginning we gave him a share of the licence fees that we received.

In March 1956 we celebrated the twenty-fifth anniversary of the founding of Dr Ing h.c. F. Porsche GmbH. As is generally known, the company had moved into its new premises in Stuttgart at the end of 1930 and was incorporated in the commercial register on 25 April 1931. On that same day in March 1956, we were also able to celebrate the production of the 10,000th Porsche car. My youngest son Wolfgang drove this 356 off the production line. The 356, which was the base model of this particular series, had been very successful and 70 per cent of them had been exported. Even then, our most important overseas market was America, where Max Hoffman was building up a particularly vigorous operation. He had also contrived to have a new model, the Speedster, produced alongside the well-known 356.

At that time Hoffman was always anxious to have the cheapest Porsche on display in his showrooms. His price was less than 3,000 dollars, to which had to be added all the 'extras', which even included the V-belt, the tyre pressure gauge and the heating, although no cars were sold without heating! This way of doing business was actually not so unusual in the USA. The aim of course was to use the low price displayed on the car to tempt the customer into the showroom, where the salesman could then demonstrate his skills. I well remember an experience I had on my first visit to the USA in 1937. At that time the small eight-cylinder Ford cost exactly 600 dollars. However, this price did not include the bumpers, the spare wheel or the tool kit. These 'extras' pushed the price up to 680 dollars. So you can see that Hoffman's tactics were based on some distinguished precedents.

Above The Porsche 356A Speedster, a model inspired in 1956 by Max Hoffman, the American dealer. Its four-cylinder engine developed 60 PS, with which the Speedster was capable of 155 km/h (96 mph).

The Speedster was a particularly sporty model, with a sharply curved windscreen. It was a sort of roadster with an all-weather hood that could be fully lowered. The hood was considerably lower than that of the Cabriolet, and taller people found it difficult to sit upright when the hood was up. However, the car had a very sporty appearance and weighed only 760 kg (1,676 lb). It was powered by either the 55 or 70 horsepower engine and cost 3,800 dollars, including the extras.

Buyers of the 356A were offered a choice of 44, 60, 75 or 100 horsepower engines. This last option was the 1500 GS Carrera, which was powered by the four-cam engine designed by Dr Fuhrmann. This engine had first been shown at the 1953 Paris Salon

Right Porsche 356 Carrera GT of 1958 with its very powerful engine in the rear.

Above This photograph shows production of the 356 at Stuttgart-Zuffenhausen in 1961. The work was of a very high standard.

Above left and left Porsche type 356B Carrera 2, an even more powerful car with several modifications.

199

The 2 litre engine of the Carrera 2 with four overhead camshafts developed 130 PS at 6,200 rpm, a very sporting car with excellent top end acceleration and disc brakes of Porsche's own design.

in the Rennspyder, the Type 550. It made its motor racing début in the third World Racing Sports Car Championship held in 1953 at the Nürburgring. This is what H.U. Wieselmann, who at that time was editor-in-chief of the periodical *Auto, Motor und Sport*, had to say about the Carrera, as it was soon to become generally known:

'However the great surprise is the new Carrera, which was first exhibited at the 1955 Frankfurt Show. With this model, Porsche are offering the four-cam engine from the Spyder, which has countless racing victories to its credit, in a comfortable and luxurious touring car. The power of this long-established and foolproof engine has been reduced from 115 to 100 horsepower, while the compression ratio has been cut back from 9.5:1 to 8.7:1. This engine will power the Coupé to a top speed of about 200 km/h (125 mph). Of greater importance, however, is the acceleration; some idea of what it is like can be gained from the following figures: in second gear the Carrera is capable of a speed in excess of 75 mph (120 km/h), while in third it will reach about 106 mph (170 km/h). And in city traffic the engine runs easily at 2,000 rpm or less. It produces its best performance at 6,200 rpm, its highest torque at 5,400 rpm and for short periods the four-cam engine will run at 7,200 rpm... Its handling, combined with its truly outstanding engine, will give all those with the feeling for it a pure driving experience that cannot be matched by any other car that I know of!'

By the time of our next anniversary in March 1957 Porsche cars had recorded a total of 400 racing victories all over the world. This is undoubtedly an impressive record which clearly demonstrates how right we were when we began to develop our own sports car based on VW components. Only if I compare the development and testing phase of our early days with the situation today do I begin to realize how enthusiastically we set to work. At that time we had no wind tunnel. We tried to achieve optimal streamlining by sticking lots of scraps of cloth on the test car and then photographing it from a motorway bridge as it drove past at top speed below us. The photographs provided us with data for the development of the aerodynamics of our bodyshell.

It would take too long to list here all the individual stages in the development of the Type 356. However, I would like to give the following brief summary. In 1958 the Speedster was replaced by the Convertible D. The D denoted Drauz of Heilbronn who were now building the bodies for all our convertible models, while Reutter made the bodies for the coupé, the hardtop and the cabriolet. The Convertible D was exhibited for the first time at the 1958 Paris Salon. The popular Carrera was now available as the 105 hp de Luxe with a petrol-electric heating system and as the 115 hp GT (Gran Turismo).

In 1959 the distribution department and spare part store moved into a new building.

In 1950 and 1951, each of our engines was assembled by one man who etched his initials on the engine block next to the engine number. In this way it was always possible to establish who had assembled any particular engine. During the phase of rapid expansion that the company went through it obviously became impossible to retain this procedure. At the beginning of 1960 our total work force had increased in size to 1,250. Quality control was systematically improved. Every fifth worker employed in the production department was involved in supervisory tasks. For each car produced the after-sales department kept record cards relating to the engine, gearbox, vehicle inspection and other test data. By the end of 1960 we had delivered a total of 39,747 cars to customers.

At the beginning of the 1930s we had nothing more than a design office in which only engineers worked. Later, when we had set up our own experimental department, we started to employ so-called wage-workers as well as salaried staff, although of course we made no distinction between salaried and wage-earning employees. All our employees were treated equally and were paid their wages or salaries on a monthly basis. Similarly, holiday pay was the same for everybody. After the war, I wanted to retain this basic principle, which I have always advocated, but unfortunately this was not always possible because my room for manoeuvre was limited by legislation, for example on sick pay.

My attempts to put wage-workers on the same footing as salaried staff led on one occasion to an amazing discussion. After I had decided that wage-earning employees should also be entitled to sick pay from the first day of their employment with us, the staff council (representing salaried employees) came to me and wanted to know what extra benefits salaried staff would now receive. My answer to this request was as follows, 'Gentlemen, I think you have failed to understand that it is my intention to put all my employees on the same footing, without any distinction either between individuals or tasks!'

On one occasion I also got into difficulties with the union during a strike at our factory which halted production, and as a result we had to send workers home. I instructed that workers who were not union members should be paid for the days lost due to the strike in the same way as union members. This gave rise to a complaint from the union, which objected to my treating all workers alike. Despite the complaint, I was not prepared to withdraw my instruction.

In 1952 the first steps towards creating an emblem for Porsche cars were taken. Max Hoffman had been urging us to do this for some time. He cited the example of the English and said what beautiful emblems they had and that we should produce something similar. He considered this important for the American market. He made the suggestion to me one day while we were lunching together in New York and I quickly sketched out a piece of heraldry on a napkin. I said to Hoffman as I was drawing, 'If all you want is a coat of arms, you can get one from us!'

So I drew the crest of the House of Württemberg and in the middle put the coat of arms of the City of Stuttgart, the rampant horse. I wrote the name Porsche at the top. I then put the napkin away and gave it on my return to Komenda with the request that he should draw a clean copy. This he did, and we then took the design to the state government and the City of Stuttgart and requested that they authorize the design for use as our emblem. The authorities raised no objections, and so from 1953 onwards Porsche cars bore their own emblem, to the great pleasure of all concerned.

Incidentally Ferrari also use the Stuttgart horse as their emblem. This came about in the following way. Ferrari had a friend who had been a fighter pilot in the First World War. He had once shot down a German plane that had the Stuttgart coat of arms on its fuselage. The Italian pilot kept the coat of arms as a trophy, and when Ferrari founded his own racing team he suggested that he should use the coat of arms as an emblem. Ferrari accepted the suggestion gratefully, and so the coat of arms of the City of Stuttgart appears twice as an automobile trademark.

On 1 November 1960 we moved into No 3 Works, which were not far from No 1 Works and housed the sales and after-sales departments and the central parts store. Also in 1960 our turnover exceeded 100 million DM for the first time, at 108 million DM.

In the meantime, the 356A had given way to the 356B. There were now only a few components that came from Volkswagen, our association with Drauz came to an end, and two different companies began to make bodies for us. One of these was Wilhelm Karmann GmbH in Osnabrück, who made the hardtop body with the roof welded on, while the other was Anciens Etablissement d'Ieteren Frères S.A. in Brussels, who were already acting as our importers for Belgium. D'Ieteren built the Roadster body for us.

The Carrera 2 with the 2 litre, 130 hp four-cam engine was announced at the end of 1961 and deliveries began the following year. We suggested to Ate that they could produce a ventilated disc brake for us. Ate, which had in the meantime been taken over by an American company, turned down our proposal. My response was, 'Then we'll make it ourselves!', to which Ate said, 'No you won't, and if you do we'll sue you!' This is an example of what sometimes happens in business in order to slow down progress. In the end, however, Ate declared themselves willing to produce the disc brake for us.

On 1 March 1964 we took over Reutter's coachbuilding activities, while Reutter transferred the manufacture of their car seats and seat covers to a new company called Recaro. Their products were manufactured initially in the old Reutter works in the Augustenstraße in Stuttgart but they now have their own factory in Kirchheim/Teck and in Bremen, from where they supply seats to the automobile industry for, among others, the Mercedes-Benz 190.

In 1963 the 356B was replaced by the Type C, which had an improved engine and Ate disc brakes on all four wheels.

It had been clear to me for a long time that we could not go on with the 356 for ever. We had to replace it; we had after all designed the car on the basis of VW components and made certain modifications to it in the course of the years. For example, we had added a new cylinder head with valves arranged in a V, aluminium cylinders with chrome-plated working surfaces, two carburettors on each side and a lot more besides. However, all these things were basically just a temporary solution to the problem of getting better performance from the VW engine. We then designed a new engine and fitted it to the 356. This was the Carrera, a four-cylinder engine with four overhead camshafts, with an initial capacity of 1.5 litres which was subsequently increased to 2 litres. This engine had actually been developed for racing use, but we fitted it in considerable quantities into the 356.

As far as the successor to the 356 was concerned, various opinions were being voiced within the company, one of which was that we needed a four-seater. Consequently, we remodelled the 356 into various types of four-seater, including a saloon, a cabriolet and a coupé, all of which were reasonable designs. The cabriolet, for example, was only 220 lb (10 kg) heavier than the 356, which was acceptable. The coupé was also quite interesting. However, I decided that we had to build a real successor, with a new six-cylinder engine: the new car had after all to be better than the old one!

It was then suggested within the company that people were getting taller and that we should be careful not to build cars that were too small, and other such nonsense. As a result the low weight of the first prototypes was never achieved again. The new car became heavier and heavier. One of the designs had been drawn up by my eldest son, Ferdinand Alexander (Butzi). He had joined the company in 1957, and since he was very interested in styling he worked with Herr Komenda, who was responsible for bodywork, when very soon he showed considerable talent. His successor for the 356 was really a very beautiful car, a 2 + 2, almost a four-seater; it was designated the Type 7 and was very much liked by all involved. We had Herr Komenda build several prototypes on the basis of the Type 7; they were labelled Variants 1, 2 and 3 and, lo and behold, each successive variant was bigger and heavier than its predecessor. I put my foot down and restricted the wheelbase to 2.2 m (86.7 in) and laid down certain targets for the wheel suspension and the engine. Anything in excess of 2.2 m would lead automatically to a four-seater.

I then realized that Herr Komenda was not taking any notice of my proposals and that he wanted at all costs to build the cars that he and his team had designed. Moreover, he was constantly changing my son's styling to a design more in tune with his own tastes. In the course of this dispute I realized that a car body designer is not necessarily an expert in styling and that, conversely, a styling specialist cannot necessarily be considered an expert in car body design. However, both are usually convinced of their expertise in both areas. I was now faced with the question of how to ensure that a model retained the lines it had been given by the styling team when it fell into the hands of the body designers. I had to think of something.

We had recently taken over the Reutter company, which had its own design department, so I went to see Herr Beierbach, who was at that time the managing director of Reutter, and said to him, 'Herr Beierbach, here is my son's model. Can you do the engineering drawings in such a way that the styling remains unaltered?' Herr Beierbach said he could, and he had engineering drawings made from the model.

When Herr Komenda was informed of this, he was absolutely dumbfounded at first, but after a few weeks he was convinced and his team began to do the drawings. What eventually emerged was what already existed in the styling department as a 1:1 model: the 901. Reutter then adopted the shape unchanged, but dissuaded me from a few things that were topical at the time. All of them were of course implemented in later models, for example, a large rear window on the 901 that could be opened in order to load suitcases. At the time, neither Herr Beierbach nor Herr Komenda was confident of being able to make it, but it was eventually realized with the advent of the 928 and the 944.

This reminds me of the time when we were developing the 356 in Austria and then moved to Germany. In Austria, the bodies were made entirely of aluminium and were correspondingly lighter than the steel bodies made in Germany. The Austrian cars had a divided windscreen, but it was already curved. The quarterlights were also curved in order to achieve a lower coefficient of drag. However, the German factory was not yet in a position to put these windows into series production. Initially we made do with Plexiglas for the side windows. At that time we were still heavily dependent on our suppliers. Even the coachbuilding tools had to be purchased from an outside supplier. Of necessity, therefore, a new production run had to have a very long lead-time.

The 901 made its world début at the Frankfurt Automobile Show in the autumn of 1963, a year before production got under way. In autumn 1964, the French company Peugeot informed us that they held a patent on three-digit model numbers with middle zeros. As a consequence, the 901 became the 911.

The 911, with its 2 litre, air-cooled, flat six engine which produced 130 hp, was not an immediate success. At the Frankfurt Automobile Show in 1963, customers found it 'a bit too angular'. It had a significantly larger area of glass than its predecessor. Indeed, everything that was new was at first considered strange by customers. However, I was not actually worried by this, the

Ferdinand Alexander Porsche, known as Butzi, our eldest son, with the 911 (901). Butzi designed the body of the 911, a car which laid the basis of the great worldwide success of Porsche's cars, and which is responsible for the saying 'Fahren in seiner schönsten Form' — driving in its most beautiful form.

Above In 1963 the 911 followed the 356. In the background are three examples of the last version of the 356. Today the 911 holds the all-time record for production of rear-engined sports cars.

Right The six-cylinder, horizontally opposed, air-cooled engine of the 911 with 2 litre capacity and 130 PS at 6,100 rpm.

reason being my own, rather individual views in this matter. It is my belief that something that appeals enormously on first acquaintance soon loses its attractiveness. On the other hand, if a certain degree of continuity is ensured, then the appeal will last. Anything else is, in my view, merely a question of fashion. At the Frankfurt Show the 911 was on show next to the 356 to which people were accustomed; as a consequence, their reaction to the 911 was to say, 'That's not a Porsche!'

The motoring press took a different view. In the conclusion to

his test in *Auto, Motor und Sport*, Reinhard Seiffert wrote:

'There is no question about it: the new sports car that will be produced at Zuffenhausen from the end of August is one of the most interesting cars in the world. It has been conceived as a car for normal road use, rather than as a GT racing car. Despite this, however, the 901 has the air of functionalism that will guarantee it enthusiastic buyers. In this respect, it is clearly quite different from the 230 SL and four-seater sports cars such

Above The 1966 presentation of the 911S, which had several improvements compared with the standard model 911.

Left A look into the engine compartment of the 911S with its six-cylinder, horizontally opposed engine of 2 litres. The engine of this model was then enlarged to 2.7 litres, and for the SC to 3 litres.

A cutaway drawing of
the 911 engine.

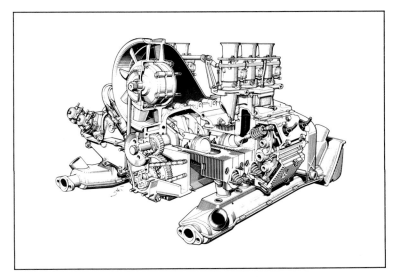

With the model I like
most, the 911.

Above The Porsche Targa type 911, the first convertible in the world with outstanding safety components like the steel roll bar to make driving in an open car as safe as in a limousine. It can also be converted to a coupé using a special hardtop.

Left For the twenty-fifth anniversary of the company, Porsche manufactured 500 examples of this 911-2.7 in a version with special equipment.

Left The Porsche type 912 was also a special version of the 911, but with a four-cylinder engine instead of the six.

The type 912 was also made in a special version for the German autobahn police. This is the 100,000th Porsche car, a 912 Targa for the police of Baden-Württemberg, the home state of Porsche.

as the Fiat 2300 S and the Alfa Romeo Sprint, which are both in the same price category. Price and performance compare with the Carrera 2, which it will succeed, but are significantly higher than the four-cylinder models. However, it is expected to be built in larger numbers than the Carrera and it is reckoned that many Porsche customers will be willing to pay the extra to get their hands on this delightful car. This assumption will probably prove to be correct.'

And indeed it did. Over the years, the 911 developed into a very successful car.

Now that my eldest son, Ferdinand Alexander, had successfully joined the family firm, the question of my other sons' careers needed to be resolved. First of all, however, I should briefly explain the structure of our business.

After the deaths of my father and Dr Piëch, my sister, Louise Piëch, and myself both ended up with a fifty per cent stake in the companies in Austria and the Federal Republic of Germany. We agreed informally that my sister should manage the Austrian operation while I looked after the German business and that we should consult each other on important matters. Hans Kern, our business manager in Stuttgart, could also be consulted on financial matters by my sister in Salzburg. In order to bring our chil-

dren into the companies, not least for inheritance tax reasons, we gave some thought to the way in which they could best become involved in the family business.

In the case of my eldest son, the decision had already been made. He was interested in styling and began his career under the direction of the head of our coachwork development department. For almost five years, Ferdinand Alexander worked in various departments in the company in order to acquire a thorough knowledge of the various aspects of the business, then in 1961 he took over the management of the studio. The first job for which he was directly responsible was the styling of the 911 body. The shape of the Turbo and Carrera models has not changed to this very day. In my office today I still have a scale-model of the 911 that my son gave me when he received authorization to put his proposals into practice. Ferdinand Alexander remained with the company until March 1972, when he left to set up his own design company in Zell am See. My sister's eldest son, Ernst Piëch, works in the import company in Austria.

My sister and I each have four children, and with each one we concluded an agreement by which each member of the family owns 10 per cent of the family business.

Gerhard Anton, my second son, loves nature and farming. He farms on his own estate at Zell am See, but has no interest in the

The type 904 Carrera GTS, the car Butzi Porsche liked most because he designed the body without any outside influence or pressure. The four-cylinder engine developed 180 PS with which the Carerra reached a top speed of 256 km/h (about 160 mph).

With my wife Dodo and our four sons (from the left) Gerhard Anton (Gerd), Peter, Wolfgang Heinz (Wolfi) and Ferdinand Alexander (Butzi).

company, although he is also a keen driver.

Peter, my third son, trained in Salzburg as an engineer and joined the company in August 1963. He also worked in different departments in order to acquire a good insight into our various activities. In December 1965 he took over as production manager and became responsible for the quality of our products, which of course is a very important factor in our international image. In the spring of 1971 he left us to pursue other interests.

Wolfgang Heinz, my youngest son, studied international trade in Vienna, obtained his doctorate there and worked for five years for Daimler-Benz. He now has the Austrian franchise for Yamaha motor cycles. He is also a member of the supervisory board of Porsche AG and Fischer Technik.

My sister's second son, Ferdinand, studied engineering in Zürich. He joined us in April 1963 and was very soon involved with the testing of the new six-cylinder engine for the 911, which he eventually developed to the series production stage. He was particularly involved with the competition cars that we used with such success in the races for the European Hillclimbing Championship and the World Sports Car Championship, including the Le Mans 24-Hours Race. We won the World Sports Car Championship in 1966, among other titles, and successfully defended that title the following year, in addition to winning the European Hillclimbing Championship, the European Rally Championship and the Trans-Am series.

From 1968 onwards, Ferdinand Piëch took on overall responsibility for development. In the same year, we won the World GT Championship and successfully defended our titles in the European Hillclimbing Championship, the European Rally Championship and the Trans-Am series. In the next three years, 1969, 1970 and 1971, we won the very important Makes Championship, in addition to a number of other international titles. Dr Piëch left us in March 1972, worked for a time as a consultant engineer, was then appointed head of development at Audi, and from 1 January 1988 Chairman of the board of Audi.

My sister's youngest son, Dr Michael Piëch, studied law in Vienna and joined the company in April 1971. Until his departure in March 1972 he worked in the administration department.

It was during this period that we became seriously involved in motor racing. Our early involvement had been on a small scale, with the 356, particularly the aluminium version made in Gmünd. Many customers had already raced in Porsche cars, even at international level. Here I will mention only Prince Metternich and Count Berckheim, who in autumn 1952 both drove the 356 in the very arduous Mexican road race, the Carrera Panamericana. Unfortunately Berckheim had to retire because of gearbox damage, but Prince Metternich, driving the 1.5 litre Porsche, came eighth in the overall classification. He was beaten only by Mercedes-Benz 300 SLs, Ferraris and a Lancia Aurelia Gran Turismo with a supercharged engine. The race was won by Kling and Klenk in a works Mercedes 300 SL.

Then came the Porsche 911, and the number of victories began to grow. Eventually we began to put all our efforts into reaching the top. In so doing, the influence of the next generation made itself felt to a very considerable degree. Our racing activities brought us both the acclaim of an international audience, but also critisism, because we were committed to racing in a way that people were accustomed to seeing only from Daimler-Benz. This happened when we started the Le Mans 24-Hours Race with six cars. In order that Porsche Stuttgart did not appear to dominate things too much, we entered three cars from Stuttgart and three from Salzburg. In fact, however, they all came from Stuttgart.

The return to Grand Prix racing

We then started to get involved also with racing cars. In 1957, a modified Spyder RS driven by Edgar Barth won the Formula 2 race at the Nürburgring. In 1958, the Frenchman Jean Behra drove a single-seat 1500 RSK in the Formula 2 contest at Rheims. This car was laid out in such a way that the driver sat in the middle, unlike the two-seater Spyders which had the steering-wheel on the left-hand side. We also won at Rheims, which inspired us to build a true one-seater during the next winter. The plan was for it to be driven by Count Berghe von Trips in the 1959 Monaco Grand Prix. What actually happened was reported in *Auto, Motor und Sport* of 23 May 1959 under the headline *Porsche's hopes and disappointments in Monte Carlo*:

> 'One great hope has now vanished. The new Porsche's first race came to an end on a wall at the Saint-Dévote curve in Monte

In 1957 a modified Spyder RS driven by Edgar Barth was entered in a Formula 2 race on the Nürburg-ring and won it, first time out.

During the winter of 1958/59, Porsche built this single-seater driven (and crashed) in the 1959 Monaco Grand Prix by the German Count Berghe von Trips.

Carlo before the Monaco Grand Prix had really got under way. The Porsche team had spent six months developing and building this single-seater from the successful 1.5 litre works racing car. It had been completed only a week before the race and the finishing touches had been applied during test runs at the Nürburgring. Only a few insiders knew that a German racing car was going to take part in a Grand Prix race for the first time in four years, provided that its driver succeeded in qualifying as one of the 16 starters allowed for the Monaco Grand Prix. This fact is of particular significance, since Ferry Porsche has decided to build a racing car again at a time when motor sport in Germany is being repeatedly subjected to wild and almost completely irrelevant attacks. It is impossible to give too much credit for this to the little Zuffenhausen company, which certainly no longer needs to publicize the quality of its products through sporting success. We are also aware that the designers, engineers and mechanics at Porsche had to set to work with a great deal of enthusiasm in order to get the single-seater finished on time. They were certainly all agreed that what emerged was more than just a racing car: it was a fresh start, a predecessor of and prototype for the new formula which will come into force from 1961 onwards.'

Count von Trips had qualified for the race in the new single-seater, taking twelfth place in practice. This was a good result in a field

In 1961 Porsche entered the four-cylinder mono-posto in Grand Prix racing. This photograph shows the finish of the 1961 French Grand Prix at Rheims. The new Ferrari V6 with Baghetti driving, beating the old four-cylinder Porsche driven by Gurney by just a few yards.

which still included 2.5 litre Grand Prix cars. Unfortunately, Trips had to retire during the second lap when he grazed a wall on the right-hand bend at the end of the Saint-Dévote straight, skidded and knocked two other cars out of the race. That can of course always happen in motor racing, but it was extremely disappointing for us. We rebuilt the single-seater just in time for the French Grand Prix at Rheims, for which a Formula 2 race had been organized. Joakim Bonnier drove the Porsche and finished third. First place was taken by a Cooper with a Borgward engine driven by Stirling Moss and second place by Hans Herrmann in a Porsche single-seater built for Jean Behra by the Italian Colotti on the basis of the RSK.

Moss then drove our single-seater in trials at the Goodwood circuit and was very taken by it. He particularly praised its road-holding and brakes, although the car was still fitted with drum brakes at a time when disc brakes were becoming increasingly popular in motor racing. At that time Moss was driving a Cooper with a Coventry-Climax engine in Formula 1 races for the private racing team of his compatriot Rob Walker. In 1960 he changed over to one of Walker's Lotus-Climax machines. We suggested to Walker and Moss that Moss should drive our new car in Formula 2 races during the 1960 season. Our offer was accepted. In the first four races of that year, in Syracuse in Sicily, Brussels, Goodwood and Pau, the Porsche single-seater made a good impression but was not yet good enough to win. For the fifth race, in addition to Moss's car, we entered cars driven by Joakim Bonnier and Graham Hill. This race was held at the Aintree circuit, which was 3 miles (4.8 km) long, and laid out within the racecourse where the Grand National, the toughest steeplechase in the world, is held each year. Aintree proved to be our big breakthrough: Moss won, Bonnier was second and Hill third. Porsche had taken the first three places.

Mercedes-Benz had had a similar success five years previously, in 1955, when at the British Grand Prix at Aintree Moss, Fangio, Kling and Taruffi had taken the first four places in the Mercedes W196. The Mercedes of course was fitted with a gearbox which contained our synchromesh system. Unfortunately Moss crashed badly during the Belgian Grand Prix in Spa-Francorchamps in a Lotus, although he was driving again only six weeks later.

Since the 1960 German Grand Prix was a Formula 2 race, the Solitude Grand Prix, which took place beforehand, almost on our front doorstep in Stuttgart, acquired particular significance as a trial run for the big race. A total of five Porsche single-seaters were entered for the race. Hans Herrmann, Bonnier and Hill were joined by the American Dan Gurney. He was driving a more recent single-seater, the aerodynamics of which had been improved by my son Ferdinand Alexander. The importance attached to this race by our rivals was demonstrated by the fact that Ferrari entered a new Formula 2 rear-engined racing car driven by Count Berghe von Trips. Indeed 1960 saw the introduction by Ferrari of a racing car with the engine mounted in front of the rear axle which he was developing for the new Formula 1 that was to come into force from 1961 onwards. Rob Walker had entrusted Moss's Porsche to the English driver John Surtees. As it turned out Count von Trips won the Solitude in the more powerful Ferrari, but Herrmann, Hill, Bonnier and Gurney took the next four places for Porsche. While the Ferrari, the Lotus and the Cooper had disc brakes, the drum brakes fitted to all the Porsches proved to be their equal in every way.

The 1960 German Grand Prix was contested over the 4.8 miles (7.7 km) of the South Loop of the Nürburgring and not, as in previous years, over the 14.17 miles (22.80 km) of the North Loop. There were 32 laps, making a total of 153.13 miles (246.4 km). Since Ferrari had decided not to race, Count von Trips was without a car, so we offered him Gurney's. Hans Herrmann drove Moss's car, since Surtees was not racing, and Edgar Barth and Graham Hill drove our other two works cars. The weather was bad and the start was postponed by a quarter of an hour. Bonnier led from start to finish, Count Trips finished second, with Hill in fourth place, Herrmann in fifth and Barth in sixth. With this victory we won the Formula 2 Constructors' Championship. This was undoubtedly a great success for us, which contributed to our decision to become involved in the new Formula 1 from 1961. The new formula was in force from 1961 to 1965 and laid down engines with a cubic capacity of up to 1.5 litres. A minimum weight of 990 lb (449 kg) for the vehicle complete with tyres, oil and coolant was also required in order to place some restriction on the extremely lightweight designs which had led to several serious accidents. The engines had to run on normal commercial petrol with a maximum octane rating of 100. Supercharged engines were no longer permitted.

On 2 October, a Formula 2 race was held at Ferrari's own track on the Modena aerodrome, 1.5 miles (2.4 km) in length, where Ferrari tested his racing cars. Naturally, the Ferrari drivers and technicians knew the circuit well, but this did not prevent us from taking the challenge. In this 100-lap race, Bonnier drove the same Porsche in which he had won at the Nürburgring. We also entered two other single-seaters, driven by Herrmann and Barth. Count von Trips drove the Formula 2 rear-engined Ferrari and Richie Ginther the front-engined Ferrari.

Right from the start, the race developed into a duel between Bonnier and von Trips. As before, our cars were fitted with drum brakes, while the Ferrari had disc brakes. The Modena circuit made very heavy demands on the brakes: while Bonnier's stood up to the punishment, those on von Trips's Ferrari showed signs of fading towards the end, so that he had to let his team-mate Ginther pass him. Bonnier won, with Ginther second, von Trips third, Herrmann fourth and Barth fifth.

The Modena race confirmed to my satisfaction that there was virtually no difference between the average speeds attained by rear-engined and front-engined cars. However, it had to be assumed that rear-engined or mid-engined cars would gradually come to dominate Grand Prix racing, simply because they had so many other advantages. The only question was which design was the more economical in achieving the same result. The Modena race also showed, incidentally, that the drum brakes fitted to the Porsche cars were still better than the Ferrari's disc brakes. After we had decided to enter Formula 1 racing in 1961, the decision on which car we intended to use depended on what our rivals were planning to do. If Lotus, Cooper and Ferrari were going to use developed versions of their 1960 Formula 2 cars, then we would do the same. However, if they intended to introduce new and more powerful engines, then we were ready for them. We were already developing an air-cooled flat eight with a cubic capacity of 1.5 litres, which was of course designed in such a way that it could be bored out for use in sports cars.

Stirling Moss did not wish to drive for us in 1961, but he did race for us twice in South Africa in December 1960 and won both times. For our 1961 works team we again hired Bonnier, Gurney, Barth and Herrmann. However, we had to use the 1960 Formula 2 car because the new car was not yet ready. Although the 1960 car was slightly modified, it did not perform well enough to beat the competition, particularly the Ferrari with its new rear-mounted V6. As a result, the 1961 World Championship was contested by the Ferrari team of Phil Hill, an American, and Count Berghe von Trips. Von Trips just had his nose in front when he was tragically killed during the Italian Grand Prix at Monza in September. Consequently Hill won the World Championship.

Our new eight-cylinder engine ran on the test bench for the first time in December 1960. As I have already said, the four-cylinder engine was inferior to its rivals, so we had to do something about it. To this end I hired the young Swiss engineer Michael May, who converted the four-cylinder engine to direct fuel injection and increased its output by 20 hp, although in a very narrow engine speed range. The new eight-cylinder engine, fitted on to a completely new chassis and a remodelled body with a significantly smaller front surface than the four-cylinder, was tested for the first time in March 1962 at Hockenheim. The four-cylinder engine with direct fuel injection was also tested at the same time. The eight-cylinder unit was used in competition for the first time in May in the Dutch Grand Prix at Zandvoort, in cars driven by Gurney and Bonnier. The four-cylinder fuel injection engine was loaned

Above Ben Pon is driving the four-cylinder Porsche monoposto with fuel injection in the 1962 Dutch Grand Prix at Zandvoort.

Left First secret test drive of the new eight-cylinder Porsche single-seater early in 1961 at Hockenheim. Driving is Herbert Linge of Porsche.

Left The new eight-cylinder Formula 1 Grand Prix car (left) next to the old four-cylinder.

Right Inside view of the new eight-cylinder Grand Prix car with the air-cooled, horizontally opposed eight-cylinder engine. Note the cooling fan on top, the gearbox behind the engine, and fuel and oil tanks right at the front of the car.

Below Dan Gurney in the eight-cylinder Porsche, winning the 1962 French Grand Prix at Rouen. It was the first Grand Prix victory for a car bearing the name Porsche.

for this race to the young Ben Pon, son of our Dutch import agent. He had already raced a few times in sports cars, but was new to Formula 1. Pon spun the car on the fourth lap, damaged the rear of the car and quit the race.

Gurney, driving a car with the eight-cylinder unit, held on to

Joakim Bonnier, also a member of the team, driving the eight-cylinder at Rouen, but who had to retire.

third place initially, but then got into difficulties with the gear lever, lost a lot of time in the pits, and in the end fell hopelessly behind the rest of the field and retired. Bonnier's engine never performed at its best and the Swede finished in seventh place, several laps behind the leaders.

We spent some time trying to solve these problems, and only Gurney, who had just returned from Indianapolis, took part in the Monaco Grand Prix. However, we were dogged by bad luck once again: right at the beginning of the race Gurney was mixed up in a shunt started off by Mairesse and collided with Trevor Taylor. The Porsche was so badly damaged that Gurney had to retire. Bonnier took fifth place in a car powered by the four-cylinder engine. This of course meant more work for us. We missed the Belgian Grand Prix at Spa and concentrated all our efforts on the French Grand Prix at Rouen-Les-Essarts on 8 July. Gurney and Bonnier were both to drive cars fitted with the eight-cylinder engine. Gurney drove despite a sore throat and fever, which in the summer heat was a considerable strain for him. Despite this, he turned in a marvellous performance and won the 48th French Grand Prix, covering the 219 miles (352 km) at an average speed of 101.9 mph (163.9 km/h). Unfortunately, Bonnier had to retire early because of engine trouble.

Gurney and Bonnier finished first and second respectively in the Stuttgart Solitude race, although this was not a World Championship race. In the subsequent World Championship events, although we notched up some good results victory eluded us, but from a technical point of view we were on the right road. However, it should not be forgotten that Formula 1 racing is a very costly business. In 1962 we took over the Reutter company. For us this was a very large investment and so in the autumn of 1962 I looked once again at the costs incurred by our Formula 1 activities. After a thorough study of the situation and lengthy deliberation on the matter, I came to the conclusion that we could not actually afford Grand Prix racing at all and that we should put an end to our involvement, which is what we did after the American Grand Prix.

As far as I was concerned, there was no doubt that sports car racing was more important for us and for our customers, since it is more closely connected with our products than pure racing cars. Nevertheless, we were able to use the experience we had gained with the Grand Prix cars in our sports car programme.

—————— 21 ——————

World fame for our sports cars

Image-building is not the only contribution that motor racing makes to the Porsche company. Technical discoveries made during our racing activities have a direct impact on our production cars, since using our cars in races and rallies helps us to improve the technical quality of our series products. The technicians involved in our sporting activities acquire priceless technical experience which is of immense value in our everyday work, and not least, motor racing motivates Porsche engineers to an extent that could not be achieved in any other way. A few months, often just a few weeks or even days, of competitive use usually reveals whether the particular technical solutions adopted are the correct ones.

Diversity of experience is another reason for the wide range of sporting activities in which Porsche has always been involved. Our endless list of victories in the World Championships of makes, the European Rally Championships and the many national and international hill-climbing championships are proof of this, as are our successes in the Le Mans 24-Hours race, the legendary Targa Florio, on the difficult Northern loop of the Nürburgring and the Monte Carlo Rally. We have also demonstrated our abilities in races outside Europe. I shall mention here only the CanAm series with their powerful competition sports cars. All this shows the diversity of Porsche's sporting activities which has brought our company great respect throughout the world.

I am of the opinion that sports cars actually foreshadow innovations, and that this was true in the past as it will be in the future. Sports cars will never of course be produced in large numbers. It is logical therefore to use them to implement and test new ideas before they are put into series production. Being a lover of sports cars, that is of fast two-seater cars, has nothing to do with the fact that these cars have a top speed of 125 or even 180 mph (200 or 290 km/h). The top speed is actually the result of mechanical efficiency and air resistance, and is thus a merely automatic process. It is not of course necessary to drive at these high speeds, but it is possible if one wants to, and that is probably the reason why many people consider sports cars to be unnecessary.

Many different types of cars use our modern motorways, includ-

Myself with Raymond Loewy, the famous American styling expert during the Le Mans 24 Hours race in 1954.

ing saloons which can travel at speeds in excess of 125 mph (200 km/h). Despite this, the average speed of cars travelling on the motorways in Germany is about 75 mph (120 km/h), an indication that most car drivers do not travel at excessively high speeds. For example, I grew up with cars, but on a busy motorway I do not drive at 150 mph (240 km/h), but rather at 85 mph (136 km/h) or 95 mph (152 km/h) or, if conditions require it, only 60 mph (96 km/h). There is no law that requires owners of fast cars always to drive at high speeds.

The 356 and the 911 have been used in many different versions by racing drivers all over the world. Here is a racing sports car completed in 1956, the 1.5 litre 550 Spyder with Richard von Frankenberg at the wheel on the Nürburgring.

Our customers had already achieved sporting success in races and rallies with their production Porsches before we began to develop our own competition machines. The impulse to build our competition cars actually came after the war from our Frankfurt dealer Walter Glöckler, who died at the beginning of 1988.

Above The Porsche type 718 RSK Spyder as raced at Sebring (Florida) in 1958. Its 1.6 litre, four-cylinder engine developed 150 PS.

Left Count Berghe von Trips racing the 718 RSK in the 1959 1,000 km race at the Nürburgring, here passing through the Südkehre (South curve). Von Trips was killed at Monza when driving a Formula 1 Ferrari in September 1961.

Left Stirling Moss also drove for Porsche. Here he is in the 718 RS61 at the Karussell during the 1961 1,000 km race at the Nürburgring.

225

In collaboration with his works manager, the engineer Ramelow, he developed a lightweight Spyder, which he equipped with our 1.1 litre engine modified to develop 58 hp. Walter Glöckler drove this car to victory in the 1950 German Championship. Inspired by the Glöckler-Spyder, our engineer Wilhelm Hild developed the Type 550, which was also a Spyder. The two-seater's aluminium bodyshell was made by Weidenhausen in Frankfurt, who had also made the body for Glöckler's Spyder. The 550 was fitted with a tuned version of the 1.5 litre engine, converted to run on alcohol, which produced more than 75 hp. A coupé roof was added to two of these cars used in the 1953 season which were then entered in the Le Mans 24-Hours Race where they won the 1.5 litre class. In the autumn of 1953, after a very successful European season, two of these 550s were entered for the famous Carrera Panamerica in Mexico. One car dropped out after it had proved itself to be the fastest 1.5 litre car in the race, while the other won its class.

For the 1954 season we equipped the Spyder, which I had designated the 1500 RS, with the new four-cam engine designed by Dr Fuhrmann. In this way the foundations were laid for the successful participation of Porsche works competition cars in the most important international races.

The eight-cylinder engine developed for the Formula 1 racing car was bored out to give a cubic capacity of 2 litres and shortly afterwards was used in the competition cars. Its cubic capacity was later increased to 3 litres. A 12-cylinder engine was also derived from it. Finally, we used the same engine as the basis for a 16-cylinder engine, which was never actually used.

One racer of particular interest was the Type 904 Carrera GTS, which also introduced a new chapter in the development of our sports cars. This was a mid-engined car with a steel boxed-rail chassis and was the first Porsche to have a fibreglass body. My son Butzi was in charge of the styling, and he had a particularly close association with this car, since this time nobody tried to interfere with his work. The deadlines we had set for the completion of this GT car were so tight that there was simply no time for lengthy discussions about styling. The 904, fitted with the 160 hp Carrera engine, was used in competition for the first time in the 12-hour Sebring race in Florida, where the Americans Cunningham and Underwood easily won their class. We subsequently built more than 100 of these cars, since a series of at least 100 had to be produced if the car was to gain homologation in the GT class. The 904 was sold to a number of customers who used it with great success in races and rallies. This version was powered by the four-cylinder four-cam engine whose output had been increased to 185 hp.

For our factory team cars we used the 904, a six-cylinder version known as the 906 and an eight-cylinder version known as

The Porsche Carrera 2000 GS-GT, another of the company's successful Gran Turismo cars in 1963, with a four-cylinder, 2 litre engine of 155 PS.

the 908. In addition, the 904 provided the basis for very light, manoeuvrable cars for speed hill-climbing which proved very successful. In this connection, I would particularly mention the Type 910 Bergspyder.

In 1967, the FIA, the governing body of international motor racing, changed the engine capacity limit for the World Championship of makes, increasing it from 3 to 5 litres on 1 January 1968. At first we thought we would be able to manage with our 3 litre eight-cylinder, but we discovered that our rivals were planning to use 5 litre engines and so we decided to develop a more powerful unit. From our efforts emerged the Type 917, which had a 12-cylinder engine with an initial cubic capacity of 4.5 litres which was increased in the course of its working life to 4.9, 5 and finally 5.4 litres.

I mention the 917 because, after 19 years of impressive class vic-

In 1966 the type 906 Carrera 6 was introduced with the six-cylinder engine giving 210 PS. It had a plastic body.

Actor Steve McQueen
driving a Porsche 908 at
the 12 hours of Sebring
in 1970 together with
Peter Revson; they
finished second overall.

An all-round
automobile for motor
sport, the 911 in its
different versions was
ideally suited for hill-
climbs, circuit races,
rallies, endurance races
and the safaris, in all of
which it obtained many
victories.

The Porsche 917
Langheck (long tail)
was powered by an air-
cooled, horizontally
opposed, 12-cylinder
engine of 4.5 litres. At
Le Mans in 1970, a 917
driven by Attwood/
Herrmann won the race
outright for Porsche for
the first time after
racing for 19 years.

tories, it brought us our first overall win in the Le Mans 24-Hours Race. In 1970 the British driver Attwood and Hans Herrmann from Stuttgart drove a 917 to victory at an average speed of 119 mph (192 km/h). In addition, we were placed first in the index-based assessment, the fuel-consumption rating, the sports car class and the GT category.

In that year of our greatest success at Le Mans, the organizers of the race, the Automobile Club de l'Ouest, had made me honorary starter. The year before, in 1969, the organizers of the famous Targa Florio in Sicily had bestowed upon me the title of honorary president, and in that same year we at last won the coveted Targa challenge trophy. This prompted me to donate a new challenge prize. I was very moved by the title I received in Sicily, since the race was particularly closely associated with the name of Porsche, my father having written his name into its history.

I shall mention here only the Sascha of 1922 and the victory of the supercharged Mercedes in 1924, to which my father made a significant contribution. Then in 1959, Barth and Seidel won the overall classification for Porsche for the first time. In 1969 came our ninth victory in the Targa Florio.

However, the overall victory at Le Mans was an event of quite exceptional importance for Porsche and reason enough for the whole family to gather at the track. The racing team was once again lodging in our old accommodation near Téloché, while the family stayed in a nearby château whose owners were great motor racing fans. Their enthusiasm for the sport was such that, in the brief periods of rest I allowed myself during the 24 hours of the race, they slipped a piece of paper under my door every half hour in order to keep me up to date with the race situation, announcing each one with a discreet knock at the door!

Above Myself with the Targa Florio Cup given to the company in 1969 after the team's ninth victory in this race.

Below The Porsche 917/30 with 5.4 litre engine and exhaust turbocharging developed 1100 PS and had a top speed of more than 370 km/h (230 mph).

The evening after the race we were joined by the drivers and engineers for a victory celebration in the château. The evening before, a further honour had been bestowed upon me in Le Mans, when I was dubbed a 'Chevalier de la Compagnie de Mousquetaires d'Armagnac'. The same honour was, incidentally, conferred upon my friend Auguste Veuillet, who, with his compatriot Edmond Mouche, had won his class at our first Le Mans race in 1951.

We won the World Championship of makes three times in succession, and then we withdrew from the competition because the regulations were changed again, with cubic capacity being restricted to 3 litres. In the meantime we had taken part successfully in the CanAm series of races held in the USA and Canada. This success was particularly important to us, because the USA was still our most important export market. In 1972, we used the Type 917-10 for the first time in this competition; it was equipped with a turbocharged engine which developed 1000 hp.

However, the exhaust gas turbocharger is capable not only of achieving considerable increases in performance, but also of improving the efficiency of the engine and thus saving fuel. The technology involved was nothing new to us when we came to use it in competition cars, since we had already used it during the war in our air-cooled diesel engines for tanks. Having been subjected to rigorous tests in our competition cars, the turbocharger then found its way into our production cars. In the same way, our company developed the air-cooled engine to a very high level by testing and proving it in countless rallies and races.

The first series application of the turbocharger was in the Type 930 Turbo, which we showed for the first time at the 1974 Paris Salon. It was the fastest sports car in Germany and the culmination of the 911. The trade press enthused over the car; the British magazine *Motor*, a leading trade publication in England, called it the 'finest driving machine'. The Turbo accelerated from 0 to 60 mph in 6.3 seconds, a performance which made it a very safe car in traffic. However, it was not only the car's performance that impressed the journalists, but also its motoring luxury and, particularly, the sheer enjoyment to be had from driving it: 'motoring at its most beautiful', as we at Porsche like to say, an expression that has always been the touchstone of the philosophy underlying all our work.

We sold the car in the USA as the Porsche Turbo Carrera at a price of $25,850. The demand for this vehicle exceeded our expectations and by May 1976 we had already sold twice as many as we had anticipated.

It goes without saying that various versions of this car were also used in competition, where it was as successful as its predecessors. I am sometimes asked to explain the thinking that lies behind

Opposite top Another powerful car was the Martini Porsche type 935. Martini was the first sponsor to race this car in the World Championship for Makes. With exhaust turbocharging, its 3 litre six-cylinder engine developed about 600 PS. It is a car obviously based on the famous 911.

Opposite bottom The Porsche 917/16 cylinder Spyder of 1969/70. This was a test car for 16 cylinder engines of different capacities from 6 litres and 770 PS to 7.2 litres and 880 PS. It was used purely for experimental purposes and never raced.

Above The Porsche 911 turbo, with 260 PS power output, one of the most beautiful Porsches to drive is seen here in Targa and convertible form.

Right The six-cylinder engine of the 911 turbo delivers 260 PS. It is a traditional horizontally opposed air-cooled engine. Despite the performance the car also offers a very comfortable ride.

Right Porsche type 936, another advanced racing sports car with space frame and plastic body removable in three pieces and six-cylinder engine with KKK turbocharger.

Above In 1976 Porsche could claim a dual World Championship; for Production Sports Cars and for Racing Sports Cars. Here is a 935 Turbo, descended from the 911, with the winning type 936 from Le Mans. In the centre (from the left) are drivers Manfred Schurti, Rolf Stommelen, race manager Manfred Jantke and drivers Jochen Mass and Jacky Ickx.

Left Porsche 956 C Coupé finished first, second and third overall in the 1982 Le Mans 24-Hours Race. Number 1: Ickx/Bell; number 2: Mass/Schuppan; and number 3: Holbert/Haywood.

Left Another overall victory was in 1987 with the 956C and Stuck/Bell/Holbert. The six-cylinder, four-valve, 2.65 litre turbo engine developed over 620 PS.

Above In 1988, after 25 years the Porsche type 911 had been successful in all categories; as a sports racing car and as a universal sports car for both the amateur and for the professional race driver.

Right The Porsche type 908 normally aspirated racing engine: eight-cylinder, horizontally opposed, air-cooled with two valves per cylinder, 2997 cc displacement and 350 PS at 8,400 rpm.

our unswerving commitment to motor racing. One of our primary considerations is that it is always an incentive for young engineers to be able to work in this area, and for this reason we always recruit young engineers for our racing activities. At the same time of course it provides good training for young people. For races and rallies, the car must always be ready by a specific date, and that is usually the coming Sunday. One cannot just say 'we'll get on with it on Monday', because on Sunday the car has to be in per-

234

The 12-cylinder normally aspirated engine, air-cooled, horizontally opposed, two valves per cylinder, 4494 cc displacement, giving 580 PS at 8,400 rpm, powered the type 917.

fect condition, and this teaches an engineer a great deal. He discovers how to save time and sometimes has to improvize in order to be able to achieve what is required of him.

A great many people also wonder why there should be so many Porsche customers in America where there is a speed limit of 55 mph (88 km/h) (60mph (96 km/h) on freeways). Well, in America we have a Porsche Club with 30,000 members. I would not like to say that they buy a Porsche simply as a piece of jewellery or

Even a 16-cylinder engine was installed into a prototype of the type 917 Porsche. It was an air-cooled, horizontally opposed design of 7166 cc capacity and a weight of 320 kg (705.6 lb). It developed 880 PS at 8,300 rpm. It was a normally aspirated engine.

This 12-cylinder turbo-charged (the turbo-charger is in front of the engine) engine, powered the 917/30; two valves per cylinder, air-cooled, horizontally opposed, driven by the exhaust gases, 5374 cc displacement, 1,100 PS at 7,800 rpm.

a status symbol; rather they buy one because it is a pleasure for them to drive such a car. A speed limit of 60 mph may be important for America, for whatever reasons, but in my estimation it is impossible to keep such a large country as the USA so completely under control that someone, somewhere does not sometimes 'give his horse the spurs'!

22

Decision for the future

On 1 March 1972 the Porsche company was reorganized. My aim was to prepare the company for the next generation. Another factor in the change, however, was that the next generation was already waiting in the wings to join a structure in which each individual did not believe that he alone was the boss. This meant that this generation was either capable of working with each other or it was not. After I had ascertained that the necessary harmony and co-operation could not be created, I drew the inevitable conclusions and said, 'Then nobody's going to be boss!'

In my view, none of the representatives of the next generation was mature enough to be trusted to get to grips with the task that lay ahead of him. Of course, each of these young people had proved his ability to a certain extent, but that alone was not enough to direct a company like ours. For that a wide range of different abilities is required. For example, I need to have an instinct that tells me whether decisions that are taken will pay off in the end. As an engineer I cannot simply indulge myself by pursuing improbable ideas that prove later to be worthless. A company cannot survive like that. I have always said, 'The greatest successes in racing can only be achieved if the production cars are marketable and do not take us into the red. If the company is not making money, I cannot get involved in racing, because I would then go bankrupt, even if I were to win every race!'

Even Ferdinand Piëch had not really understood that. And as far as my son Ferdinand Alexander was concerned, the young man who styled the 911 and thus proved his ability in this field was not in a position at that time to manage my company, since he now has his own very successful company. But that is how it was at that time with the third Porsche generation.

People of course hold widely diverging views. An American, for example, builds up a company and, if all goes well, he sells it when it is at its most valuable and starts another company with the proceeds, and he will do exactly the same thing with the new company. That is not how we do things at Porsche. If it had been my intention to set up a company for the purposes of speculation, I would have had to give it a fancy name from the beginning, because I refuse to sell my own name. As a consequence,

At the age of 78, I was still working for the company every day.

My mother Aloisia Porsche on her eightieth birthday, with me and my sister, Louise Piëch.

something would have had to be falsely programmed by me from the start, because there had never been any doubt in my mind that I would carry on what my father had started. Quite simply I believed that was the right thing to do.

The restructuring of Porsche into a joint-stock company was done with the idea of making it possible for me to leave the enterprise whenever this seemed to be opportune. In my purely personal opinion, I cannot call myself an entrepreneur if the only reason for building up a company is to sell it when it has reached its maximum value.

I started out on my career with my father; I am still pursuing that career today and right from the beginning I was fully committed to it. As the saying goes, I 'had tasted blood' during my work with my father, and I have never escaped from this close bond with his legacy.

At the beginning of 1972 all the members of the family withdrew from the Porsche company. On 1 March 1972 our companies acquired a new organizational structure. Dr. Ing. h.c. F. Porsche KG in Stuttgart-Zuffenhausen, the VW-Porsche Vertriebsgesellschaft in Ludwigsburg near Stuttgart and the Porsche Konstruktion KG in Salzburg, owned jointly by my sister Louise Piëch and myself, came under the control of a holding company, Porsche GmbH, with offices in Stuttgart. My sister and I were managing directors, with Dr Fuhrmann being responsible for the technical side. He had worked for us as a designer between 1947 and 1956 and until 1971 had been chairman of the Goetze company in Burscheid. Our financial director was Heinz Branitzki, who had come to us in 1965 from Carl Zeiss in Oberkochem. The sales director was L. Schmidt, the development manager was H. Bott, while H. Kurtz was in charge of production and K. Kalkbrenner headed the personnel department.

The reorganization of our company was completed when it became a joint-stock company. Dr. Ing. h.c. F. Porsche GmbH became Dr. Ing. h.c. F. Porsche AG. The new company was a purely family concern with at first 10 and then 12 shareholders. I became chairman of the supervisory board, with my sister Louise Piëch as my deputy. It should be pointed out that the third generation fought tooth and nail to prevent the representatives of the older generation, that is my sister and me, from taking up such important positions.

With the establishment of the joint-stock company the supervisory board was increased in size. Today, after the passing of the law regarding the participation of employees in the economic management of the company, the board has 12 members, six from the owners' side and six representatives of the employees, four from our work force and two from the trade union. When the company was restructured into a joint-stock company it gained a board of management comprising the above-mentioned gentlemen.

I have allowed this new management complete freedom, simply because leaving the board of management to join the supervisory board and then managing the company from the latter body is unlikely, in my view, to produce worthwhile results. It is simply not on.

I had always managed the company in accordance with a definite principle. For example, I used to make regular visits to the design office, where I sometimes saw something on a designer's drawing board that I did not like. I did not then go up to the man and say to him, with all the authority of my position, 'Please change that!', but rather I would voice my criticism in such a way that the person in question would believe afterwards that

With Professor Dr
Fuhrmann (centre) and
H. Branitzki, present
Chairman of the Board.

he had thought of the better idea himself. In this way I was certain that my suggestion would be implemented. If a designer is forced by his superior to accept something, then he will no longer take pleasure in his own work and will lose his motivation.

The new management structure heralded a change of direction for the company. For many years I had collaborated closely with my father and was so deeply influenced by his ideas and his philosophy that I continued to pursue them even after his death. This means that all my work bears his imprint, the result of a deep feeling of almost innate compatibility. In 1972, when the entire family withdrew from the company, the decisions taken by the new management encroached so much upon the company's whole philosophy that they led to fundamental changes. That is a fact and there is no point in discussing whether the new direction is the right one or not. There are many ways of reaching the right destination, and with the new philosophy and the variants that have emerged from it we have found our clientele.

The programme drawn up by the new management was based on the transaxle principle, in which the engine is mounted at the front and the gearbox is linked to a live rear axle. This was nothing new to me, since my father had already used it during his time at Daimler in the design of a racing car which later became the successful W25. However, it was a complete break with our earlier design principle and no longer bore my father's imprint.

The new programme included a number of variants with simi-

Above The Porsche 928, introduced after the 911, and technically based on the transaxle system. It presented a completely new line, *not* following the old Porsche tradition with the air-cooled engine in the rear.

Left The Porsche 928 was introduced to the market in 1978. Here is the final assembly point in the new Zuffenhausen plant.

241

lar styling. There was also a new body for the 911, and the basic concept for the current Type 928, in a four-seater coupé variant with rear seats, with approximately the same dimensions as the Mercedes coupé. We were actually very satisfied with what was being proposed. For reasons of time and cost, Dr Fuhrmann and the development team suggested that the 928 variant be adopted.

They calculated that the water-cooled engine of 928 would be less expensive than the air-cooled engine used hitherto. They also calculated that the bodyshell would be cheaper because the engine was front-mounted, which meant that the soundproofing for the rear-mounted engine could be dispensed with. In the end the supervisory board agreed to the 928 variants. The first life-size models and prototypes were then built. The life-size models had as much space in the rear as the Mercedes coupé, but during the development process the space in the rear was gradually reduced.

The automatic gearbox was larger than planned, and another portion of seating space was taken away. Then came the legislation making it compulsory to fit rear seat belts, and another bit of seating space was eaten away. So instead of lengthening the car or seeking some other solution, we finally made the rear seats very small and so got away from the 911.

At the same time, however, we had omitted to keep the 911 up-to-date, since it was generally thought that it was going to be discontinued. The new management had no relationship with the 911: it was not their car. Only later did it emerge that the 928 was not the right car to succeed the 911.

At that time I had had drawings made for a four-wheel drive vehicle in the same mould as the Range Rover. This vehicle also had a front-mounted engine. I could not bring myself to like the transaxle principle, because with a front engine and rear drive, it must be virtually impossible to fit four-wheel drive. The four-wheel drive Passat was also sketched at this time.

There is still some dispute as to the desirability of a fixed four-wheel drive system. On many terrains it is not necessary at all, and it simply makes the car more expensive. The whole subject sometimes seems to me like a debate about whether we should supply refrigerators to Eskimos. However, we did have considerable experience with four-wheel drive as a result of our involvement with the VW amphibious vehicle and other designs. If my proposals for a comfortable off-road vehicle that could equally well be used on normal roads and a four-wheel drive Passat had been adopted, we would have been way ahead of the Japanese who are now making a great deal of money from this sector. I am also sure that the 928 would have sold even better if it had been longer and had offered the same degree of comfort as the Mercedes. Similarly, the 928 had to be aimed at a completely new clientele: people who drive Jaguars or Mercedes.

The first transaxle vehicle to be included in our programme was the 924, which had been developed for Volkswagen as a cheaper successor to the 914. VW then decided not to build it, largely because of the energy crisis, and we took it over again. Our collaboration with VW was already running into difficulties, and it was planned to equip the 924 with an engine of which it had to be assumed that it would not remain in series production for very long. If the Audi five-cylinder engine had been available at that time, we could have used that. As it was, we had to build our own four-cylinder engine, and since the new management was proposing that we should proceed in accordance with the *Baukastenprinzip*, literally the building-block principle, and make a four-cylinder and an eight-cylinder engine, this was what was decided.

When Piëch joined Audi, he suggested taking the five-cylinder engine for the 924 and using two of them to build a 10-cylinder engine for the 928. However, our relationship with Audi was not close enough to allow us to accept the proposal. If we had adopted that course of action, we would have been even more heavily dependent on the VW organization.

So the 928 was fitted with a V8 engine of our own design which had a cubic capacity of 4.5 litres and produced 240 hp. Options included a five-speed gearbox or an automatic four-speed box from Daimler-Benz. The new management invited a few journalists to

The Porsche 924 was another coupé based on the transaxle concept, first developed by Porsche for Volkswagen, then, after VW dropped it from the programme, taken back by Porsche and produced for Porsche at the Audi Neckarsulm plant.

Above The Porsche 944 was another transaxle car, developed on the basis of the 924, but with more power — 163 PS at 5,800 rpm. It was also available in a turbocharged version of 220 PS.

Right The engine of the 944 Porsche is a water-cooled, four-cylinder of 2.5 litres with a power output of 163 PS at 5,800 rpm.

comparative tests at the Nürburgring, in which the 928 was compared with the 911 on the Northern loop. However, there was virtually nothing to compare, since the two cars represented completely different philosophies. As a result, we had to find a completely new customer for the 928. As I have already mentioned, we have now found that new type of customer. Incidentally, the new 928 was no faster at the Nürburgring than the older 911.

Myself, as Chairman of the Supervisory Board, with American Peter Schutz (right) Chairman of the Board, who left the company in 1987.

The 928 and 928S are now outstanding cars with better road-holding and more powerful brakes than the 911. They will form the basis of our model range for a long time, since there is no doubt that they still have much development potential. The V8 engine in the 928 can be increased in size to 6 litres: if I can make a 3 litre unit out of the four-cylinder engine, why should I not make a 6 litre variant of the eight-cylinder engine?

The 924 is no longer in the model programme, whereas I feel that the 944 should be retained for as long as possible. I have already described the origins of the 924. The way in which VW had costed it made it too expensive. If we had been able to cut the price by 20 per cent, it would have found its proper niche in the market. Moreover, it is my opinion that, as an exclusive make, we should no longer bother with anything smaller than a six-cylinder model. The 944 with the exhaust-driven turbocharger is an exception and should remain in the range.

I was once quoted in the press as saying that I must have a new board of management every few years, and indeed at the beginning of the 1970s one journalist even wrote that I dismissed my chief designers one after the other. That is of course totally untrue. Take our chief designer, Senator Karl Rabe, for example. He was

245

with us at the beginning and spent his entire working life at Porsche: not much of a turnover there. Similarly our current technical director, Professor Bott, has been with us for 35 years, and as far as the chairmen of the board are concerned, there have only been two in the past 15 years up to 1987, namely Professor Fuhrmann and Peter Schutz. In the same period other car manufacturers have had five or six different chairmen.

Throughout my life, I have always sought employees able to work as part of a team. To this end, I have recruited people from America, usually Germans who had been working for some time in the USA. Strange to say, these people tend to forget during the journey home that such a thing as teamwork actually exists, so I was very happy when I discovered Peter Schutz. Our collaboration with him got off to a very good start, but it would appear that even an American forgets how to work in a team if he spends any time working in Europe. In our early years together, Schutz spoke repeatedly of the need to discuss everything in order to be able to reach an understanding. This is certainly a sound management principle, but over the years he heeded it less and less. There is no doubt that Schutz was successful in his work, but with increasing success he became less willing to listen to other people, and in the later stages of his career it seemed to me that he changed completely. There came a point at which he would no longer listen to what his colleagues on the board had to say if their opinions differed from his.

I do not wish to overlook the human factors that may have contributed to this development, because recently I had the feeling that Schutz's trip to America was for him a sort of return home. I suspect he was simply suffering from homesickness. This was certainly a very human side of Schutz and a very understandable one. When the storm clouds began to gather, he did not feel comfortable with us any more and was perhaps no longer happy to shoulder the responsibility. If he had been prepared to continue in harsher times, he might have preferred to move in an American direction. I discussed this sort of strategy at the beginning of the chapter.

Of course Peter Schutz rendered very valuable services to the company. For example, he halted the decline of the 911 by building a cabriolet and remained adamant that the 911 should not simply be allowed to die, and I say quite openly that we would be in a very bad position today if the 911 had been discontinued. I am absolutely clear in my mind about that. On the other hand, however, he did not develop a range for the future, preferring to rely totally on the 911 and 928. When the dollar exchange rate was high there was no problem with the American market and so there was no reason for him to change course. However, there had been periods in the past when we had reduced exports to America in order not to become too dependent on that market. At the time of the stock market crash in October 1987 we exported 62 per cent of our production to the USA. We had usually made every effort to keep that figure under 50 per cent.

Together we will overcome this difficulty, but contemplation of our general position today provides me with much food for thought. Those entrepreneurs who, after the total devastation of the war, took it upon themselves to shoulder all the risks, are depicted by many people as 'exploiters', despite the fact that the state takes most of their profits in taxes. There was indeed no other way of financing the social measures introduced in the post-war period, which we welcome. Large sections of the population have achieved a degree of prosperity that has never before existed in the history of our country. For this reason, I simply do not understand those demagogues and political groups which deliberately stir up discontent, spread uncertainty and create wholly unnecessary tensions based on false premises.

In our supervisory board we now have co-determination on the basis of parity of representation; in other words, responsibility is equally shared by owners and employees. This is right and proper, but at the same time it means that we, owners and employees, are jointly responsible for the existence and future of the company. We should all be aware of this.

On my seventy-fifth birthday in September 1984, I received this four-seater version of the 928S from the people of my company as a present. (From left to right, first row behind the car) Peter Schutz, then General Manager and Chairman of the Board, Rudi Noppen, Helmuth Bott, myself, Heinz Branitzki, Heiko Lange, M-Jon Nedelcu.

Modern technology supplies us with information from all parts of the world. We know, for example, that millions of people are still living and starving in the most wretched conditions. But I often wonder whether the Western industrial nations, for all their prosperity, are prepared to subordinate their own wishes to the needs of these starving millions? When all is said and done, our economic system in the West, with its capacity for organization and its modern technology, is alone capable of producing enough to provide real assistance to the starving millions. However, we are more concerned with increasing our own prosperity and reducing the amount of work we do. Is this all our future will consist of?

The greatest challenge in my life to date was to start from scratch again when everything lay in ruins after the war and, with my colleagues and employees, build up an automobile factory, because until that time we had only been development engineers.

23

Weissach — an engineering service from project to product

What is Weissach? For me personally it is simply the realization of a dream; I shall explain later why this is so. In modern terminology, the Weissach development centre is described thus:

> 'Speedy racing cars on the world's famous racetracks and the powerful Leopard combat tank demonstrate the wide range of Porsche's development activities. At the Weissach development centre the latest high technology is used to develop vehicles and components. Our engineers and technicians are involved in the testing of modern materials such as magnesium, titanium and fibre-reinforced plastics for use in lightweight construction and in the planning and development of complex systems. The many projects realized here include the Leopard system, which is not only a weapons platform but also an armoured recovery vehicle and a carrier for bridge-laying equipment.

When Zuffenhausen became too crowded the Weissach Development Centre was built. The Sextagonal units of the 'think tank', extended test facilities and complete short test track are the modern realization of everything which began on Kronenstrasse in Stuttgart during 1931. The goal remains unaltered: technology in the service of mankind.

'The centre's work is based on a delight in innovation, an unconventional approach to development projects, smoothly functioning information systems and a project management system that keeps costs within the budget and ensures deadlines are met.

'These basic elements are complemented by facilities for computation, CAD, prototype construction and testing with the aid of computer-controlled systems, a centre for environmental protection and a large wind tunnel. There is a test area where vehicles can be put through their paces on the track and across country.

'With its comprehensive facilities, the Porsche Development Centre can tackle planning and development tasks in a way that will meet the exacting demands of the future!'

So much for the present-day description of Weissach's facilities. It all began in 1930 in the Kronenstraße in Stuttgart with one of the first consulting engineering companies, an institution already known in America. However, pure consultancy can hardly be described as an ideal case. In practice it all looks different.

If you turn up at an automobile company as the representative of a consulting engineering practice and present your drawings to the technical people there, they will reject them on principle, because they believe that they can do things better than those whose services have to be bought. Moreover, it is much more difficult to impress the sales people ·vith drawings, because they just say, 'We don't understand them at all!'

In order to run a proper consulting engineering practice, one really has to be in a position to show the finished product. Everybody understands that, and both sides, engineers and sales people, can begin to see what one is driving at. That is the reason why, in the Kronenstraße in Stuttgart, I was already dreaming of a development centre such as the one we now have at Weissach. As you have already read in this book, back in the 1930s we were trying to run a proper consulting engineering practice when we began to build our first cars in the garage of our house in the Feuerbacher Weg, and then set up a development centre in Stuttgart-Zuffenhausen.

However, there is an enormous difference separating Zuffenhausen from Weissach. Weissach in all its complexity is a reflection of the motor industry as it is today. Projects begin with the engineering drawings, which are much more complex and detailed than they were before the war. At that time, the drawings were not as complete as they are today. Nevertheless, an automotive craftsman was capable of converting them into a working part. He was truly a multi-skilled worker. He could turn, mill, plane, weld, in short do everything necessary to produce the part. Today several people are required to do the same job, one working on the lathe and another on the milling machine. It is hardly ever possible today to have everything done by the same craftsman.

Despite computer-aided design, we did not take any longer to design a car in the early 1930s. In the case of the six-cylinder Wanderer, for example, we started on the drawings shortly before Christmas and delivered the completed design together with the parts list on 1 April. Of course we used existing components to a certain extent, which simplified the whole business.

After the war, we developed the 356 sports car in Gmünd, which was of course based on the VW Beetle. The development of such a car today would require a centre like Weissach. Of course there were wind tunnel facilities before the war, but they were then destroyed and had not been rebuilt at the time that the 356 was developed. As I have already described, we used strips of wool and photos taken from the motorway bridge as a substitute. In this way we ascertained where the airflow broke away. Today at Weissach we have one wind tunnel for models and one for real cars, which can be tested with moving or stationary wheels.

Are modern cars so much better as a result? I cannot say. Before the war we almost caused a sensation when we created the Volkswagen, a car which could be driven for hours on the autobahn at full speed without seizing up. I remember the report written by the well-known British motoring journalist Gordon Wilkins, who, as representative of the specialist magazine *The Motor* and together with his no less famous colleague Laurence Pomeroy, was the first foreign journalist to be allowed to drive one of the Volkswagens manufactured by Daimler-Benz during a visit in 1938 to the site of the Wolfsburg plant which was then under construction. He wrote:

'The streamlined shape is very advanced, but we were surprised by the simplicity of the interior, with its cheap cloth upholstery and bare metal dashboard relieved only by a speedometer and a large round glass gear-change diagram. There is not even a petrol gauge, only a piece of bent pipe that is used to switch over to the reserve petrol tank. The ride on poor roads was certainly more pleasant than in British small cars of the period, most of which were fitted with rigid axles and leaf springs. Acceleration is leisurely and accompanied by a fierce roaring emanating from the rear, largely from the cooling fan. However, when we drove at top speed on the autobahn, we began to respect the car's 'motorway durability', in other words, its capacity for being driven all day long at full speed without the driver having to worry about a breakdown. British cars are designed to accelerate more rapidly and tend to cause problems if they are driven for a long time at full speed!'

251

However, contrary opinions were expressed. When some British officers sent a VW saloon to England after the war and suggested appropriating the ownerless factory in Wolfsburg, they received the following memo from the committee that examined the VW:

'This German car is ugly, too noisy, its rear engine is a dubious innovation and the whole design is some sort of joke that provides absolutely no justification for incorporating the factory into the British occupation zone, possibly putting money into it and hoping it will develop into something big!'

As we know, Major Hirst and his colleagues did not follow this recommendation and they decided to have a few cars built. What became of their project is well known.

Certainly cars have become more advanced. However, several people are now needed to do what, in earlier times, an engineer sketched and put into effect himself. Firstly the stylist comes up with an idea which then has to be tested by the technical boys, and what finally emerges is quite different from the original idea, perhaps because of different results obtained in wind tunnel tests or on account of the ventilation or for installation reasons. There has been a general trend in automotive engineering towards a significantly higher degree of specialization. As a result, the efficiency of individual engineers has been reduced, since the all-rounder who knew something of everything has all but disappeared.

In the interests of fairness, however, I should point out that Weissach is not involved exclusively in the motor industry. The world is our customer and our projects range from helicopters to specialist fire-fighting vehicles. There is hardly an industrialized country in the world for which we have not worked, including the Soviet Union.

I can do no better than to quote *Auto, Motor und Sport* which, under the headline *From Alfa to VW: Weissach plays host to the motor industry,* had the following to say:

'The Weissach development centre is a port of call for the automobile industry throughout the world. According to Horst Marchar, Porsche's outside project manager: "It is easier to list those car-makers who have not yet been in touch with us!"

'At Weissach, customers' worries, both major and minor, are of course handled with discretion and a non-disclosure clause is included in all contracts. However, it is well known in the automobile world who the customers are. The largest single project handled at Weissach was commissioned by the Soviet state enterprise Lada. Between 1980 and 1983, Porsche worked on the development of a new front-wheel drive car (codenamed Gamma) with a transverse four-cylinder engine. The vehicle's outer shell was already determined, but Weissach was given *carte blanche* to develop the rest of the vehicle.

'Another, somewhat smaller, commission was the design of three- and four-cylinder engines for SEAT of Spain. Of course Porsche also does a great deal of work for their former exclusive customer VW. Whether it is a question of preparing the Golf Mark II tyres to be fitted for series production or of developing the concept of the synchro-four-wheel drive, engineers are very much involved with what goes on underneath the skin of Wolfsburg products. Their expertise in all-wheel engineering is also tapped by BMW.

'Randomly selected development commissions show that the Weissach client list reads like a *Who's Who* of the international automobile business. The centre is currently working for Renault on fuel-injection versions of well-known engines; for Ford on a digital engine management system for four-cylinder power units; and for Alfa Romeo on a catalytic converter engine with a lambda control system based on an Alfasud unit. It is developing a turbo opposed piston engine for Lancia and helping Volvo to fit four-valve engines in their 7 series cars. Peugeot entrusted the development of the 505 turbocharged engine to Porsche engineers and even Rolls-Royce were not too proud to go to Porsche for assistance with the testing of fuel-injection engines.'

We reduce the harmful emissions from engines for Italian, French, German and American companies. We conduct investigations into the use of synthetic materials and wind tunnel tests. All the facilities at Weissach are used for the further development of the automobile, because far from having completed the task of making the motor car as environmentally sound as possible, we have hardly begun. However, we are proud of having introduced many things before they were required by legislation. For example, before there was any hint of legislation in the area, our steering columns were designed in such a way that, in the event of an accident, the driver could not be impaled on it. In fact, we are always a few steps ahead of the law. That is one of the reasons why Weissach welcomes very prominent customers from all over the world. I would not like to mention any names, but always say, 'They're all my customers!', since I do not want to give the impression that individual companies cannot achieve things as well. Under certain circumstances, however, it is obviously cheaper for us to investigate the same question for three or four customers than if each company were to go it alone.

For an automobile designer, it is always an historic moment when he receives a commission to design a new car from scratch without having to take into account equipment already in existence. This was the case, for example, when we created the Volkswagen. The impressive post-war success was achieved despite the doubts expressed at the time, and it was world-wide success on a scale never before seen.

We built on this foundation at Porsche when we set up our own car factory. It was not until the Type 356 gave way to the 911 that we produced a completely new design. This car was and is very successful. This shows that technology is capable of extraordinary achievements if it is allowed the necessary freedom of manoeuvre. Of course the commercial side lays down certain limits which have to be respected if one wishes to be commercially successful. Occasionally, however, the engineer is permitted to realize his dreams, at least to a certain extent. The Type 959 is a good example of this. In this instance, we created a car into which we packed everything made possible by the very latest technology. Only a limited number were built, because of the price, but the fact that this car was built and sold at all made it possible for the engineers to introduce innovations that may subsequently find their way into larger production series.

It is my personal opinion, however, that an engineer should always try to solve a problem in the simplest possible way. That has always been the guiding principle behind my engineering activities. Under no circumstances should an engineer seek to prove, for example, that he could build a lift on Mount Everest. It may well be possible in theory, but there is little point in doing it. For me, the simple solution is always the best, and the Volkswagen is a clear illustration of that.

24

One hundred years of the automobile

In 1986, the automobile celebrated its one hundredth birthday. As a child I lived through the early years of the age of the automobile. Unfortunately, however, I was not taken to school by car but in a coach pulled by horses. I started school in 1915 and during the First World War there was no petrol available for use in private vehicles.

In the early days, the motor car gave a few privileged people the chance of greater mobility. Technical and industrial development over the next hundred years made it possible to produce cars more cheaply, with the result that today it has virtually become a vehicle for use by all.

People today have a very close relationship with their car because it gives them a feeling of freedom. Those who own a car can avail themselves of this freedom at any time, for all they have to do is fill the tank with petrol and they can then go wherever they wish. This was impossible until the advent of the motor car.

There are still railways, it is true, and the establishment of rail systems was also a major advance, but they did not give the traveller the same degree of freedom as the car. People wishing to travel by rail are constrained by timetables and have to share their carriage with other people, usually strangers. With a car, on the other hand, the individual is completely free and it is my contention that this freedom has actually changed people, making it easy for us to leave our immediate environment and become acquainted with other countries and their inhabitants.

At the same time, the motor car represented a great social advance. A married man with children and a modest income could suddenly afford to take his family on holiday. In conjunction with economic progress, the Volkswagen made a significant contribution to this change. In the 1920s, for example, it would have been impossible for a working-class family to go to Italy or Austria. Only Henry Ford with his Model T gave Americans on modest incomes the chance to acquire a car and travel long distances in it because it was so cheap to run.

Of course I am not forgetting that the motor car has also created problems which must be resolved. Despite great efforts, we have not yet succeeded in creating anything perfect, but we have made considerable progress in our attempts to make cars safer. We are developing methods of managing traffic flows in such a way that traffic will be safer, and we have succeeded on a technical level in considerably reducing the environmental damage caused by cars.

We should not forget that the motor car today is not only a pleasure vehicle but also performs many other functions without which our modern world could hardly exist. It is only a small minority that seeks to spoil the motor car for the great majority of people, without of course considering what would happen if, as a result of their actions, automobile production were to be restricted or even brought to a complete halt. I also have the impression that those who condemn the motor car do not much care whether people are really free and feel themselves to be free.

Quite apart from that, the economic importance of the motor industry should not be overlooked, and indeed this fact is repeatedly alluded to in public debate. Moreover, the motor industry is, as we know, very export intensive and makes a significant contribution to our trade balance.

The German automobile industry is one of the strongest in the world and its products are of the highest technical quality. However, its markets are different from those of the American automobile industry, for example, and as a consequence it has different production volumes.

The Japanese motor industry, which throughout the world presents us all with serious competition, is slowly beginning to be more cautious in its pricing policy, because wages are also rising in Japan and workers' claims have to be met, and this is actually a trend which is causing us some concern as well. The Porsche Company, with its top-quality products, may be less affected, but the remorseless increase in costs can only be met by the introduction of more modern and less costly production techniques.

Producing cars in larger volumes and selling them at lower prices can no longer be considered as a solution, because it leads to excess capacity and the production of vehicles that suddenly cannot be sold. The consequence is unemployment which in turn forces the state into increased expenditure. The resources needed to finance this extra expenditure can only come from the taxpayer, who in consequence no longer has as much disposable income available for consumption.

One can look at the issue from whatever angle one likes; it is a vicious circle which cannot easily be broken. If we decide to produce in larger volumes in order to keep prices low, we will be faced one day with another problem, namely the fact that the limits of car ownership have been reached and the market is saturated. This can be seen in Los Angeles, for example, where this limit is already visible, since there are more cars than people. There are many people there who own two, three or even four cars. Of course the owner can only drive one of his cars at a time, but virtually every holder of a driving licence drives a car, and in this way the upper limit of car ownership has been reached. Lorries and motor cycles are not included here.

The Americans have tried to keep pace with this development and have created the necessary road network, while in Europe we did not begin to modernize the road network until the early 1930s, and it is not complete today. There are still large areas of Europe where there are no motorways or similar roads, and in those countries where there are motorways, these roads are hopelessly congested, particularly during the holiday period.

This difference becomes obvious when one flies from Los Angeles to Frankfurt. In California there is a modern road network, while in Frankfurt there is only one four-lane section near the airport. To the best of my knowledge, this is the only such stretch of road of any length in Germany, and after a few kilometres it leads into a two-lane section. This leads to bottlenecks which of course create constant problems. Between Los Angeles and San Diego, for example, four-lane highways have been built to cope with the increase in traffic. In the Frankfurt area, however, which is after all a very important centre for international travel, the existing roads can no longer cope adequately with the traffic that uses them.

It would appear that the will to eliminate does not exist. Arguments are constantly being put forward against it, so much so that one can easily get the impression that it is not the elimination of these problems that is being considered, but rather ways of making the situation even worse! The aim would seem to be to make people despair of the situation so that they no longer wish to drive their cars. There are countless examples of this. I have no objection to pedestrian zones in areas where there is plenty of space for traffic as well, but where that is not the case they are simply inappropriate. In any case, it can hardly be a solution to make main roads into pedestrian zones.

For example, the planning authorities in Stuttgart, a city where the automobile industry and its suppliers contribute a great deal to the local economy and which is surely grateful for the taxes paid by these companies, do not take sufficient account of the motor car. I would even go so far as to say that the traffic policy adopted is not exactly welcoming to the motor car. Efforts are being made to reduce the amount of space available for traffic, rather than increase it.

The automobile industry is a very important sector of German industry which provides employment for hundreds and thousands of people. I sometimes wonder what the politicians in charge would do if the situation in the industry were to deteriorate or if individual firms were to go bankrupt. Of course the constantly increasing volume of private traffic creates problems for which solutions must be found, but reducing the amount of space available for traffic is not the answer.

One sometimes gains the impression that politicians and the government do not care if it takes people half an hour or an hour to get to their places of work, although this represents a waste of manpower and, in the final analysis, of national wealth as well. Much of what the Greens, for example, are seeking would lead to a reduction in the national wealth. We aspire, quite rightly, to a higher standard of living, but we are not willing to lay the foundations of increased prosperity. Workers would be better off, and healthier into the bargain, if they gained half an hour a day for early morning exercises or gardening instead of sitting in their cars in a traffic jam.

In America people think differently. A highway is built between two towns because it is calculated that it will save a certain number of people a certain amount of time. Time is money, but when a road is planned in Europe, the first question is 'How much will it cost?' and not 'What benefits will it bring?' That is not discussed at all.

Measures taken by government threaten to make motoring so unattractive that there will be serious economic consequences.

We Europeans are not really so different from each other, but let us take Paris as an example. They still have a traffic problem there, but in the last 20 years they have invested heavily in new roads and are even talking now of building roads under the city. Where in Germany is there a city where so many new roads have been built? I do not know of one.

Already a lot of people are wondering whether it is not better to fly on holiday instead of going by car. The media have been talking mockingly for some time of the 'metal avalanche'. This is not of course an optimistic scenario for the future of the motor industry. The lengthy traffic jams develop because there is not enough space for all the cars, thus reducing speed drastically. To make an analogy, traffic is no different from a liquid being conveyed through a pipe: if I pump the liquid through quickly, a large volume will pass through, whereas if it flows slowly, proportionally less liquid will be conveyed.

Some politicians suggest that we switch over to rail travel and make more use of suburban rail networks. Once again, I would like to take America as an example. In America, parking places in large cities are just as rare and expensive as here. Consequently, a lot of people who work in New York but live outside the city travel to work by rail. However, they use their cars in conjunction with the train by availing themselves of the well-known park-and-ride system. They go by car to the nearest station, park their car there and take the train into New York. In this way they retain the freedom that their car gives them. We also have modern suburban rail networks linking city centres with suburbs, but do the stations have adequate car parks where commuters can leave their cars all day? No, they do not, and this surely represents a failure of the planning process. So long as we are not in a position to offer a reasonable combination of road and rail transport, the suburban rail networks will remain underused.

We will not solve the problems on the motorways and enable the traffic to flow more freely unless we eliminate the bottlenecks. We ought to do this for economic reasons alone, because the stop-start traffic jams give rise to some enormous losses. At the same time, moreover, freely flowing traffic causes much less environmental damage. This is a lesson that should be learnt by all those campaign groups which oppose any extension of the road network, however reasonable it may be.

If one cites America as a positive example, one repeatedly hears the counter-argument, trotted out to support a disapproving attitude, that Europe is too densely populated and that what America can afford is not possible in Europe. I do not agree with this, but rather that meticulous planning is most required in those areas where there is a shortage of space. What is the use of a large-scale motorway exit if the traffic passing through it gets stuck in a bottleneck after a few hundred metres, creating a traffic jam? The black spots are well known, and a tape-recorded message is all that is required for the traffic announcements on the radio, since the traffic jams almost always occur at the same places.

In fact, we should take nature as our model in designing motorways and lay them out in a way similar to our great rivers, so that with each stream that flows into it the main river increases in size, only to part again where the river grows weaker. Let us take as an example the Munich-Salzburg autobahn, which needs several lanes until the Innsbruck turnoff, after which it divides and needs fewer lanes.

There seems to be a trend in politics today to take individual people as targets, because they are less able to defend themselves than large associations or organizations. The car owner is a good example, an individual person who is not organized in a large association. Since the motor car has been declared environmental enemy number one, who will defend the motorist with equal force? The motoring organizations? Hardly, because they have other interests apart from motoring.

If one follows the public debate or the activities of citizens' pressure groups in environmental issues, one may well wonder who is actually concerned about the environmental damage caused by aeroplanes — not about noise pollution, but that caused by exhaust gases. Could this be because most airlines are state-owned?

I often think about what can be done to reduce environmental damage. What measures can be taken, for example, to improve the air in holiday areas and to reduce the amount of pollutants? Provided that electrically driven vehicles can be developed to a point where they can be operated at relatively low cost, electric cars could be used for urban transport in spas and other health resorts. In Baden-Baden, for example, car parks would have to be built on the edge of the town for visitors arriving by car, who would leave their own vehicles and hire electrically driven cars to take them into the centre of the town. The city fathers would then have further grounds for proclaiming the quality of the air in Baden-Baden.

To summarize, it can be said that the Americans have coped better than the Europeans with the increasing volume of traffic. It may be argued that American traffic police enforce the law very rigorously, but in my view American traffic police are no stricter than their German counterparts. It is just that American drivers have been more successful than the Europeans in adapting their behaviour to the prevailing traffic conditions. Moreover, the Americans recognized the problems much earlier and planned their road-building programme accordingly.

In the Federal Republic of Germany in 1987, there were 28.3 million registered motor vehicles; if we take the Shell forecast as the basis for our calculations, this figure will rise to over 30 million by the year 2000. At that point, it is predicted, a plateau will have been reached and a certain degree of stabilization will ensue. Most new registrations will then be replacements for old vehicles.

Competition in the motor industry will become harsher and will force us to rationalize still further. The Japanese are now beginning to produce high-quality cars in increasing numbers, while the Koreans are taking over those sections of the market with which the Japanese established their world-wide success. Other countries will follow the Koreans. The high-quality sports car will still have its place, but it will be very important for the entire European motor industry to succeed in maintaining the attractiveness of its products.

Even if people continue to use aircraft for their holiday travel, there is no doubt that tourists will continue to want a car to be available at their destination so that they can explore their surroundings. If their holiday destination is in a warm country, then they may well consider hiring a convertible or open-top sports car. Since more and more people are spending their holidays in far-away places, increasing numbers of tourists will wish to hire a car at their holiday destination.

Even the major political parties have realized that motorists are also voters and that they will lose votes if they ignore the problems of this section of the electorate.

The motor car has enhanced the lives of many people, and it is scarcely credible that these same people will be prepared to give it up. Reason and a willingness to find answers to the problems that exist will do more to maintain the appeal of the motor car than excessive state control.

25

What will the future bring?

The last hundred years have seen more changes than any comparable period in history. We have witnessed the development of technology to a point that would have been considered inconceivable at the beginning of this century. Who could have imagined then that we would be able to orbit the earth or land men on the moon? These are events that bear witness to an unprecedented level of economic success. They have influenced our lives and had an effect on many areas, including the motor industry. In all this, it is interesting to observe the direction in which the motor car has developed under the pressure of external influences. The oil crises which pushed up the price of petrol had a positive effect on the development of diesel engines, while efforts are being made to develop even more economical cars. Engines are being made more efficient and a low drag coefficient has suddenly become an important way of reducing fuel consumption. At the same time, however, there is an increasing number of vehicles in a special category in which coefficient of drag plays no role at all and which are bought by people who do not actually need them. I am talking here of the trend towards four-wheel drive, off-road vehicles.

Both developments are taking place side by side. On the one hand, a lot of money is being spent on advertising cars with as low a coefficient of drag as possible, while on the other hand advertisements extol the practical virtues of off-road vehicles. Many people who buy such cars do not really need them, since they neither go hunting nor run a farm. They may perhaps need them in winter if they travel in deep snow to St Moritz, but for this type of application it is wrong to promote a design that runs counter to a trend generally recognized as essential.

On the other hand, the constant search for the optimal body shape may well lead to certain practicalities being ignored. For example, the rain channel that was an integral part of earlier designs of car roofs is now being eliminated, because it has a negative effect on the coefficient of drag. As a consequence, rain drips on to the seats if the door is opened when it is raining, or the occupants of the car may even get rained upon. It may be argued that this is all something of an exaggeration, but the problem does exist. In any case, the point I am making is that there is no such thing as a perfect solution in automobile design; here, as in so many other areas, compromises have to be made. In the future, such compromises will give rise to a trend towards smaller cars made necessary by the decreasing amount of space on the roads. It is also likely that an increasing amount of long-distance travel will be transferred to the air, although as mentioned already, travellers will still need to have a car available at their destination so that individual mobility remains unimpeded.

With the products that we make, namely sports cars, we at Porsche are actually on the right road. It is true that this is not generally recognized by most people, and indeed sports cars are sometimes considered to be unnecessary vehicles, but it is a fact that statistics show that sports cars are the best used vehicle of all. According to the statistics, 90 per cent of all passenger cars only carry two people. With the exception of those driving two-seater sports cars, therefore, everybody else is driving around in cars that are actually too large for their needs. In my opinion, the small car, possibly with two occasional seats in the rear, will be much more common in the future than it has been up to now.

Environmental awareness will continue to grow, and as a result of the difficulties that individuals experience when travelling on holiday or simply in everyday traffic, the motor car will continue to be a subject of controversy and debate. In this respect, the motor car is in a particularly difficult position, since there is no party, except in Switzerland, which really represents the interests of motorists with any degree of vigour although recently two parties for motorists have been established in Germany.

The earth's reserves of raw materials and energy are finite, and consumption of them has increased considerably. As engineers, therefore, we have to consider how we can make cars more durable, more resistant to corrosion, in order to preserve such an important economic good. A great deal of progress has already been made in this area. The use of galvanised steel, of aluminium alloys and plastics represents a considerable advance. Through improved designs and the use of new materials it will be possible to make cars lighter and thus reduce fuel consumption.

At the same time, the use of new materials brings with it new arguments about waste disposal. Iron is no problem since it can be recycled, as can aluminium and its alloys, but plastics are a different matter since they cannot be disposed of so easily. They do not rot away, and recycling is not yet sufficiently developed. True, we are working to solve this problem, but this example clearly demonstrates that when using new materials we also have to consider their disposal. How do we get rid of plastic when it is no longer needed? What are we to do with the increasing proportion of plastic used in cars when a car is scrapped? What about all-plastic bodies?

263

Nuclear technology provides a good and very topical example of the problems involved. We were quick to harness nuclear energy, both for military and peaceful applications, but we still do not know how to dispose of the hazardous waste. Nobody has yet come up with a solution that could be considered definitive. In my opinion, it is no solution to build vast storage facilities in the bowels of the earth or to accumulate vast stocks of potentially lethal waste.

It seems to be part of the spirit of our time to relegate the most important issues to second place in our list of priorities. Whole new districts are built in our cities, and only afterwards are the drains laid; a hotel complex is built on the coast, effluent is discharged straight into the sea and it is only after the sea has been badly polluted that consideration is given to ways of saving it. We must do things the other way round. Much can be achieved with modern technology, and it undoubtedly benefits us all, but we must also acknowledge the risks involved and learn how to control them.

Neither the diesel nor the petrol engine has been developed as far as is possible. It is particularly interesting for me to see that the air-cooled engine is closer to its future design than the water-cooled engine. I myself have witnessed the development of the air-cooled engine in many different areas of application from its very beginnings to the present day. Researchers are looking at the use of materials in engines which can withstand higher temperatures than hitherto, such as ceramics, for example, in order to improve engine efficiency. During the war we looked at these things in connection with turbine engines, the efficiency of which is very dependent on operating temperature. The main reason why turbines are not yet used in road vehicles is probably that they consume too much fuel. A higher operating temperature in the combustion chamber would represent a considerable step forward in the search for a solution to this problem, but suitable materials are still sought, and much work still needs to done in this area. The higher the operating temperature in a turbine engine, the greater the efficiency, so that as new materials are developed turbines might possibly become a genuine alternative to the normal piston engine.

Of course the operating range of an engine in a road vehicle is completely different from that of an aero engine. In an aeroplane, where turbines have for a long time been used to good advantage, whether in turboprops or turbojets, the engine control cycle is relatively simple and unchanging. Full load is required for take-off, then the aircraft cruises at a reduced engine speed and also lands at a similarly reduced speed. A car is completely different, since the cycle is constantly changing. This means that in traffic the engine has to be regulated almost constantly. Many proposals have already been put forward and much development work carried out on ways of compensating for these constantly changing demands on the turbine by means of an electrical drive system. In this way the turbine, operating at a constant speed, could generate an electrical current and the engine could be regulated by the electrical part of the mixed drive system. This is a method with which we already have a great deal of experience, although less with a turbine as the current generator, but rather with petrol and diesel engines, for example in the Maus (Mouse) tank. The problem is not the use of the turbine as the current generator, but rather — as described above — the improvement of engine efficiency.

Another problem is the diesel engine, which has been the subject of much debate recently because of the solid particles contained in its exhaust gases. A fundamental point needs to be made here, one which is often overlooked in the often heated debate. This is that it is only in the post-war period, and really only in the last 10 years or so, that we have begun to investigate the effects that pollutants have on the environment and on human beings. What actually damages human beings?

In the case of the diesel, there is a relatively large group which supports the use of this kind of engine, because its emissions contain relatively few pollutants. On the other hand, there is another not exactly small group which is of the opinion that diesel exhaust gases, particularly the particles of solid matter or soot that they contain, are carcinogenic. It should be pointed out that, in the modern diesel engines used in cars, the proportion of soot particles in the exhaust gases is very low. Until now it has been maintained that the soot particles are carcinogenic only in much higher concentrations than normally occur in traffic. Here, therefore, we have a conflict of opinion. However, as long as this uncertainty prevails, some wonderful engine may be developed that will provide a positive answer to a lot of the questions currently being asked, but it will not be built because some people believe that it causes cancer.

I can remember a good example from the days when we were developing the Volkswagen. The heating system in the VW worked by leading air over the exhaust pipe, where it was heated and then conveyed into the interior of the car. This gave rise to a debate, probably instigated by our competitors, in which it was maintained that this was a very dangerous procedure, since the occupants of the car could well be poisoned if a leak developed between the heating and exhaust systems. So we drilled a hole 2 mm in diameter in the exhaust pipe and measured the exhaust gases that built up inside the car. The volume of poisonous fumes was less than if two people had been smoking cigarettes in the car. This shows that pollutants have long been a subject for public debate, but that debate is more heated today than ever before. Sound, wide-ranging research may help to clarify the issues and point the way towards a solution.

Many alternatives to the conventional internal combustion engine are being investigated, as are alternative fuels. Let us take electric power as an example. It is no secret that the problem here is that of developing a suitable energy storage device that is considerably lighter than conventional batteries and can also store enough electricity to give the car the same kind of range on one tankful as a petrol or diesel engine. Moreover, the cost of such a storage device must be economically justifiable.

In this connection, I remember a competition organized during the Third Reich for the invention of a battery of the same weight as a conventional type but capable of storing many times more energy; the prize was fixed at 20,000 Reichsmark. At that time, 20,000 Reichsmark was a lot of money, but I said to the people organizing the competition, 'If I were to invent a battery like that, I wouldn't sell it to you for 20,000 marks, because it would make me a millionaire several times over!' This episode says most of what there is to say about electrical power systems for cars.

We have also investigated hydrogen-powered engines, not for cars but in connection with wind power plants that we were developing. The same problems occurred as with electric power for cars, namely how to store the electrical energy generated in order to have it available when it is required. One way of doing this is to use the electricity generated to make hydrogen and store it in containers so that it is available at any time to drive the generators. This is basically similar to the way in which hydro-electric power stations in the Alps function. During the night, when most industrial plants are not operating, the water used to generate energy is pumped up again into the reservoir so that it is available again to generate electricity during the day, when factories are working. As with the hydrogen stored in the wind power plants, a circular system is created by means of which electricity can be generated when it is needed.

As far as cars are concerned, it is still my opinion that we are unfortunately not yet in a position to design the ideally shaped car. To me, that means reaching a standard where the customer no longer asks, 'Where is the engine?' It should actually be of no consequence at all whether the engine is mounted at the front or the rear. In this connection, I always think of the car with an under-floor engine that we developed for Volkswagen. That was very close to the ideal shape, and if in future engines become even smaller, it should be fitted wherever it takes away least space from the car interior.

In our debates on car design, the position of the engine still plays a very important role, and this debate, which should no longer be the focus of interest as far as the car of the future is concerned, always reminds me of the old steam locomotive whose chimney always had to be in the same position so that one knew which was the front. With respect to cars, too much importance is still attached to things which are actually of no interest to consumers such as accessibility or ease of repair, since they are largely ignorant of such matters. Who today wants to know how the movement of a watch works? For this reason, I think that the questions on the functioning of the car that still form part of the German driving test are outdated and completely superfluous.

The example of atomic energy in particular shows us that all great technological discoveries involve a certain degree of danger, in that while they can be used for the benefit of mankind they can also be harmful. Thus they are equally good and bad, and it is understandable that there are people who completely reject nuclear technology on the grounds that it might tempt an irresponsible government to use it to blackmail a neighbouring state.

In taking stock of a long life, I have to conclude that mankind has indeed gained a great deal of experience and expertise, but is not, in the final analysis, any the wiser for it; if this were not the case, then the world would not be as it is today. People wish to maintain and further develop a functioning economic system, or see endless wage claims fulfilled, which will at a certian point start to menace our competitiveness in the world market and thus threaten the foundations of our prosperity and ultimately our standard of living.

We have to contend today with an increasing tendency towards selfishness in our society. I consider this to be a misunderstand-

Receiving the title of an Ehrensenator (Senator of Honour) from the University of Stuttgart on 24 May 1985. It was presented by Professor Dr Zwicker (right), the Rector of the University. Besides this title, I already had the titles Professor and Dr Ing. h.c. (honoris causa).

267

Above For the twenty-fifth anniversary of the 911, in summer 1988, Porsche presented a new top model of the type, the Porsche 911 Carrera 4. This outstanding car has four-wheel drive. Although the car is called the 911 Carrera 4, the company type number is 964.

Right Rear view of the Porsche 911 Carrera 4. The rear spoiler with cooling grill (above the Carrera 4 badge) folds flush with the engine compartment lid at low to moderate speeds and rises to its fully extended height as the car reaches speeds at which it can have significant influence on downforce.

ing of the meaning of democracy: we should not think primarily of ourselves, but rather of society as a whole. We should ask ourselves, for example, whether an airport is necessary for the community as a whole and not seek to prevent it being built simply because we happen to live in its vicinity. This way of thinking should guide us in all important decisions. It is my opinion that many politicians today act in the way they think most likely to guarantee their own re-election, even if that means making con-

cessions for which responsibility cannot actually be accepted.

Basically, however, I am an optimist, and as far as the future is concerned I follow the example of my wife who, when asked about the future, would say, 'It'll never be as bad as we fear nor as good as we hope!'

Unfortunately my wife Dodo died on 27 July 1985. With her realistic judgement, but also with a strong optimism, she was my companion for almost the whole of my life, and supported the attainment of my goals with enthusiam. We laid her to rest in our chapel at the family estate at Zell am See.

In 1988 we celebrated the twenty-fifth anniversary of the Porsche 911, which better than any of our other models embodies the company motto, 'Driving in its purest form'. We marked this anniversary with the introduction of a new model in the 911 series, the Type 911 Carrera 4, in which the 4 stands for four-wheel drive. The new model has been designated the Porsche 964. With dynamically controlled four-wheel drive, a new chassis, improved aerodynamics and a partially enclosed 250 bhp engine, this version of the 911 complemented the Porsche model range from 1989 onwards.

Porsche were using four-wheel drive technology even at the time that my father was in charge. We showed a four-wheel drive version of the 911 at the 1981 International Motor Show in Frankfurt. In 1984 a four-wheel drive Carrera became the first sports car of its kind to take part in the famous Paris-Dakar rally and was driven to victory by René Metge. The rally of the Pharaohs in Egypt in the same year saw the first successful competitive use

Note that here, at speed, the rear spoiler of the 911 Carrera 4 is extended. The Carrera 4 uses a viscous coupling-controlled Ferguson-type epicyclic central differential that directs 31 per cent of the engine torque to the front wheels and 60 per cent to the rear.

of the Porsche 959 with computer-controlled, variable-torque-split, four-wheel drive. In 1986, the three Porsche 959s entered for the Paris-Dakar rally took first, second and sixth place, and in 1987 production of the exclusive Porsche 959 series for road use began, followed in 1988 by the introduction of the Porsche 911 Carrera 4 with a more highly developed version of the four-wheel drive system.

The Carrera 4 is actually a variant of the Type 959 of which a small number were built as a sort of development vehicle. The road version of the 959 incorporated some of the more valuable discoveries made from our experience with the earlier version, but we did not make use of everything included in the development vehicle. All this work finally gave birth to the four-wheel drive vehicle designed for sale to customers. It embodies a great deal of experience acquired from the development vehicle. Thus the Carrera 4 does not contain all the complicated mechanics used in the Type 959. It is powered by the most normally aspirated engine ever used in the 911 series. The introduction of the Carrera 4 was preceded by eight years of technical development and testing in competition. As early as our four-wheel drive cabriolet study of 1981, we had combined four-wheel drive with the rear-wheel drive concept in a sports car for road use. In this design, an additional drive shaft leads from the gearbox on the rear axle to the front axle. This shaft is housed in a tube which forms a stable link between the front and rear axles and has its roots in the transaxle principle. This arrangement was maintained in all the four-wheel drive vehicles developed on the basis of the 911.

The Porsche 959 competition version. This coupé with four-wheel drive was a technical development platform, from which the road version was derived. This racing version of the 959 finished first and second in the Paris-Dakar Rally of 1986.

If I look back again at the developments of our Porsche 911, this type undoubtedly represents a controversial concept, which even today many people do not regard as an optimal design. As an unswerving defender of the concept, the almost unprecedently long life of this model and the fact that new variants with a few modifications will ensure its survival into the future make me very proud that I have kept faith with my opinion.

The road version of the 959 did not have all the mechanical parts of the racing version. It was a 'civilized' version of the racing model, but was still a very powerful car, manufactured in a small series and sold for a very high price. One of the customers was conductor Herbert von Karajan.

271

26

A necessary postscript

The headlines that accompanied the reports on Porsche published in various newspapers and magazines in the course of 1988 caused me to reflect. I read things like 'Blue funk in Zuffenhausen', 'Ready about!' 'The great race against time — Porsche intends to survive' and much more in the same vein. Well, there can be no question of Porsche 'not surviving'. I do not deny that we have got into difficulties as a result of heavy reliance on the American market and the falling dollar exchange rate, but it has meant that we have been able to clarify the goals that we should strive after in the future. It must be our aim to plan for a future in which we shall use two basic types to concentrate entirely on the exclusive and expensive end of the market. The technical expertise that has been acquired by dint of hard work over the years should not be used to eliminate this or that model from the range overnight, so to speak. Investment that has already been made should not be allowed to remain unused but must be translated into new products, and this product can only be an exclusive car. I leave open the question of whether we should emphasize the sporting or the luxury aspect, since that must be answered by the market. Porsche should also put more resources into contract development work at Weissach. Our activities at the development centre represent a great challenge for us engineers, but are at the same time a very delicate matter which require a high degree of confidentiality. Our customers must be sure that they can have complete confidence in our handling of the tasks with which they entrust us. The guarantee of confidentiality is important for every company, because in the final analysis every car-maker suffers if a new project is made public too early. However, this means that we cannot advertise who we are looking for. It is the customer who, in the end, pays for breaches of confidentiality, and in any case, it is no use to a company or a customer if we tell them about products that they will not be able to buy for five or 10 years. Our development centre at Weissach, and I can say this with a great deal of pride, is virtually unique and is used by customers from all over the world.

In 1988 we also opened a new car-body works in Zuffenhausen which also sets standards and which — I would particularly like to stress — was wholly financed by us without resort to bank loans. The total investment made by Dr. Ing. h.c. F. Porsche AG amounted to 125 million DM. This new plant will not only help us to maintain our high standards of quality, but also to improve them still further.

I am also convinced, and I can say this quite safely, that the introduction of a younger generation on to the board of management, a process which has been in full swing since the summer of 1988, will also help us take the right decisions in the future. We have a successor to Herr Bott, Herr Bez, who worked for us for several years some time ago, we have a new financial director, Herr Walter Gnauert, who takes over from Herr Branitzki, who has become chairman of the board. Our next task is to find a successor for Herr Branitzki, but in this case we still have a few years in which to conclude our search.

I have no fears about the future of Porsche if we just remember what it was that made our company great. The new car that we introduced in 1988 is actually the 1963 model that has formed the basis for an outstandingly successful series of models and which today, in the form of the Carrera 4, incorporates the most modern technology despite the age of the basic concept.

Our activity as consulting engineers understandably tempts us to show that we can master anything. It is of course important for our own products that we develop and manufacture what the market expects of us. In this respect, we were perhaps a little mistaken with the variants which differ from the 911 concept.

Since the family and the third generation left the company in 1972, I welcome the fact that my youngest son Wolfgang has joined me on the supervisory board, and with him the continuation of the tradition established in 1930 is guaranteed.

I have always understood the Porsche to be more than just a car. It is my philosophy of the automobile which has found devotees throughout the world.

Appendix

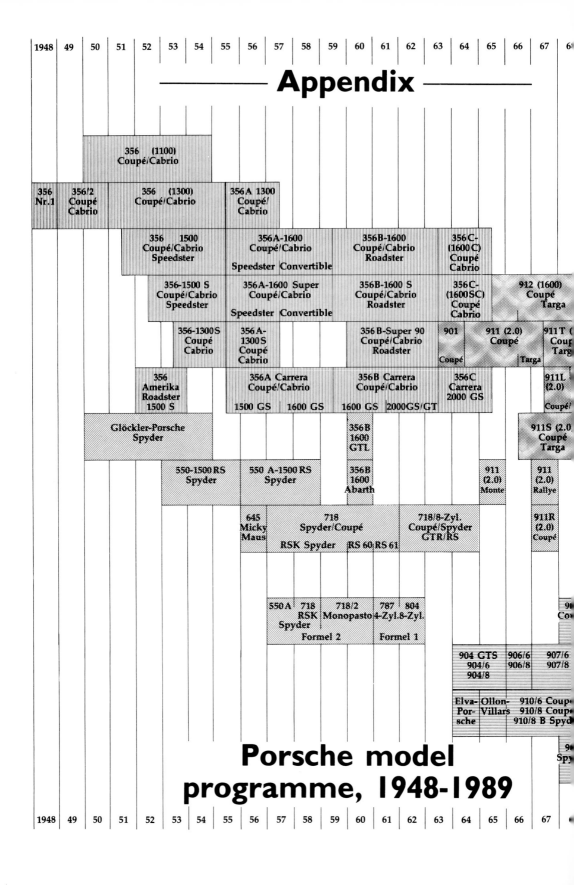

Porsche model programme, 1948-1989

69	70	71	72	73	74	75	76	77	78	79	80	81	82	83	84	85	86	87	88	1989

944 Turbo 2.5 Coupé

914/8 3.0 | **914/6 GT 2.0** | **916 2.4**

944 GTP Le Mans   **944 2.5 Coupé**   **2.7**

914/4 1.7 | **914/4 1.8**   **924 SCCA** | **924 Carrera GT GTS/GTR**   **944S Coupé 2.5**   **3.0 Cabrio**

914/6 2.0 | **914/4 2.0**   **924 2.0 Coupé**   **924S 2.5 Coupé**

912E (2.0) Coupé   **924 Turbo 2.0 Coupé**   **944S Turbo Coupé**

911T 2.2 Coupé Targa | **911T 2.4 Coupé Targa**

928 4.5 Coupé

911E 2.2 Coupé Targa | **911E 2.4 Coupé Targa** | **911 2.7 Coupé Targa**   **928S 4.7 Coupé**   **928S4 5.0 Coupé**

911S 2.2 Coupé Targa | **911S 2.4 Coupé Targa** | **911S 2.7 Coupé Targa**

911 2.2 Rallye | **911S 2.2 Safari** | **911S 2.5 Coupé** | **911 2.7 Carrera Coupé/Targa** | **911 3.0**   **911 SC (3.0) Coupé/Targa** | **Cabrio**   **911 Carrera (3.2) Coupé/Targa/Cabrio**   Speedster

911S 2.3 Coupé   **911 Turbo (3.0) Coupé**   **911 Turbo (3.3) Coupé**   Targa/Cabrio

911 2.4 Proto   **911RS Carrera 2.7 | 3.0**   **934 Gruppe 4 (3.0)** | **911 SC Safari**   **911 SC-RS**   **911 Carrera 4 Coupé**

08/02   **908/03 Spyder**   **911RSR Carrera 2.8/3.0**   **935 Gruppe 5 2856 ccm | Moby Dick**   **911 4 × 4**   **959**   **959 Coupé**   Paris-Dakar

917 Coupé   **911 RSR Turbo**   **935 (1.4) Baby**   **961 Coupé IMSA/GTX**

917PA Spyder | **917/10 Turbo Spyder**   **936 Spyder Gruppe 6**   **956 Coupé Gruppe C**   **962 Coupé Gruppe C**

917/20 Spyder | **917/30 Spyder**   **2708 CART**

69	70	71	72	73	74	75	76	77	78	79	80	81	82	83	84	85	86	87	88	1989

Index

Figures in *italics* refer to illustrations. FP = Ferry Porsche. Makes of cars are listed under the general heading 'Cars', and races under 'Races'.